Empires Beyond the Great Wall

THE HERITAGE OF GENGHIS KHAN

Natural History Museum of Los Angeles County
Inner Mongolia Museum of China

太
祖
皇
帝

即成吉思汗諱帖木真

EMPIRES BEYOND THE GREAT WALL

THE HERITAGE OF GENGHIS KHAN

by Adam T. Kessler

CONTRIBUTORS

Shao Qinglong
Wen Shanzhen
Hung Xueying
Zhang Wenfang
An Li
Ding Yong

TRANSLATION BY

Bettine Birge

PHOTOGRAPHY BY

Marc Carter

Natural History Museum of Los Angeles County

Published in conjunction with the exhibition
Genghis Khan: Treasures from Inner Mongolia

NATURAL HISTORY MUSEUM OF LOS ANGELES COUNTY
March to August 1994

AMERICAN MUSEUM OF NATURAL HISTORY, New York City
September to November 1994

TENNESSEE STATE MUSEUM, Nashville
December 1994 to March 1995

ROYAL BRITISH COLUMBIA MUSEUM, Victoria
March to September 1995

DHL Worldwide Express and Japan Airlines have provided
international transportation for the exhibition.

Assistance with international travel for personnel was provided
by Singapore Airlines.

Natural History Museum of Los Angeles County
Los Angeles, California 90007

Copyright © 1993 Natural History Museum of Los Angeles
County, Natural History Museum Foundation. All rights reserved.
Map on page 147 © 1993 Robert Marshall; courtesy of University of California Press.

LC 93-087480

ISBN 0-938644-34-3 hardcover
ISBN 0-938644-33-5 softcover

Printed in Singapore.

EXHIBITION PERSONNEL FOR THE
INNER MONGOLIA MUSEUM OF CHINA

Exhibit Designer: Shao Man
Conservators: Xia Hexiu, Chief Conservator; Ge Liming;
 Liu Chunbo; Eng He
Collection Managers: Fu Ning, Ding Yong, Zhao Aijun,
 Su Dong
Translator: Su Dong
Statue Maker: Zhang Heng. Statue Maker's Assistants:
 Xiong Jianman, Yang Yibin, and Jia Yifan
Model Makers: Bai Rui, Ba Hong
Sketch Artist: Gao Mei
Administration: Man Yong
Driver: Tao Xishun

EXHIBITION PERSONNEL FOR THE
NATURAL HISTORY MUSEUM OF LOS ANGELES COUNTY

Exhibit Designer: Jane Herwegh-Hellwitz
Registrar: Marin Jones
Taxidermist: Timothy A. Bovard
Sculptor: David Robert Cellitti
Costume Maker: Kevin Bennett
Exhibition Installation: Charles R. Fischer, Lauren M. Tawa,
 Renee Tedesco, Elliot White, Allan Matsumara,
 Donald J. Cocke
Facilities Support and Crafts Division: Robert Janeck, Supervisor
Exhibition Tour Coordinator: Barbara J. Rolfes
Publicity: Brett Henry
Administration: Elsa Garcia-Naveira

FRONT COVER: Gold-gilded bronze funerary mask. Liao dynasty,
907 to 1125. Collection of the Zhelimu League Museum.

BACK COVER: Cast gold pendant of a kneeling horse. Xianbei, Eastern Han to Western Jin eras (second to third centuries A.D.).
Collection of Zhelimu League Museum.

ENDSHEET: Provinces of the People's Republic of China. The
leagues of the Inner Mongolia Autonomous Region, and two of its
major cities—Huhehaote, its capital, and Chifeng—are shown.

FRONTISPIECE: Portrait of Genghis Khan in his sixties. Painting by a
Chinese artist on stretched silk. Courtesy of Palace Museum,
Taipei, Taiwan.

PAGE 6: Gold statue of a Qidan Apsaras (female spirit). Liao dynasty, 907 to 1125. Detail of Figure 71. Collection of Zhelimu
League Museum.

Contents

Foreword

THE NORTH AMERICAN TOUR of archaeological treasures from Inner Mongolia is an event of historical significance. The exhibition is the second organized by the Natural History Museum of Los Angeles County in an effort to focus attention on a mysterious and important part of the world—the ancient Silk Road of Eurasia, which has remained substantially forgotten in the West since the middle part of our century. As one of the earliest established museums on the Pacific Rim, we are firmly committed to the promotion of East/West scientific and cultural exchange. It is our expectation that this exhibition from the People's Republic of China will encourage development of international cooperation to advance archaeological work and field exploration in the century to come.

In mounting the exhibition, we have had assistance from a number of institutions and individuals. The Board of Governors and Trustees of the Natural History Museum has given approval and support for the endeavor at each critical stage in planning, as has the Board of Supervisors of the County of Los Angeles; Michael D. Antonovich, Supervisor of the Fifth District, and William A. Mingst of the Board of Trustees have been especially helpful. Peng Qingyun, Vice Director of the Bureau of Cultural Relics of the Chinese central government in Beijing, was instrumental in obtaining central government approval for the exhibition's tour to other museums in North America. Ambassador Ma Yuzhen, Former Consul General of the People's Republic of China to Los Angeles, was very helpful to us in the early stages of our negotiations. And we are indebted to Jiao Xuedai, Director of the Inner Mongolia Department of Culture, and the Vice Director there, Zhao Fangzhi, for their help with logistics and their gracious hospitality to our delegations to Huhehaote.

The exhibition was assembled for transport by the Inner Mongolia Museum of China in Huhehaote and contains a great number of objects from this museum's collections; but it also contains material from the Archaeology Research Institute of the Chinese National Academy of Social Sciences in Beijing and from eight other institutions in Inner Mongolia: the Cultural Relics Management Bureau of Ningcheng County, Chifeng; the Chifeng Municipal Museum; the Balinzuo Banner Museum,

Chifeng; the Ordos Museum, Dongsheng; the Zhelimu League Museum; the Cultural Relics Work Station of Wulanchabu League, Jining; the Hulunbeier Cultural Relics Work Station; and the Wengniute Banner Cultural Relics Management Office. We are grateful to Shao Qinglong, Director of the Inner Mongolia Museum of China, and his staff and to the directors and staffs of the other museums for their cooperation.

Officials of the state departments of the United States and the People's Republic of China gave us a great deal of assistance. We thank Wang Xuexian, the Chinese Consul General of Los Angeles, and Xiang Xiaowei and Liu Jikang, the former and current Cultural Attache of the Los Angeles Chinese Consul General's, for their support. I am also grateful to Eugene A. Nojek, Cultural Affairs Officer of the U.S. Embassy in Beijing.

Adam T. Kessler has served as curator for the exhibition, selecting objects and exploring their histories and interrelationships for this book and the exhibition and working tirelessly to make the complex cultures that the objects represent come alive for their new Western audience. Catherine Krell, Deputy Director of Marketing and Public Affairs, has overseen the public programming related to the exhibit for the Natural History Museum, and James D. Olson, Chief of Exhibitions, has administered the exhibition's design and tour. Robin A. Simpson, Head of Publications, edited the book and coordinated the photography and book production effort of an excellent team. Jane Herwegh-Hellwitz, Exhibit Designer, has created a dramatic and compelling installation for the exhibition.

Lee Yukuan provided important background information on a number of the relics in the exhibition and also facilitated arrangements at several key points in the exhibition's creation, and we are most appreciative of his involvement.

The museum has received assistance with international transportation from the exhibition's national sponsor, DHL Worldwide Express and Japan Airlines; we are grateful to L. Patrick Lupo, Chairman and Chief Executive Officer of DHL International Ltd., for his commitment to this important project. We thank our colleagues at the American Museum of Natural History in New York City, the Tennessee State Museum in Nashville, and the Royal British Columbia Museum in Victoria for their efforts on behalf of the exhibition's North American tour.

I am very pleased to present this exciting exhibition to the people of the United States and Canada, and I thank everyone who contributed to its realization.

CRAIG C. BLACK
Director, Natural History Museum of
　Los Angeles County

Cultural relics from the Inner Mongolia Autonomous Region of China are being exhibited for the first time in North America. This event is the result of joint effort on the part of museum staffs of China, the United States, and Canada, and it is an achievement that deserves celebration. I take this opportunity, as a representative of the staff of the Inner Mongolia Museum of China, to express our deep thanks to our American counterparts for their sincere and enthusiastic support, and to express our admiration for the fruits of their efforts.

The Inner Mongolia Autonomous Region is situated on China's northern border. A beautiful and richly endowed area with a long history, it has been the stage upon which nomadic peoples acted for millennia. From the beginning of their civilized history we can see how well-known confederations of tribes of the Eurasian steppe—such as the Eastern Hu, Xiongnu, Wuhuan, Qidan, and Mongols—developed, expanded, merged together, or disappeared. They came like travellers; arriving on horseback, one after the other, and departing with a flourish of their whips, they each contributed to an important chapter of Chinese history. In particular, Genghis Khan of the thirteenth century established a Mongolian national entity that had a profound effect on China and the world. Inner Mongolia is presumed to have been the birthplace of Genghis Khan and is now homeland to more than 3 million people of Mongolian descent, who are important members of China's polity.

Since the founding of the People's Republic of China, archaeological excavations in Inner Mongolia have yielded important discoveries. With each succeeding field expedition, more magnificent cultural relics of the northerners have become known, reflecting the elegance and unusual creative abilities of these people. In particular, the Neolithic cultures of the north and the cultures of the Xiongnu, Xianbei, Qidan, and Mongols have aroused admiration and are becoming the subject of international research.

Building on the many exquisite objects that have been excavated in Inner Mongolia, and thanks to the concerted effort and cooperation of the staffs of museums in both China and North America—especially those of the Inner Mongolia Museum of China in Huhehaote and the Natural History Museum of Los Angeles County, we are able to present to the people of the West the exhibition and this book, which systematically introduce research on the objects. I have no doubt that the exhibition will promote cultural exchange and mutual understanding.

The cultural relics from Inner Mongolia not only are priceless possessions of China but are important riches in the world's treasure house. This common cultural heritage brings us together. In a farewell message to an acquaintance going to live far away, the Tang dynasty poet Wang Bo wrote, "The people within the seas are intimate friends, the margins of heaven are like neighbors." We hope that this exhibit and book will create a cultural tie and a bridge of friendship between China and North America and will allow our peoples to become true friends. By studying the past we gain new insights into the present; through familiarity with the old, we can create the new and make a joint contribution to the understanding of world civilization.

ZHAO FANGZHI
Director, Archaeological Research Institute
    of the Inner Mongolia Museum of China
Vice Director of the Department of Culture, Inner
    Mongolia Autonomous Region of China

Preface

THE NORTH AMERICAN EXHIBITION of treasures from the Inner Mongolia Autonomous Region is truly a cause for celebration. The artifacts were excavated during recent decades by archaeologists laboring at sites all over Inner Mongolia, and their finds are nothing short of extraordinary. Their work is unknown for the most part in the West, and recognition of their feats is long overdue. Indeed, only in recent years has there been acknowledgment for the contributions of Inner Mongolian archaeology in China itself.

For the past several years, I have had the opportunity to travel extensively in Inner Mongolia to survey archaeological sites. Its climate has left us with an astonishing array of well-preserved ancient settlements, cities, burial sites, and artifacts. Each time that I returned, there was news of a plethora of new discoveries, significant not only for the study of the origins of Chinese civilization and the development of Chinese dynastic history, but also for a deeper understanding of the role that eastern Eurasia played in world history. I believe that Inner Mongolia is one of the remaining great archaeological frontiers. Its continued exploration in the twenty-first century promises to unlock many mysteries.

I have consulted at length with Inner Mongolian specialists about their work. In considering the conclusions of these scholars, it should be borne in mind that the modern boundaries that define the Mongolian land mass were nonexistent in ancient times, when there was only the Great Wall and the frontier (referred to in Chinese as the *sawai)* beyond it. I do not exaggerate when I report that the scholars whose work is cited in this book are among the most skilled archaeologists working in the world today. They are enthusiastic and persevering, and truly visionary. Their pioneering spirit is admirable.

Western sinologists sometimes remark that Chinese archaeologists uncritically accept their ancient texts; there has been a tendency in western circles to suspect these written records for their inherent bias against the peoples of China's northern frontier. Ancient and medieval Chinese accounts of the peoples beyond the Great Wall indeed are disjointed and often pejorative; even the names China adopted for the northerners were laden with contempt. No one better recognizes the bias than the Inner Mongolian archaeologist, who also knows that these records are nevertheless valuable sources for archaeological research. As I see it, the ancient texts have much to contribute to an integrated view of world history and to the foundation for Silk Road archaeology of the future.

I was greatly assisted in the preparation of this book by Dr. Bettine Birge, Assistant Professor in the Department of East Asian Languages and Cultures at the University of Southern California, who translated the contributions of our Chinese colleagues and reviewed the final manuscript. Peter R. Lee assisted Dr. Birge.

A few words regarding the translations: The *pinyin* system of romanization has been used for Chinese words, phrases, terms, and proper names. Except for the Mongol names in Chapter 6, the names of non-Chinese peoples have also been written in *pinyin*, with alternate spellings given in parentheses where appropriate. The reader should also know that in Inner Mongolia there are different geographic administrative divisions than in the rest of China. A banner *(qi)* is the equivalent of a county *(xian);* a league *(meng)* is a larger administrative unit that includes a number of banners or counties. The area around some major cities, such as Huhehaote, Baotou, or Chifeng, has been designated a municipal district *(shi diqu)* and has status equivalent to that of a league.

I am also indebted to Dr. Ruth W. Dunnell, Storer Assistant Professor of Asian History at Kenyan College, who reviewed the manuscript for the Natural History Museum and made a number of thoughtful suggestions and corrections. Dr. Chou Hung-hsiang, Professor of East Asian Languages and Cultures at University of California at Los Angeles, was of great assistance to me in interpretation of ancient inscriptions.

I would like to express my sincerest gratitude to the many people in China and North America who worked so hard to bring this exhibition into being. Peng Qingyun, Vice Director of the Bureau of Cultural Relics of the Chinese central government, is a man of unfailing commitment to the advancement of East/West scientific exchange. Li Quanxi, the former director of the Department of Culture of the Inner Mongolia Autonomous Region, assisted us with our initial preparations in Huhehaote; Mr. Li died recently, but I am certain that he would have been gratified to see his dream for this American exhibition come to fruition. Su Jun and Wang Dafang of the Inner Mongolia Department of Culture were untiring in their efforts to gain approval for the exhibition with the Chinese central government; they also provided me with valuable archaeological field notes.

Wen Hao, former director of the Inner Mongolia Museum of Huhehaote, gave moral and intellectual support, and his successor, Shao Qinglong, was most helpful with the final arrangements. Marc Carter worked with great dedication to photograph the exhibition's artifacts. Kong Qun, chief photographer of the Inner Mongolia Museum, also worked long hours for us, taking supplemental photographs and searching the museum archives for rare images.

I was given excellent source materials by Wu Zhanhai and Wang Zhihao, the Director and Vice Director of the Ordos Museum in Dongsheng; Chen Tangdong, Director of the Cultural Relics Work Station of Wulanchabu League in Jining; and Zhen Long, Director of the Baotou City Cultural Relics Station. Liu Huanzhen, Research Associate of the Baotou Station, shared information on the provenance of ancient artifacts and accompanied me on surveys of archaeological sites.

I would like to thank the many members of the Inner Mongolia Institute of Archaeology who provided assistance, including Li Yiyou, former director of the Institute of Archaeology; Tian Guangjin, the institute's recently retired director, and his wife Guo Suxin; and Ta La, one of the institute's administrators of field excavations.

Other valuable assistance was given by Tian Guanglin of the Research Institute of Northern Peoples Cultural Affairs in Chifeng; Xiang Chunsong, Director of the Chifeng Municipal Museum; and Jin Yongtian, Director of the Balinzuo Banner Museum.

I am grateful to my father, Dr. Jascha F. Kessler, Professor of English and Modern Literature at University of California at Los Angeles, who reviewed the draft at various stages and made a number of helpful suggestions.

I am deeply indebted to Lee Yukuan, who at 91 years of age, remains one of the foremost Chinese antiquarian experts of the twentieth century. Mr. Lee provided introduction to officials in Beijing and Inner Mongolia and travelled with us over formidable distances to the Ordos steppeland. His commitment to advancing understanding of authenticity of ancient Chinese culture is extraordinary. I am also grateful to Li Jingtai of Beijing, Mr. Lee's nephew, for his selfless assistance to me during my travels.

Finally, I am most grateful to Dr. Craig C. Black for the confidence that he has shown in me and my work and for his foresight and determination in conceiving of and administering this worthwhile project.

Introduction

THE GREAT EURASIAN STEPPE extends from the plains of Hungary in southeastern Europe far into northern Asia. Although it is bordered by a variety of different terrains, such as tundra, forest, and desert, essentially it is a vast, treeless area covered by a growth of grasses suitable mainly for animal husbandry. The Asian part of the steppe, a region of about 2.6 million square kilometers (1 million square miles), stretches from China's Xinjiang Uighur Autonomous Region in the west to the Manchurian provinces in the east, and from Siberia in the north to the Great Wall of China in the south. In the twentieth century, this area has been divided into two political entities—the state of Mongolia (formerly the Mongolian People's Republic) and the Inner Mongolia Autonomous Region, a province of the People's Republic of China.

From around 400 B.C. on, Chinese states—such as the Zhao, the Yen, and the Qin—began to erect defensive walls along portions of their northern frontier, and early in the third century B.C., the Qin dynasty constructed a Great Wall, in large part by joining the older walls. In the centuries that followed, various portions of the Great Wall were built and rebuilt—by non-Chinese states such as the Northern Wei (A.D. 386 to 534), the Liao dynasty (907 to 1125), and the Jin (1115 to 1234) as well as Chinese dynasties. Remains of many of these ancient walls, which were constructed of pounded earth or layered stones, can still be found throughout Inner Mongolia. But the Great Wall with which we are most familiar is the masonry and earth structure built by the Ming (1368 to 1644), which extends for thousands of kilometers from the Yellow Sea deep into central Asia.

The Great Wall was primarily intended as a barrier against incursions from the north. The recent discovery of a series of ancient cities with north-facing wall fortifications in Inner Mongolia indicates that the concept of a northern line of

Opposite: The Mongols employ a siege engine in attacking a city. From a manuscript of Jami' al-tawarikh, by Rashīd al-Dīn. Courtesy Bildarchiv Preussischer Kulturbesitz, Berlin.

13

TIME FRAME	CHINA	PEOPLES BEYOND THE GREAT WALL
50,000 years ago to 3rd millenium B.C.	Paleolithic, Neolithic, Pre-dynastic	Ordos Man; Dayaocun Man; culture types: Xinglongwa, Zhaobaogou, Hongshan, Laohushan, Xiajiadian Lower Period.
3rd to 2nd millenium B.C.	Xia (c. 2050-1650 B.C.) Shang (c. 1650-1100 B.C.)	Xunyu, Guifang

11th to 2nd centuries B.C.	Zhou (c. 1100-881 B.C.)
	  Spring and Autumn (722-481 B.C.)
	  Warring States (403-221 B.C.)
		Rong, Di, Linhu, Loufan, Eastern Hu, Xiongnu

2nd century B.C. to 2nd century A.D.	Qin (221-207 B.C.) Western Han (206 B.C.- 8 A.D.) Xin (8-23 A.D.) Eastern Han (25-220 A.D.)	Xiongnu, Wusun, Yuezhi, Wuhuan, Xianbei

2nd to 6th centuries	Three Kingdoms (220-280 A.D.)
	Western Jin (265-316 A.D.)
	Sixteen Kingdoms (301-439 A.D.)
	Southern Dynasties (317-589 A.D.)
	Northern Dynasties
	  Northern Wei (386-534 A.D.)
	  Eastern Wei (534-550 A.D.)
	  Western Wei (535-556 A.D.)
	  Northern Qi (550-577 A.D.)
	  Northern Zhou (557-581 A.D.)
		Wuhuan, Xianbei (founded Northern Wei), Rouran, Zhi, Qiang

6th to 9th centuries	Sui (581-617 A.D.) Tang (618-907 A.D.)	Tujue (Turk), Huigu (Uighur), Tuyuhun, Mohe, Xi
9th to 13th centuries	Five Kingdoms (907-960 A.D.) Liao (907-1125 A.D.) Northern Song (960-1127 A.D.) Southern Song (1127-1279 A.D.) Jin (1115-1234 A.D.)	Qidan (Khitan; founded the Liao dynasty), Nüzhen (Jurchen; founded Jin dynasty), Dangxiang (Tangut; founded Xixia state, 1032-1226 A.D.)
13th to 14th centuries	Yuan (1279-1368 A.D.)	Mongols
14th century to 1911	Ming (1368-1644 A.D.) Qing (1644-1911 A.D.)	Mongols, Tatars, Manchus (founded the Qing dynasty)
1911 to 1949	Republic	
1949 to present	People's Republic of China	

Chronological Table

defense had precedents in ancient China that date as far back as the third millenium B.C. Although the Great Wall was never completely successful in repelling the invasion of northerners, it was nevertheless a daunting obstacle in the era before the widespread use of incendiary devices. But the Great Wall is perhaps best understood as a demarcation of the frontier between two very different ways of life—the agrarian existence of central China and the pastoral nomadism of the steppelands to the north.

MONGOLIA, CHINA'S INNER MONGOLIA, and several geographic features of the eastern steppelands derive their names from the Mongols, one of the most influential and certainly the best-known of the nomadic confederations of tribes to have emerged from beyond the Great Wall. At the close of the thirteenth century, the Mongols had campaigned in regions as far apart as Poland, Palestine, and Japan. The Mongolian empire—which extended from Hungary to Korea and included most of Asia and good portions of eastern Europe—was the largest that has existed in human history, vaster by far than that of Alexander the Great.

The Mongols built their empire through conquest, and their military feats have been studied and admired for generations. Trained from their early years to hunt from horseback, they were superlative equestrians and archers. In their traditional annual hunting expedition, called the *nerge*, a vast ring of mounted hunters

14

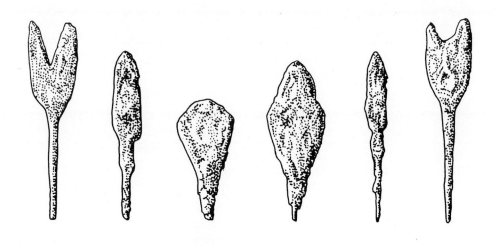

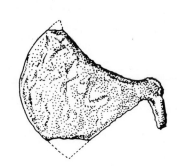

tens of kilometers in circumference would coordinate their movements to contract around and gradually corral all the wild game before them. This exercise was in every respect a practical training for military situations.

During war time, every male under the age of 60 was responsible for military service. The Mongols thus had available a well-trained force of cavalry that could be swiftly mobilized (Morgan, 1986). Even in peace time, all able-bodied men were under military orders (Sinor, 1981).

The Mongol warrior was always well-equipped. As with his ancestral predecessors, his foremost ally was his horse, which was related to the Przevalsky *(Equus przewalskii poliakoff)*, one of the only breeds of wild horse to have survived into modern times. This stocky, pony-like animal was tough and nimble and could travel at a good speed and endure long journeys (Sinor, 1981). Its dense coat and its ability to forage beneath snow made it ideal for winter fighting. It was also very obedient and even-tempered, even in the midst of the clangor of battle. Each Mongol soldier had a string of about five horses available to him during a campaign (Morgan, 1986).

The Mongol warrior's primary weapon was the compound bow, which had a pull of about 70 kilograms (160 pounds) and a range of more than 180 meters (200 yards). The arrows he employed (carried in bundles of thirty in separate quivers) included lightweight missiles with small sharp points for long-range firing and heavier ones with broad heads for close combat (Turnbull and McBride, 1980). Studies of extant arrowheads have shown that the Mongols also used armor-piercing arrows (Alekseev, 1989). Other Mongol weapons included small battleaxes and a long lance fitted with a hook for pulling enemies from their saddles. Although records differ in their accounts, it appears that the Mongol fighter wore leather armor that was weatherproofed with a covering of crude lacquer made from pitch. In Yuan times (1279 to 1368), he wore a metal helmet (Turbull and McBride, 1980).

The Mongol warrior was robust, capable of riding days on end and nourishing himself without cooked food: he consumed dried milk curd, millet meal, and meat that he cured by placing it under his saddle, and he drank blood from an incision cut into the neck of his horse. When the army paused to hunt, the men would eat dogs, wolves, foxes, horses, rats, mice, lice, and even the afterbirth of their mares (Turnbull and McBride, 1980).

Although the actual size of the Mongol army is a matter of debate, it at times contained at least 125,000 men and was organized according to a decimal system, with the largest unit, a *tumen,* corresponding to a modern division (10,000 men). Transfer from one unit to another within the army was forbidden, and it was by creating ethnically diverse units that Genghis Khan broke up the tribal associations of the nomadic groups that he conquered and enforced obedience to his house (Morgan, 1981).

Discipline was severe and pragmatic: desertion and failure to follow the bold

Top : Examples of iron arrowheads *(left)* and the head of a socketed battleax retrieved from Kara Khorum, the site of the Mongol capital from the time of Genghis Khan's son, Ögödei. From Phillips, 1969.

Right: A *paizi,* a metal plate issued by the Mongols to officials or other travelers to serve as a diplomatic passport. Facsimile of the bronze piece with raised writing in the Mongol 'Phags-pa (*Baisiba*) script housed in the Gansu Provincial Museum, Lanzhou. A comparable piece of iron with silver inlay with Mongol 'Phags-pa (*Baisiba*) script has recently been acquired by the Metropolitan Museum of Art.

in an attack or to rescue members of one's unit that had been captured by the enemy were punishable by death (Sinor, 1981), as were plundering without permission or sleeping while on guard (Phillips, 1969).

The Mongols made use of sophisticated military tactics. For example, in their conquest of the Jin dynasty in north China, they were minutely scrupulous in preparation of their materials; they also gathered information by spying and scouting, and they exploited the Jin's internal political conflicts by courting defectors (Zhu Qingze and Li Penggui, 1983).

The Mongols' system of long-distance communication permitted rapid contact between the most remote parts of their immense empire. This network, called the *Yam* in Turkish, was established by Genghis Khan's successor, Ögödei, for use within the territory of his own khanate and was later extended throughout the empire. Post stations were placed every 40 to 50 kilometers (25 to 30 miles—about a day's travel on horseback); each station was supplied by local inhabitants with a stock of horses and fodder for the use of travelers carrying a tablet of authority (*paizi* in Chinese, *gerege* in Mongolian). Express couriers, who carried the documents entrusted to them upon their person throughout their journeys, wore belts of bells or carried horns to signal their approach to a post station; upon their arrival their remounts would be waiting and ready. In emergencies, these messengers strained their endurance to the utmost, sometimes covering over 300 kilometers (almost 200 miles) in a single day (Morgan, 1986).

Remains of pounded-earth defensive wall built by the Zhao state from 306 to 300 B.C. located at Wusutu Village, north of modern-day Huhehaote. The Zhao wall stands approximately 1 to 2 meters (3 to 6.5 feet) tall, and its pounded-earth layers are each about 10 centimeters (4 inches) thick.

Mongol forces were capable of coming together with remarkable speed and would advance in organized columns, coordinating their movements by signalling with flags by day and with lanterns raised and lowered in the dark of night. Scouts were sent ahead, not just to gather information but to test the opponent: if outnumbered, they would draw the enemy warriors into pursuit and lead them directly into the hands of the main Mongol group. Light cavalry would dash through openings in the front ranks of the heavily equipped forces, showering the opposing soldiers with arrows and javelins and working to encircle them; when the foe was in disarray, the heavy cavalry would take over the attack (Turnbull and McBride, 1980). If necessary, the Mongols resorted to various strategems; they staged fake retreats, during which fleeing warriors would turn backwards in their saddles and shoot arrows at the enemy, and they obscured the battle area and confused their opponents by burning reeds to create smoke screens or stirring up clouds of dust.

The Mongols were not successful in every military encounter, and they were quick to realize their own limitations and to adopt new forms of technology. For example, one of their first attempts at besieging the Xia capital in 1209 ended in failure: they tried to flood the city and instead inundated their own encampment. To deal with such unfamiliar problems as the siege of a fortified city, the Mongols began to employ technicians from China (and later the Middle East) to plan and supervise their attacks. These experts procured siege catapults for the Mongols; the siege machines were operated by twelve to twenty-four men pulling ropes and could hurl projectiles such as rocks, clay balls, or incendiary devices hundreds of paces.

Although we acknowledge that "Rome was not built in a day," Westerners are quick to assume the spontaneous generation of a historical phenomenon such as the Mongols. There is, moreover, a tendency to shroud the cultural heritage of a steppe empire like that of the Mongols in a mysterious and impenetrably dark past. Over the last 45 years, however, archaeologists of the Inner Mongolia Autonomous Region of the People's Republic of China have made remarkable strides in studying the cultures of the Mongols and earlier peoples of the eastern Eurasian steppe. Their work has given us opportunity to test the veracity of ancient Chinese records of these societies as well as to deepen our understanding of the interplay between nomadic and sedentary cultures in the context of world history.

Their discoveries emphasize the value of viewing the Mongol conquests not as an isolated phenomenon but as the culmination of a continuous historical process. From this perspective, we can see that the Mongols were but the last in a long series of steppe empires to emerge from east Asia. They were truly the inheritors of a rich past.

SINCE THE TURN of the twentieth century, scholars have scrutinized archaeological remains from the Eurasian steppe in an effort to learn more about the origins of the nomadic pastoralism that developed there. As Sevyan I. Vainshtein points out (1989), the evidence seems to confirm the prevalent theory that tribes of farmer-herders living in demanding ecological conditions turned increasingly to animal husbandry, grew steadily more migratory, and by 1000 B.C., became what are now typically recognized as pastoral nomads.

Qiao Shaoqin (1992) sees a similar evolution in northern China. He maintains that nomadic culture originally developed in regions where grassland was juxtaposed to cultures that had long persisted through a mixed economy of agriculture and animal husbandry. Qiao believes that alterations in climate provided the stimulus for a specialized pastoral nomadic economy.

Ancient Chinese inscriptions and texts use various appellations in describing the populations of nomads living along the northern frontier of China in ancient times. Central China constantly contended with these peoples during the late Shang and early Western Zhou dynasties (circa fourteenth century to 881 B.C.), and from that time through the Spring and Autumn and the Warring States eras (722 to 221 B.C.), the northerners were referred to in Chinese as the *Rong* and the *Di* (generic names applied to groups who lived in various locations). At the turn of the twentieth century, the great Chinese scholar Wang Guowei analyzed the character *Rong* and concluded that it derives from "armor" and "spear." He considered it a general name for weaponry that therefore labelled the northern people as aggressors or bandits who with weapons in hand encroached upon Chinese imperial lands. Wang interpreted the term *Di* to mean peoples of "distant or far away lands" (Wang Guowei, 1959).

We have learned much about the steppe empires from accounts of the sedentary societies that struggled with them. Given the adversarial relationship between the nomadic powers and settled Chinese civilization, however, it is not surprising that records of sedentary states describe the material culture of their "barbarian" neighbors in vague, disjointed, and often disparaging terms. As a consequence, archaeologists have made tremendous efforts to supplement our knowledge of the peoples of the north. It is a worthwhile endeavor because the political confederations that the ancient peoples of Inner Mongolia and the steppe formed came to play a critical role in the developments of Chinese dynastic history. Furthermore, the influence of those confederations often extended into portions of Eurasia connecting China to the West, and they were important in promoting East/West cultural diffusion in the ancient world prior to the perfecting of maritime travel.

Like the Mongols, the earlier nomadic confederate states of the Eurasian steppe are particularly interesting because of the superiority of their military organization and tactics. Before the advent of gunpowder and firearms, their combination of horsemanship and archery, as well as their sophisticated deployment of superb cavalry, presented a deadly menace to the sedentary societies of the ancient world.

Cavalry warfare in Eurasia came about through a long process of historical evolution. Based on analysis of the wear of horse bits, David W. Anthony and Dorcas R. Brown (1991) maintain that horsemanship was practiced by Indo-

Yang Kuei-fei mounting a horse, by Ch'ien Hsuan. Yuan dynasty, 1279 to 1368. Courtesy Freer Gallery of Art (57.14), Smithsonian Institution, Washington, D.C.

European peoples of the Ukrainian steppes as early as 4000 B.C. Although there is contention over the question, it is likely that the horse had been domesticated in China during the late Neolithic era (circa third millennium B.C.), when it was harnessed to chariots as well as used as a draft animal. The technique of mounted warfare appears to have penetrated the east Asian steppe rather late.

Chinese records indicate that the Di rode horses as early as the Spring and Autumn era (722 to 481 B.C.; Ma Changshou, 1962). By the time of the Warring States (403 to 221 B.C.), the nomadic use of mounted men had become a form of warfare so powerful as to inspire emulation: the Zhao king Wuling ordered his militia to abandon the chariot warfare and weapons heretofore used in China and to adopt the nomads' way of deploying archers on horseback. As of the fifth century A.D., the combined use of saddle and stirrup had markedly improved the mobility and striking power of cavalry from the empires of the northern steppe (Karl A. Wittfogel and Feng Chia-sheng, 1949; Qi Dongfang, 1993).

Through Inner Mongolian archaeology, we have gained insight into the basic integrity and continuity of culture beyond the Great Wall. Many of the features that contributed to the Mongols' military might had origins in the steppe empires of east Asia that preceded them. For example, Chinese texts describe the training of Mongol youths to hunt on horseback from an early age in terms almost identical to those used to outline the training given to Xiongnu youths who lived some 1500 years earlier (Sinor, 1981). The steps that Genghis Khan had taken to reorganize the militia and break up tribal allegiances that might threaten his authority were similar to those used by the Xianbei leader, Tuoba Gui, in forming the Northern Wei dynasty (A.D. 386 to 534). The hunting exercises, military organization, and battle tactics of the Mongols were largely present in a sophisticated form among the Qidan people who established the Liao Dynasty

(A.D. 907 to 1125). In fact, some of the Mongols' most important military advisors were Qidan officials who had defected from the Jin Dynasty (A.D. 1115 to 1234). The Mongol post system and the tablets of authority that their messengers carried were also derived from the Qidan, who had instituted such a communications network during the Liao dynasty (Morgan, 1986).

I N THE EARLY PART of this century, the surveys and excavations of western archaeologists such as Peter Kozloff of Russia, Aurel Stein of England, and Sven Hedin of Sweden first brought the ancient civilizations of the steppe to the attention of the West. In recent years there has been resurgence of interest among westerners in the trade routes across the Eurasian landmass because of the advances in political and economic contacts between China and the West that they fostered (Wilford, 1993).

Many Western scholars formerly believed that key aspects of Chinese material culture were derived from people to the north or west, carried along the trade routes and anciently imported. In some matters as yet unresolved, such as the question of the origin of blue and white porcelain, this diffusionist notion is still strong. However, the accumulation of archaeological discoveries from within China, particularly in the last two decades, indicates that many components of Chinese material culture originated there, independent of outside influence. These discoveries put us in a position to study the impact that China's accomplishments had on the peoples beyond the Great Wall, and through them on societies farther to the north and west.

Siege engines used by the Mongols; these were ballistae for throwing stones or other heavy objects at the enemy. After Phillips, 1969.

The question of contacts between Asia and the West is therefore of considerable interest to Inner Mongolian scholars. Tian Guanglin (1992) points out that one of the oldest of the many routes connecting China to the West passed through Inner Mongolia and discusses the cultural diffusion that such routes fostered. For example, recent archaeological discoveries challenge the long-held notion that the bronze culture of the Ordos area of Inner Mongolia had its origins elsewhere on the Eurasian steppe, pointing instead to the impact that the dynastic civilization of central China had on the early development of bronze technology in the Ordos. In fact, because of these finds, Tian Guangjin and Guo Suxin (1986) have proposed a thorough reevaluation of the influence of the Ordos on the rise of the bronze cultures of Siberia and the Black Sea region.

T HE TRADE ROUTES between east Asia and Europe are collectively known in the West as "the Silk Road," because in ancient dynastic times silk was one of China's main exports. Chinese records, and archaeological retrievals such as the woven silk fabrics uncovered in the late 1950s at the Neolithic Qianshanyang site in China's Zhejiang province, indicate that at least as early as the second millennium B.C., China had already mastered the production of silk.

Various recent isolated archaeological finds have offered tantalizing evidence of the spread of Chinese silk products to the West. Remains of silk cloth dating as far back as the sixteenth century B.C. have been found in the distant regions of what was formerly Soviet central Asia (Campbell, 1986). The discovery of silk in the hair of an Egyptian mummy dating from about 1000 B.C. has stirred excitement among western scholars (Wilford, 1993); scientific analysis supports the notion that this silk was Chinese in origin (Lubec, et al., 1993). Silk embroidery dating from the fifth century B.C. found at the Pazyryk site in the Altai mountains of Siberia appears to be Chinese (Artamonov, 1965), and Chinese silks have also been retrieved from seventh century B.C. graves in Germany and fifth century B.C. burials in Greece (Campbell, 1993).

Men in cangues (neck pillories) are led off by their Mongol captors. From a manuscript of Jami' al-tawarikh, by Rashīd al-Dīn. Courtesy Bildarchiv Preussischer Kulturbesitz, Berlin.

The Mongols have intrigued westerners in part because of a strange fascination with accounts of their ruthlessness. Hundreds of thousands, perhaps millions, died at their hands. A notorious example of their cruelty was the custom of setting captives taken from recently conquered cities in the front rank of an assault, forcing the besieged to kill their fellow countrymen as they defended themselves.

East Asian contacts with the West gained impetus during the Western Han dynasty (206 B.C. to A.D. 25), in large measure because of struggles between the Han dynasty and the Xiongnu, who formed one of the first powerful steppe empires along China's northern frontier. After defeats suffered at the hands of the Xiongnu, the Han maintained tentative peace with them through marital ties and the payment of annual tribute of large quantities of Chinese products, of which a great amount was silk. The Xiongnu had conquered vast territories in northern and central Asia, and it is thus understandable that silk and other Chinese products should subsequently have made their way westward across Eurasia, as evidenced by twentieth-century discoveries of Chinese cultural products in Xiongnu burials in Mongolia and Siberia (Tian Guanglin, 1992).

The westward relocation of another people, the Yuezhi, during the Han also fostered China's contacts with the West. The Yuezhi, who had lived since time immemorial on the periphery of China—in the region between the Qilian Mountains and Dunhuang in modern-day Gansu province, were expelled far into central Asia during the Xiongnu conquests of the early second century B.C. and finally forced into the northern reaches of Afghanistan. In the late second century B.C., the Han court sent an emissary, Zhang Qian, to the distant Yuezhi to seek an alliance against the Xiongnu. Zhang Qian, who reached the Yuezhi only after being held a Xiongnu prisoner for many years, was unsuccessful in convincing them to join forces with the Han, but he returned with information critical to the Han's westward expansion and trade. Lin Meicun (1989) finds reason to believe that the Yuezhi were instrumental in bringing the famous jade stones of the distant Hetian oasis in central Asia to dynastic China; as he astutely points out, the role of the Yuezhi people in the initiation of East/West cultural exchange is one of the principal issues to be addressed in studies of the ancient Silk Road.

After their expulsion into northern Afghanistan, the Yuezhi founded the Buddhist Kushan state. Tang Xizi (1982) concludes that, from the time of the Eastern Han dynasty (A.D. 25 to 220), they were playing a crucial part in the transmission of the Buddhist religion to China. The introduction of Buddhism into China interests the Inner Mongolian specialist because many early Buddhist cultural relics have been uncovered in Inner Mongolia as well as in Chinese central Asia (Chen Sixian, 1979).

The Buddhist religion had gained great prominence in northern China by the fourth century A.D., when the Xianbei people founded the Northern Wei dynasty (A.D. 386 to 534). Several centuries before the birth of Christ, these people—tribes of the Eastern Hu confederation—had fled from the might of the Xiongnu empire, retreating into the Xingan Mountains of the northeasternmost regions of Inner Mongolia. But late in the first century A.D., the Xianbei were able to defeat the Xiongnu and gain control of their lands. Bu Yangwu and Cheng Sai (1992) have studied Xianbei bronze and iron cauldrons found in Inner Mongolia and determined that one of the earliest prototypes for such vessels is an Eastern Hu piece dating from the Warring States era (403 to 221 B.C.). Many similar vessels have been retrieved in Siberia, southern Russia, and especially Hungary, but these pieces date from several centuries after the birth of Christ (Maenchen-Helfen, 1973). These later objects, products of the Hunnic culture, raise intriguing questions: Is the presence of this type of vessel in eastern Europe related to the expansion of the Xianbei and their rise in power in northern and central Asia? Although few scholars still believe that the Huns were descendants of the Xiongnu, the issue of their connections with the material culture of eastern Eurasia remains.

The Xianbei conquered vast areas of western China and northern and central Asia, and their Northern Wei dynasty established garrisons to govern such outlying territories. The Northern Wei capital of Pingcheng (at modern-day Datong in northern Shaanxi province) was close to the Ordos and the steppe lands beyond the Yinshan mountains in Inner Mongolia. During the Northern Wei era, contacts with the West flourished over the Silk Road. In recent decades, archaeologists working in Gansu province and Inner Mongolia have found a great many artifacts of western provenance, such as coins and gold and silver artifacts from Constantinople and the Sassanian empire of Persia. These goods may have arrived in the East through the trade efforts or other western contacts of the Xianbei peoples (Tian Guanglin, 1992) and may be further evidence of the political power and influence of the Xianbei in central Asia.

A great expansion of East/West cultural contact along the Silk Road began during the Tang dynasty (A.D. 618 to 907) and continued during the Song (960 to 1279) and into the Yuan (1279 to 1368). Scholars of Inner Mongolia believe that the Qidan, who established the Liao dynasty (907 to 1125), the Dangxiang, the founders of the Xia state (1032 to 1226), and finally the Mongols all played critical roles in this process.

Inner Mongolian archaeology has made important contributions to our understanding of the ancient world as a whole—to the emerging picture of historical development in northern China as well as to the larger study of cultural contact between Asia and the West. I expect that during the twenty-first century, Inner Mongolian and western archaeologists will work together on the study of the Silk Road to further advance knowledge of the origins and development of ancient art and technology.

Bronze *fu* (cauldron) with twin lugs. Xianbei, Northern Wei (386 to 534). Unearthed from a tomb at Lingpi Village, Helingeer County, Huhehaote Municipal District. Height 51.7 cm; diameter of mouth 35 cm, of footring 13 cm. Each of the cauldron's round lugs has three mushroom-shaped ornaments.

1

Origins

Ⓘ N 1922 LOCAL GUIDES helped the Frenchman E. Licent carry out surveys in the Sjxara-osso-gol (Salawusu) River valley in southwestern Inner Mongolia. During the work, Licent uncovered various animal fossils and retrieved by surface collection three quite fossilized bones of human limbs. Excited by these preliminary discoveries, he teamed up with the biologist Teilhard de Chardin and in 1923 conducted a comprehensive survey of the area known by the Mongolian name *Ordos,* the northern grasslands that are bounded by the middle Yellow River and extend into eastern Ningxia, northern Shaanxi and northwestern Shanxi provinces, and southwestern Inner Mongolia. Licent and Chardin discovered ancient stone tools and fossilized vertebrate bones in two important locations: at Shuidonggou in eastern Ningxia and at Xiaoqiaopan near the banks of the Sjara-osso-gol River.

After the surveys, as they were sorting through the fossil remains of antelope teeth and fragments of ostrich eggs collected in 1922, the two scientists discovered a thoroughly fossilized left incisor tooth of an eight to nine year old child. Dr. Davidson Black of the Peking Xiehe Hospital studied the specimen and named it "the Ordos tooth." Since the 1940s, Chinese specialists have used the name "Ordos Man" to refer to the assemblages of human fossils and stone tools uncovered at Shuidonggou, Xiaoqiaoban, and other sites.

In the mid-1950s the Chinese archaeologist Wang Yuping conducted three separate surveys of the Sjara-osso-gol region looking for Paleolithic remains. At Dishaogouwan Village, approximately 4 kilometers (2 miles) west of the area Licent had surveyed in 1922, Wang—aided by a local boy—was fortunate to collect two more human fossils: the parietal portion of a skull (the part that forms the top and sides of the cranium; Fig. 1) and a femur (thigh bone). Between 1978 and 1980, teams of Chinese researchers retrieved another seventeen human fossils from the Sjara-osso-gol region, including a lower jaw bone (maxilla inferior); six of

Opposite: Pottery *li* (vessel with three bagged legs) with polychrome decoration. Xiajiadian Lower Period, 2300 to 1600 B.C. Unearthed in 1974 at the Dadianzi city site, Aohan Banner, east of Chifeng. Height 21.5 cm; diameter of mouth 6.3 cm. Collection of China National Academy of Social Sciences, Archaeology Research Institute.

Figure 1 (below). Fossil of the parietal portion of a human skull (external, *top*, and internal views). Retrieved in mid-1950s, Dishaogouwan Village, Sjara-osso-gol (Salawusu) River Valley, in the Ordos. Collection of Ordos Museum, Dongsheng.

This cranium fragment and twenty-two other human fossils collected in this region are the remains of "Ordos Man," who lived and hunted in southwestern Inner Mongolia approximately 35,000 years ago.

Figure 2 (right). Archaeologists at the Dayaocun site, approximately 33 km northeast of Huhehaote, circa 1973: From left to right are the eminent paleontologist Pei Wenzhong (1904 to 1982), Lu Zun'e, Professor of Archaeology at Beijing University, and Wang Yuping of the Inner Mongolia Museum. Courtesy of Inner Mongolia Museum, Huhehaote.

these human fossils were retrieved from geological strata. To date, a total of twenty-three fossils of young and mature, male and female Ordos Man have been found.

Many of the human fossils and cultural remains of Ordos Man have been retrieved from the Sjara-osso-gol River banks, which rise 70 to 80 meters (230 to 260 feet) above the river's water level. On the basis of a study of the geological strata from which six human fossils were retrieved during the 1978-1979 expeditions, it has been determined that Ordos Man lived during the late Pleistocene epoch. Carbon-14 tests further show that these people prospered in southwestern Inner Mongolia approximately 35,000 years ago.

Study of the morphology of the fossils has revealed Ordos Man to be *Homo sapiens sapiens*. While the cranial bone of Ordos Man appears to be somewhat thicker than those of modern people, it is thinner than that of the *Homo erectus* found in China. The facial curvature—the nonprotruding forehead and area between the eyebrows—is quite comparable to that of modern Mongols. Based on the fossil remains uncovered in the Sjara-osso-gol region, Wu Rukang (1958) has concluded that "Ordos Man's overall form appears to be closer to modern man's than that of his counterpart, the Neanderthal Man of Western Europe—indeed he appears to be the direct ancestor of the modern [Mongolian people]." Of particular interest to physical anthropologists is the fact that Ordos Man's incisor tooth has a shovel-shaped depression (as does Peking Man's) and that the parietal fossil found by Wang Yuping in the 1950s exhibits impressions of the major cranial arteries, the positions of which differ from those of modern humans.

During the late Pleistocene era, the Sjara-osso-gol region was moist and thickly vegetated. The climate was considerably warmer than it is today, and drought was infrequent. It is possible that a great deal of water flowed down from the mountains to form lakes in this area, and that in the vicinity of the banks of the

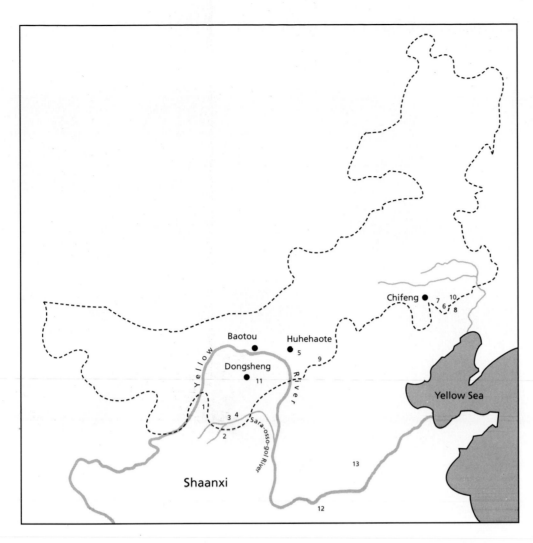

Archaeological sites, Paleolithic through early Shang dynasty.

1. Shuidonggou, Lingwu County, Ningxia Autonomous Region.
2. Xiaoqiaopan, Jingbian County, Shaanxi province.
3. Dishaogouwan, Wushen Banner, Yikezhao League.
4. Dagouwan, Wushen Banner, Yikezhao League.
5. Dayaocun, Huhehaote Municipal District, Wulanchabu League.
6. Xinglongwa, Aohan Banner, Zhaowuda League.
7. Zhaobaogou, Aohan Banner, Zhaowuda League.
8. Dongshancui, Kezuo County, Liaoning province.
9. Laohushan, Liangcheng County, Wulanchabu League.
10. Dadianzi, Aohan Banner, Zhaowuda League.
11. Zhukaigou, Yijinhuoluo Banner, Yikezhao League.
12. Eritou city site, Erlitou Village, Yanshi County, Henan Province.
13. Yinxu city site, Xiaotun Village, Anyang County, Henan Province.

Sjara-osso-gol River there were grasslands and forested areas. A variety of animals flourished in these conditions, as is evident from the tremendous quantity of animal fossils collected in the area since 1922. Among the forty-five kinds of vertebrates represented (thirty-four mammals and eleven birds) are the most complete fossil skeletons of a wild ass *(Equus hemionus* Pallas) and a rhinoceros *(Coelonta antiquitatis* Blumenbach) found within China to date.

Ordos Man subsisted in this rich environment principally as a hunter, and the Ordos Man of the Sjara-osso-gol employed flint and quartz—materials not particularly plentiful near the region—to make stone tools. Past scholars have maintained that these tools, which are relatively small in size, can be closely compared to the Perigordian and Aurignacian stone tool types of western Europe. However, with the accumulation of new evidence, Huang Weiwen and Wei Qi (1981) have determined that Ordos Man's tools can be more appropriately compared to those retrieved in the Zhoukoudian cave site (#I location) of Peking Man.

Ordos Man preyed upon such animals as wild boar *(Sus scrofa* L.), red deer *(Cervus elaphus* L.), Ordos Big Horn Deer *(Megaloceros ordosianus* Young), the so-called Wangshi Bison (named after a local woman killed in an accident during the Licent and Chardin surveys), and a variety of rodents and birds. Of interest are the discoveries made at the Shaojiagouwan site, which was first surveyed in 1923 by Licent and Chardin, who found a set of stone tools and smashed animal bones there. Over 300 antelope or gazelle horns *(Procapra picticaudata przewalskyi* Buchner) and *Gazella subgutturosa* Guldenst) have subsequently been retrieved from the site. From these discoveries, it is clear that the antelopes of the Sjara-osso-gol grasslands were one of Ordos Man's main prey. Moreover, these horns appear to have been broken from the antelopes' heads, lending credence to the notion that Ordos Man collected the horns to use as tools.

Figure 3. Tortoise-shell-shaped stone scrapers, Quaternary period, 50,000 to 10,000 years ago. Retrieved from Dayaocun site, approximately 33 km northeast of Huhehaote. Photograph by Kong Qun.

These late Pleistocene scrapers have thick, heavy bodies; they are domed on one side and flat and even on the other. The domed sides were worked from the edge of the core up, leaving a ridge line along the center of the scraper; some pieces appear to have been worked from as many as four different angles. In use, they were probably held with the fingers pinching toward the center of the domed side and pushed in a forward motion in skinning animals, cutting meat, or working animal hides.

Some of the smashed animal bones from Shaojiagouwan were burned and found in association with charcoal fragments. These facts can be considered together with the discovery of an oval ash pit by Wang Yuping in the late 1950s at the southwestern part of the Dagouwan site, approximately 15 meters (50 feet) above the level of the Sjara-osso-gol River: over thirty smashed and burnt animal bones were uncovered within the pit. In a word, it is evident that Ordos Man used fire to cook his food (Wang Yuping, 1961).

Another significant achievement of Inner Mongolian archaeologists in recent years is the uncovering of Paleolithic stone tool workshops up and down the Daqingshan mountain range. One of the most extraordinary of these is the Dayaocun site (Fig. 2), located approximately 33 kilometers (20 miles) east of the Inner Mongolian capital of Huhehaote. The site was discovered in 1973 and was thoroughly surveyed and excavated in 1976, 1979, and 1983. The excavations yielded over a thousand stone tools and revealed a Paleolithic stone tool workshop with a surface area of almost 2 million square meters (500 acres). Based upon the well-preserved stratigraphy uncovered at this site in 1983, Chinese geologists and paleontologists have determined that this stone tool workshop was in operation as early as 50,000 years ago and continued to be used even into the early Neolithic era. Although stone tool workshops have also been uncovered in Guangdong and Shanxi provinces, those sites date from the Neolithic, not the Paleolithic era.

Unlike in the Sjara-osso-gol area, the materials for stone tools are abundant at Dayaocun. The site is located along the southern foothills of the Daqing Mountains, which were formed in the Archaen (i.e., pre-Cambrian era) and are made up primarily of coarse granite and light and dark gray colored flint. The flint, which can be retrieved from the top half of the hills, is tough and tensile, making it an

ideal material for tools. Among the stone artifacts retrieved at Dayaocun are dish-shaped and prismatic cores, multisided choppers, scrapers, and handaxes. One of the most common stone tools uncovered is a scraper struck into a tortoise-shell-shaped core (Fig. 3). The way these scrapers were made and their special features suggest that they were used to pare or trim along a flat surface, such as when skinning an animal or working on a hide. Chinese geologists and paleontologists have determined that 50,000 to 60,000 years ago the area around the Dayaocun site was a richly vegetated terrain. Numerous animal fossils, some of which appear burned, indicate that—like the Paleolithic people of the Sjara-osso-gol area—the Paleolithic man of the Dayaocun was a hunter who cooked his prey.

Figure 4. Design of an unusual pottery *zun* ("jar"). Zhaobaogou culture type, circa 4500 B.C. Retrieved from Xiaoshan site, Aohan Banner. From Tian Guanglin, 1989.

    The motif is of supernatural creatures—a pig with a snake-like body and a flying deer with an extended scaly snake-like body below a horned head. These designs are being studied as examples of China's earliest images of the dragon.

S INCE THE ESTABLISHMENT of the People's Republic of China in 1949, Chinese archaeologists and historians have stepped up efforts to study the origins of Chinese civilization. The results, a plethora of extraordinary archaeological finds, are recorded in volumes of articles in scholarly journals. These discoveries have brought the understanding that while the material culture of ancient Chinese civilization seems to have had many different sources within China, it had already coalesced by the second millennium B.C. into the mature institutions characterizing China's first dynasty, the Xia (circa twenty-first to seventeenth centuries B.C.). Study of archaeological discoveries dating from the predynastic and Neolithic eras extending back 4,000 to almost 8,000 years has profoundly strengthened the hypothesis that the material culture and systems of belief of ancient China are autochthonous, stemming from an even more remote past.

    The discoveries made in the northern parts of China, particularly in the Inner Mongolia Autonomous Region from the 1970s on, deserve recognition for their relevance to the emerging picture of the origins of Chinese civilization. Over a hundred different sites belonging to the Neolithic, predynastic, and dynastic eras have been found within Inner Mongolia. These sites, which are located in widely separated areas, vary in size from settlements to walled cities. The sites in the northeast around Chifeng City (northeast of current-day Beijing) and those in the Ordos below the northern bend of the Yellow River are especially significant.

    Around 10,000 years ago (at the beginning of the Holocene era) the fauna of the Pleistocene became extinct and a different climate came into being. During subsequent millennia, the climate grew warmer and moister. It is in that context that we see the emergence of agricultural society in Inner Mongolia. In the 1970s and 1980s, archaeologists excavated a series of settlements on the hilltops and in elevated flat areas near the Xilamulun River (north of Chifeng) that date from approximately 6000 B.C. These remains have been termed the Xinglongwa culture type, the model site of which is in Aohan Banner (County), east of Chifeng.

    The Xinglongwa settlement in the southeastern region of Aohan Banner is well organized and spread across an area of approximately 20,000 square meters (5 acres). Over a hundred semisubterranean rectangular houses are lined up in

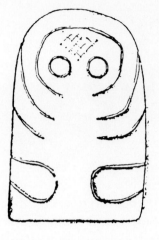
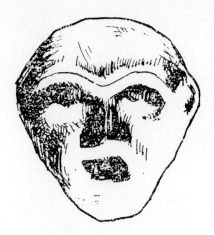

Figure 5 *(left)*. Sketch of a granite human figurine. Xinglongwa culture type, circa 6000 B.C. Retrieved from southeastern Aohan Banner. From Tian Guanglin, 1989.

This pillar-shaped statue is 10 cm high and has a smooth, glossy surface and a flat bottom. Incised lines depict an abstract figure of a person kneeling with arms extended over the chest. The head is disproportionately large; cross-hatched lines above the large round eyes represent hair.

Figure 6 *(right)*. Sketch of a pottery ornament representing a human head. Zhabaogou culture type, circa 4500 B.C. Retrieved at Xiaoshan site, Aohan Banner. Height 5.1 cm; width 4.5 cm. From Tian Guanglin, 1989.

The bridge of the nose is long, and slender and curving eyebrows extend over the large eyes.

rows, surrounded by an uneven oval-shaped protective ditch. The houses vary in size from about 20 to 140 square meters (200 to 1,500 square feet).

The majority of the agricultural tools uncovered at the Xinglongwa settlement in Aohan Banner are made of stone. The most representative of these tools has an angle of construction and striation marks that indicate it was a hoe used to dig up earth. At the beginning of the Holocene, the area around Aohan Banner was forest and rich grassland, and the shovel-shaped stone tools, axes, and adzes (a cutting tool with a thin arched blade set at a right angle to the handle) were used for cutting grass and clearing trees. From the discovery in the site's houses of milling stones used for husking, it is evident that grain was harvested at that time. The animal bones and bone tools uncovered show that the people of that era supplemented their diet by hunting and fishing and practicing animal husbandry (raising mainly pigs).

A variety of coarsely constructed pottery has been uncovered from the Xinglongwa settlement in Aohan Banner. After comparing the pottery of this and other Xinglongwa sites to pottery from contemporaneous sites of central China, Chinese experts believe that the Xinglongwa culture developed along its own indigenous course.

Discoveries from the successor to the Xinglongwa culture, the Zhaobaogou culture (also excavated in the 1980s), have stirred tremendous excitement both within China and abroad. Dating from approximately 4500 B.C., the Zhaobaogou culture type is named after discoveries made at Zhaobaogou Village in Aohan Banner. Since 1988 over sixty Zhaobaogou culture-type sites have been found by Chinese archaeologists. The settlement in Aohan Banner, which covers almost 15,000 square meters (4 acres), is organized very much like the Xinglongwa settlements, although no protective ditch surrounding the houses was uncovered. It is clear from the stone artifacts retrieved that during Zhaobaogou times the most representative agricultural tool was a stone plow.

The pottery of the Zhaobaogou era was more sophisticated than that of Xinglongwa times. Apart from pottery clearly made for daily use, vessels of some special significance, painted with most unusual animal designs, have been uncovered on the elevated southern portion of the site at Zhaobaogou Village (to date, only two other Zhaobaogou culture-type sites have yielded such pottery). The designs of supernatural creatures—a pig with a snakelike body and a flying deer that appears to have an extended scaly snakelike body below a horned head (Fig. 4)—are being studied as examples of the earliest images of the dragon, one of China's most ancient and important symbolic creatures. The Zhaobaogou pig-dragon design in particular may be a precursor to images in jade uncovered at sites of the Hongshan cultural type of a later time.

Another Zhaobaogou design is of a bird with round eyes, a long hooked beak, and some sort of crest or crown. This image has also been studied closely,

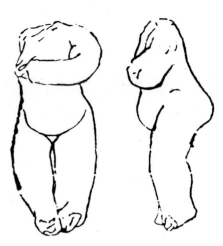

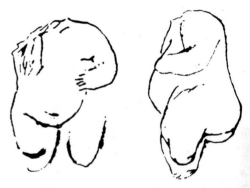

for several reasons. In the early Xia dynastic era, people in this area were known as the Niaoyi (or "Bird Tribes"). Moreover, there are various legends of birds associated with the ancestors of the founders of the Shang dynasty (circa 1650 to 1100 B.C.). The names of several predynastic lords of the Shang who lived during and served under the Xia dynasty appear in ancient inscriptions with associated bird marks or images. One legend purports that the son of the founder of the Shang dynastic line, Xie, was conceived when his mother ate the eggs of a black swallow with supernatural powers. According to the modern scholar Jin Jingfang, before moving south into central China, Xie's son Zhaoming lived in Inner Mongolia, somewhere near the upper portion of the Xilamulun River northeast of Chifeng (Wang Huide, 1990).

One other fact about the Zhaobaogou and Xinglongwa excavations deserves mention: they have yielded some of the earliest human images uncovered within China to date. An elliptical or pillar-shaped statue with a flat bottom, found at the Xinglongwa settlement in Aohan Banner, is an abstract depiction of a kneeling figure with round eyes (Fig. 5). The Zhaobaogou image is that of a human face; the chin points down, the bridge of the nose is long, and there are extended slender and curving eyebrows over large eyes (Fig. 6). These two images from the seventh to fifth millennia B.C. are important to the study of cultural remains in Inner Mongolia because, as Zhang Nairen, Tian Guanglin, and Wang Huide (1989) point out, they appear to be females and are perhaps precursors of ritual statues of women found at altar remains dating from the Hongshan cultural era of the fourth millennium B.C. The Zhaobaogou facial image is similar to images of very ancient provenance found carved on rocks in the Chifeng area. Such masklike facial images have a tradition throughout the history of the peoples of northeastern Inner Mongolia.

Cultural remains dating from approximately 5000 to 3000 B.C. have been uncovered in southwestern and southeastern Inner Mongolia and categorized into a series of different culture types. From about 5000 B.C. on, a good climate in these areas was an impetus to the rapid development of agriculture, with a great flourishing of this economy occurring around 4000 B.C. One of the most significant discoveries dating from this era is the remains of the Hongshan culture type, which has been known since Japanese archaeologists conducted excavations in the Chifeng City area in 1935.

To date, Hongshan culture-type sites have been found in an area centering on the Xilamulun and Laoha rivers (north and east of Chifeng) but extending on the southwest to Zhangjiakou in Hebei province, on the east to the middle portion of the Liao River in Liaoning province, and on the north into the Daxing Mountain Range. This culture developed and flourished in this area from about 4500 to 3000 B.C. Most of the Hongshan sites have been found on the hilltops or in flat elevated areas on both sides of rivers. Like the structures of predecessors

Figure 7 *(left)*. Structures at the Niuheliang site, on the border of Lingyuan and Jianping counties, western Liaoning province. Late Hongshan culture type, circa 3500 to 3000 B.C. Photograph courtesy of Liaoning Institute of Archaeology.

These structures, which include burials but are otherwise comparable to those at the Dongshancui site in Liaoning province, are thought by some scholars to represent ritual obeisance altars.

Figure 8 *(right)*. Sketch of pottery figurines of pregnant women. Hongshan culture type, circa 3500 B.C. Retrieved from Dongshancui site, Liaoning province. From Zhang Xiying, 1993.

The piece at top was recovered east of the site's round stone ritual altar.

in this area, Hongshan structural remains are semisubterranean, rectangular in shape, and of various sizes. The largest house found at the Xishuiquan site near Chifeng, for example, is almost 12 meters (north to south) by 9 meters (30 by 40 feet), and the pathway from its south-facing door slopes downward.

An examination of its pottery remains and stone tools shows Hongshan to have been an advanced society. The red pottery is refined and yet hard and solid, and the various different kinds of vessels were used to hold water or to store foodstuffs; a separate kind of brown pottery was used for cooking. A large number of specially shaped stone plowshares and unusually large milling stones points to the fact that Hongshan culture had a well-developed agricultural economy.

The discoveries made at Hongshan culture-type sites since the 1970s are of unprecedented significance for study of the origins of Chinese civilization; of particular importance are the finds dating from the late Hongshan era—a period that bridges the Neolithic and pre-Xia dynastic developments of the third millennium B.C. Taken as a whole, the archaeological discoveries made in the Inner Mongolia Autonomous Region and adjacent areas in the last few decades have given scholars the opportunity to reconsider traditional accounts of "legendary" figures of those times.

In the 1980s, a site dating from the late Hongshan era was excavated at Dongshancui in eastern Liaoning province, revealing what are considered China's earliest known ritual obeisance altars. Over 2,000 square meters (21,000 square feet) have been unearthed to date, and both round and rectangular altars have been found. Artifacts associated with these structures have convinced specialists that they were used for ritual ceremonial purposes (Fig. 7).

The rectangular altar in the central portion of the Dongshancui site is flat and approximately 10 by 12 meters (30 by 40 feet). Within this area are three

Figure 10. Gray pottery *jue* (three-legged wine vessel). Xiajiadian Lower Period, 2300 to 1600 B.C. Unearthed in 1974 at Dadianzi site, Aohan Banner, east of Chifeng. Height 17 cm; top opening 11.5 by 4.8 cm. Collection of Institute of Archaeology, Academia Sinica.

separate piles of large pointed stones with flat bottoms. In the vicinity, in addition to other kinds of pottery vessels, were large cylindrical vessels that have no bottom; these appear to have been used to store on-site offerings of food. Also found was a jade *huang* ("semicircular") plaque depicting two dragon heads.

Protective walls constructed of brown-colored stones were erected on the eastern and western sides of the Dongshancui site. In the southern part of the site is a perfectly round area 2.5 meters (about 8 feet) in diameter that is surrounded by grayish-white stones. Within the circular altar and in its vicinity, archaeologists found pottery statues of female deities, varying in size from small figures to pieces almost life-size. More than twenty of these statues have been retrieved from the Dongshancui site; several of the figures are of naked pregnant women (Fig. 8).

The Dongshancui finds add to our understanding of the origins of Chinese ritual beliefs. Scholars are now speculating that the altars were used for the worship of Heaven and Earth and to pay homage to ancestors; from the many animal bones uncovered it appears that animal sacrifices were also carried out. This is remarkable, because it means that the traditional Chinese concepts of representing Heaven as round (circular and all-encompassing) and Earth as square (enclosed within the four cardinal points) may have roots in high antiquity (Chen Sixian, 1989). Given the advanced stage of agricultural society evident from the late Hongshan finds, the image of a pregnant woman representing a deity is comprehensible: ritual obeisance to such a deity would have represented prayers for prosperity. The goddess figures also suggest acknowledgment of the important role women played in the development of agriculture and animal domestication.

Hongshan culture-type sites have yielded a great number of jade artifacts, including carvings in shapes of jade ritual objects from later dynastic times (such as a *bi*, a flat round disc with a hole in the center). China's earliest known jade

31

images of swallows, turtles, and dragons have come from Hongshan sites. The dragons are semicircular and have the head of a pig and the body of a snake (Fig. 9; as mentioned above, such an image appears painted on the pottery from the earlier Zhaobaogou culture).

The jade dragons are considered by Chinese specialists to be Earth deities. The fact that the dragons have a pig's head is consistent with the importance of animal husbandry during Hongshan times. The animal bones uncovered at Hongshan culture-type sites have demonstrated that people of that era raised mainly pigs, as did the early people of the Xinglongwa culture. Furthermore, ancient Chinese textual accounts depict the dragon as a kind of water snake. As Sun Shoudao and Guo Shaohui see it, this is consistent with the fact that the raising of pigs is a form of "wet animal husbandry" (Guo Shaohui, 1988). During the predynastic era of the late third millennium B.C., the traditional figures involved in flood control were named after the dragon. Because the founder of the Xia dynasty, Yu, solved the flooding problems, the dragon became an emblem for the dynasty. In other words, such figures were deified because they were able through their acts to bring Earth back to a peaceful state and return agricultural society to prosperity.

In studying the origins of Chinese ritual beliefs, however, these finds present us with a more profound question: What were the roots of ancestral worship, one of Chinese civilization's most ancient traditions? In light of the new finds, it is useful to reconsider some of China's oldest legendary accounts.

According to Chinese legends, at some time in the early predynastic era there existed the woman called Nuwa. Among other things, Nuwa was famous for establishing ritual laws for marriage, which delineated proper family relations, thereby preventing the production of inbred children and of course creating family names. The establishment of a system of family names made possible the tracing of lineage, and hence ancestral genealogy. (It is interesting that the Chinese character for "surname," *xing*, derives from a "woman" radical, *nu*, and the character for "to be born.")

Ancient Chinese records describe Nuwa as a supernatural figure who put Heaven and Earth in order; she is also traditionally depicted as having a snakelike lower body with scales. Thus there is reason to believe that ritual obeisance altars at the Dongshancui site were not merely for worship of Heaven and Earth but were also for ancestral worship—or worship of Nuwa herself, whose lawgiving made possible ancestral genealogy.

The predynastic era of the third millennium B.C. was characterized by the warfare of kings vying for power and authority. It is in the context of such conflicts that one would expect to see the emergence of fortified cities in China. Indeed, in recent years archaeologists have surveyed and excavated a great number of walled cities in Inner Mongolia dating from this era. The earliest of these city sites found to date is the Laohushan site located at Liangcheng south of Daihai Lake (an area southeast of Huhehaote).

Built on a hill facing south, the Laohushan site covers approximately 130,000 square meters (32 acres) and is completely surrounded by a stone wall. The northern portion of the wall, the best preserved, is approximately 600 meters (2,000 feet) in length. The house foundations uncovered within the city show that the houses were built to fit the sloping terrain and that most were semisubterranean. The earliest structures are rectangular in shape with rounded corners; later houses appear to have been constructed using a white plaster for the walls, a technique similar to that found in the houses cut into hillsides at the contemporaneous Yuanzigou site (directly north of Daihai Lake). The remains of pottery kilns outside the southwestern city wall at the Laohushan site indicate that a distinct pottery industry had already emerged here.

Figure 11 *(opposite)*. Bronze *yan* (three-legged vessel with enlarged upper body). Shang Yinxu Period, circa fourteenth to eleventh centuries B.C. Unearthed in 1973 at Tuchengzi, Keshenketeng Banner. Height 54 cm; distance between handles 28.8 cm; weight 11.75 kg. Collection of Inner Mongolia Museum, Huhehaote. Photograph by Kong Qun.

The vessel was cast from a three-piece mold and exhibits conspicuous seams; the body and the bowed legs are adorned with string design. In form, this artifact closely resembles a bronze unearthed from an early-Yinxu-period tomb at the late Shang capital at Anyang, Henan province.

The Laohushan site dates from approximately 2800 to 2300 B.C. and thus covers roughly the entire era of the predynastic Sage kings prior to the emergence of the Xia dynasty. As Tian Guangjin points out (1992), during this era rainfall in the area near Daihai Lake was at a peak; unlike today's conditions, it was ideal for agriculture.

A number of walled cities comparable to that at Laohushan have been uncovered to its northwest (north of the Yellow River near Baotou City) and southwest (east of the Yellow River near Qingshuihe County). Of these cities, the Baotou Ashan site is notable because remains of ritual obeisance altars similar to the ones of the Hongshan era have been discovered there.

Over a hundred city sites that date from approximately 2300 to 1600 B.C. have been uncovered by archaeologists in southeastern Inner Mongolia and also in the western portions of Liaoning province and the northern sections of Hebei (north of modern-day Beijing). These sites belong to what is known as the Xiajiadian Lower Period culture type, an advanced agricultural society that had nascent bronze technology.

The cities excavated thus far vary in size, the largest covering an area of almost 100,000 square meters (25 acres). Since these cities were built according to the strategic nature of the terrain, they are irregular in shape—rectangular, circular, or oval. The city walls were constructed entirely with stones or with piled-up earth covered with stones. Most of the walls that remain stand between 0.2 and 1.5 meters (0.5 to 5 feet) in height, with the tallest between 2.1 and 3.5 meters (6.8 to 11.5 feet); most are about 1 meter (3 feet) thick, although the thickest are between 6 and 13 meters (20 to 40 feet).

The houses uncovered within the Xiajiadian Lower Period cities are usually above ground, circular, and constructed with stones. The larger houses are always found in the central and relatively flatter areas of the sites. Although smaller cities contained 60 to 70 houses, 216 have been found at the largest site surveyed; counting the houses already destroyed, specialists estimate that this city had over 600 structures inside its walls.

From the discoveries at one of these sites, the Dadianzi city site in Aohan Banner, it is evident that Xiajiadian Lower Period culture had close ties to the culture of central China during the Xia dynasty. Many of the finds at the site, which is located directly east of Chifeng, can be closely compared to objects retrieved in the last 30 years at the site of a Xia dynastic capital, the Yanshi Erlitou site in Henan province. Liu Guanmin and Xu Guangji (1981) have described the close similarities between stone tools and pottery vessels retrieved from Xiajiadian culture-type sites and the Erlitou site. Liu Guanmin (1992) notes that pottery vessels retrieved from tombs at Dadianzi (Fig. 10) are quite close in appearance and form to those from Erlitou. Liu also notes that buried in a great many tombs are numerous shells and shell-shaped objects carved from other material. This is a burial practice prevalent at the Erlitou site, where imitative shells carved of stone and bone have been found.

The construction of the Dadianzi site's city walls is also noteworthy. Unlike the walls of many contemporaneous counterparts in the Chifeng City area, those of Dadianzi are made of pounded earth (hangtu). This is a critical point, because pounded earth is one of the principal architectural techniques found at sites in Henan and Shandong provinces dating from the Xia and Shang dynastic eras. Further, directly southeast of Aohan Banner on the western fringes of Liaoning is the Xiajiadian Lower Period culture-type city site of Shuiquan, which has pounded-earth building foundations. Wang Huide (1992) concludes that the Shuiquan foundations are comparable to those unearthed at the Erlitou site.

The Xiajiadian finds add a new dimension to the study of early Chinese civilization. They demonstrate that there was a flourishing civilization in southeastern Inner Mongolia from immediately prior to the establishment of the Xia dynasty to as late as the early period of Shang dynastic hegemony. One critical fact about these city sites is that they were built along an east/west line—an orientation essentially parallel to that of the Great Wall of China erected in the area in later times. Wang Huide (1992) concludes that this orientation, and the moats and sturdily built northern city walls, indicate that these cities acted as a confederated defense against incursions from the north.

After the fall of the Xia dynasty, a number of changes led to the gradual decline of Xiajiadian Lower Period culture. First of all, sometime around 1500 B.C. the climate changed in Inner Mongolia, making many areas less suitable for a successful agriculture. This led to a gradual relocation of agricultural society from southeastern Inner Mongolia southward toward northern Hebei. From that time on, agricultural subsistence in southeastern Inner Mongolia began to be infused with a pastoral nomadic economy.

The trend toward a pastoral animal-rearing existence appears to have been widespread in Inner Mongolia, and the discoveries in the southwest—at Zhukaigou in the Ordos area—substantiate this conclusion. Zhukaigou is the site of an early bronze-age culture that emerged during the late predynastic era, flourished during the Xia dynasty, and persisted until the latter part of the early Shang dynasty. After extensive analysis, Tian Guangjin (1992) has determined that the climatic changes around 1500 B.C. in the Ordos area marked the decline of agricultural society and the rapid growth of a pastoral economy. In later times, while the economy of southeast Inner Mongolia retained a strong agricultural component, pastoralism became the principal mode of subsistence in the Ordos area.

Another factor that undoubtedly affected both southeastern and southwestern Inner Mongolia after the fall of the Xia dynasty was the political power of its successor, the Shang dynasty. The Xiajiadian cultural remains from north of Beijing show that, during the Xia dynasty, these people were a component of a confederation that had its northern line of defensive cities in the Chifeng area. The eminent archaeologist Zhang Zhongpei (1990) believes that the Xiajiadian cultural remains of northern Hebei from this era can be identified with ancient Chinese records of a large powerful clan, the Youyi. The worsening climatic conditions in southeastern Inner Mongolia during the early Shang era forced people to move south to northern Hebei. During the reign of the late Shang-era king, Wuding, however, the Shang dynasty moved its capital north to Anyang in northern Henan province, and Wuding initiated military actions against various clans to the north of the new capital, which was called Yinxu. Wuding led vigorous campaigns to vanquish defiant clans in northern Shanxi, in Shaanxi, and north and south of the Yellow River in Inner Mongolia. And as Zhou Heng (1980) points out, operations were also mounted to reassert Shang hegemony in northern Hebei.

The discovery of large bronze ritual vessels (Fig. 11) north and northwest of Chifeng dating from the early era of the Yinxu capital shows that Shang civilization left its mark on southeastern Inner Mongolia. Although the vessels are crude, and there is reason to believe that they were made with the bronze technology of the indigenous Xiajiadian culture, vessels of this size have not been uncovered from Xiajiadian Lower Period cultural sites (i.e., predating the Yinxu era). Based on the inscriptions on some of these vessels, Su He (1982) concludes that they probably belonged to local families enfeoffed as nobility by the Shang dynasty.

When King Wu founded the Western Zhou dynasty (circa eleventh century to 771 B.C.) after the fall of the Shang dynasty, northern Hebei and southeastern Inner Mongolia came under the dominion of the Duke of Zhao's fiefdom of Yen. During the Zhou dynasty, the northern peoples who inhabited these areas (known generally as the Rong and the Di) became a powerful enemy of central China.

2

The Eastern Hu and the Xiongnu

IN PRE-QIN CHINESE RECORDS, the general names used for the peoples living along China's northeastern frontier during Zhou times were the *Di* or the *Hu*. According to China's first dictionary, the Han-era *Shuowen Jiezi*, the character *Hu* derives from "meat" *(rou)* and refers to a cow's wattle. Some scholars believe that the character derives from "moon" *(yue,* which is similar to the "meat" radical) and implies that the northerners—like the people of central China—followed a lunar calender. The Hu peoples who lived in southeastern Inner Mongolia were called the Eastern Hu.

By the time of the Warring States (403 to 221 B.C.), the Eastern Hu were a thriving bronze-age culture and a powerful political force along China's frontier to the north and east of modern-day Hebei province. The Eastern Hu were the ancestors of such peoples as the Xianbei, the Qidan, and the Mongols, and the comparative study of the material culture of all these groups helps us understand the continuity of practices and beliefs in northern China during ancient times.

In the last several decades, a great variety of remains believed to be of the Eastern Hu have been uncovered in southeastern Inner Mongolia and in western Liaoning and northern Hebei provinces. These remains have been termed Xiajiadian Upper Period culture. Although such ancient materials were first unearthed by the Japanese excavating near Chifeng City in Inner Mongolia in 1935, they were not well understood at the time. The majority of the hundreds of Xiajiadian Upper Period cultural sites have been found since 1960.

Most of the Xiajiadian Upper Period cities faced south and were on elevated flat areas next to the banks of rivers. The cities, which were near modern-day Chifeng, were approximately 20,000 to 30,000 square meters (5 to 7 acres) in size, and the houses were either above ground or subterranean, and round or rectangular. The round structures were approximately 3 to 5 meters (10 to 16 feet) in diameter and had walls of stone and piled earth and living areas of pounded

Opposite: Ram's head dagger pommel. Detail of Figure 15.

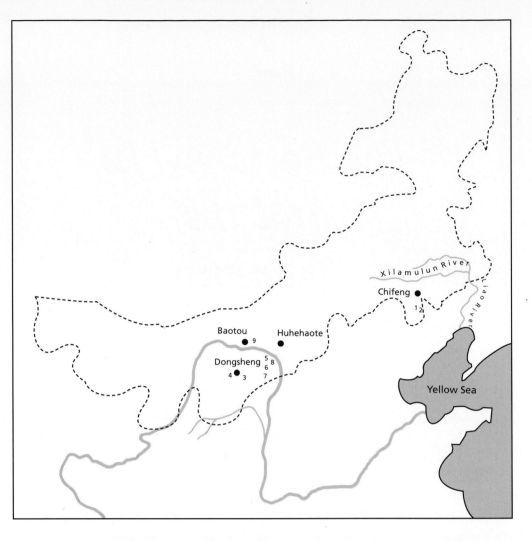

earth. In most of the houses, a large post was erected in the center, and a stone-paved pathway led away from the south-facing door. Some houses were surrounded by stone walls.

The Xiajiadian Upper Period sites are distinct from the Xiajiadian Lower Period settlements often found buried beneath them. The differences in these sites support the theory that, after the fall of the Xia dynasty (circa sixteenth century B.C.), the change to a colder and dryer climate in southern Inner Mongolia forced people to abandon agriculture as a major source of subsistence and to gradually adopt an animal-rearing economy. A great number of animal bones appear in both Lower and Upper Period sites (although the Upper Period sites include bones of some animals, such as the horse, that are not seen in the Lower Period sites). However, as Liu Guanmin and Xu Guangji point out (1981), the quality of pottery in Upper Period sites is inferior to that of the agriculturally flourishing Lower Period. Most of the Xiajiadian Upper Period pottery is made of coarse red or brown-red clay fired at relatively low temperature (Fig. 12). In a word, pottery had become qualitatively less important in Xiajiadian Upper Period culture.

The same decline in quality is not seen in the large number of bronze objects uncovered at Xiajiadian Upper Period sites. Not only do these bronzes technically far outstrip the pieces found in Lower Period sites, but they have a range of shapes and sizes and exhibit unusual features. A great many of these bronze artifacts have been unearthed from Xiajiadian Upper Period tombs, which are usually in graveyards located on south-facing slopes or on elevated flat areas near rivers.

At least as early as the Xia dynastic era, southeastern Inner Mongolia had important cultural exchange with central China, and the connections continued into the late Shang and early Zhou dynasties, when central China went on military campaigns to secure hegemony over northern Hebei as well as subdue vari-

Figure 12. Burnished red pottery pot. Xiajiadian Upper Period, circa eleventh to fourth centuries B.C. Unearthed in suburbs of Chifeng. Height 11 cm; maximum diameter of body 19 cm. Collection of Chifeng Municipal Museum.

ous defiant northern peoples. During the Spring and Autumn eras, the Di people often attacked and plundered the Chinese states that occupied northern China. This was one of the principal ways in which traditional ritual bronzes from China found their way into Xiajiadian Upper Period sites and northern bronzes came to be deposited in dynastic Chinese sites.

A Chinese *gui* food vessel was retrieved in 1975 from a hoard along the Huolinhe River in Zhalute Banner, some 300 kilometers northeast of Chifeng. On the basis of its inscription, Zhang Bozhong (1982) dates the bronze to the late Western Zhou and early Spring and Autumn eras; he maintains that it was a ritual vessel of the Xing state of northern Hebei. Another bronze ritual *gui* vessel (Fig. 13), unearthed in 1985 from the Xiajiadian Upper Period Xiaoheishigou site in Ningcheng County, south of Chifeng, bears an inscription comparable to that of the Zhalute Banner piece. In the latter half of the seventh century B.C., a confederation of Di tribes made major incursions into northern China (Ma Changshou, 1962). It is possible that these *gui* vessels were taken into Inner Mongolia during this era by the Di peoples.

The peoples of the north greatly valued and were influenced by Chinese ritual bronzes. Some bronzes found in the north have shapes characteristic of central China but incorporate uncommon design elements. A bronze piece from the Xiaoheishigou site (Fig. 14) is similar in form to traditional Chinese *yi* vessels, which are shallow ewers with spouts that were used for ritual purposes during dynastic times. However, the Xiaoheishigou piece has unusual feet that may be an elaboration by northern artisans.

Cultural exchange between central China and the Eastern Hu was by no means one-sided. A late Shang-era bronze dagger (Fig. 15) has a shape (and particularly, a curvature) that is characteristic of others unearthed at Xia and Shang

Figure 13 *(opposite)*. Bronze *gui* (deep circular vessel used for serving grain) with dragon-head handles. Xiajiadian Upper Period, eleventh to fourth centuries B.C. Unearthed in 1985 at Xiaoheishigou site, Ningcheng County, south of Chifeng. Height 24.5 cm; diameter of mouth 21.4 cm; base 21.5 cm square. Collection of Cultural Relics Bureau of Ningcheng County.

The vessel is adorned with vertical string design. The inside bottom of the bowl bears a fourteen-character inscription *(this page)*.

cultural sites; but its ram's head pommel is typical of bronze daggers crafted in the north. As Wu En (1985) points out, ram's head daggers have been retrieved from the late Shang-era capital at Anyang in Henan province; these were perhaps taken by the Shang during their northern campaigns.

Some of the most significant discoveries of Eastern Hu culture have been made at the Nanshangen site in Ningcheng County south of Chifeng, in a tomb labelled #101. The tomb is rather large and oval-shaped, and its walls are lined with stones. A layer of decayed wood dust at the tomb's base, which is laid with flat stones, indicates that the interred had been buried in a wooden casket.

Among the artifacts recovered from Tomb #101 were seventy-one bronzes. By comparing the larger ritual bronze objects from this tomb with similar pieces from central China, specialists have dated Tomb #101 to the late Western Zhou and Early Spring and Autumn eras (mid-ninth to mid-eighth centuries B.C.; Northeastern Cultural Relics Team, Department of Archaeology, Academia Sinica, 1973).

The bronzes retrieved from Nanshangen include various kinds of weapons with some singular features. In the larger tombs of men from the Xiajiadian Upper Period, a bronze helmet is often found near the head, and a bronze sword—with or without a bronze scabbard—near the waist. An oval bronze helmet (Fig. 16) from the Nanshangen site has semicircular openings in the front and back and indentations on the top that indicate that leather straps were fed through an open rectangular button at the helmet's apex and tied below to secure it to the head.

One sword of superior quality workmanship has been retrieved from Tomb #101 completely intact. Chinese experts call it the "Yin/Yang" sword (Fig. 17) because of the unusual design of its hilt: one side shows a naked male figure with his arms at his sides and his hands on his belly, the other a naked female with arms

Figure 14. Bronze *yi* (shallow ewer with spout). Xiajiadian Upper Period, eleventh to fourth centuries B.C. Unearthed in 1985 at Xiaoheishigou site, Ningcheng County, south of Chifeng. Height 9.2 cm; length 16 cm; width 7.7 cm. Collection of Inner Mongolia Museum, Huhehaote.

The ewer has an animal-shaped handle and a loop beneath the spout. The rim is decorated with a series of multiple-line horse-shoe-shaped designs; beneath this band is horizontal string design. The feet resemble human legs bent at the knee.

Opposite: Bronze *lei* (wine jar with wide shoulders and narrow foot). Xiajiadian Upper Period, eleventh to fourth centuries B.C. Unearthed in 1985 at Xiaoheishigou, Ningcheng County, Chifeng. Height 28 cm; diameter of mouth 20.5 cm, of belly 26.5 cm. Collection of Inner Mongolia Museum, Huhehaote.

crossed above her breasts. The lute-like shape of the blade is characteristic of swords of this era found in cultural sites all over China's northeast. Another bronze sword from Tomb #101 has a design of two couchant tigers facing each other on the hilt (Fig. 18) and a similar blade.

Another tomb (#102) at Nanshangen has yielded a bone artifact etched with a scene of a figure hunting deer with bow and arrow and of two dogs standing among horse chariots (Fig. 19); the human figure on this piece resembles the man shown on the Yin/Yang sword. The bone carving and the Yin/Yang sword are interesting: such open representation of human male genitals is rarely seen in cultural remains from central China.

The face on the figures of the Yin/Yang sword is masklike—flat with slightly elevated cheeks—and has protruding round eyes, a long nose, and a bald head. Bronze ornaments of faces with a similar mask-like quality have been found at Xiajiadian Upper Period burials in western Liaoning province, and more recently at the Xiaoheishigou site (Fig. 20).

The scene depicted on the bone slip from Tomb #102 (Fig. 19) is evidence that the Eastern Hu hunted with bow and arrow and used horse chariots. Based on this piece, and on depictions in rock art and inscriptions on Zhou era bronzes, Lin Yun (1991) concludes that at least during the entire Western Zhou era, northern peoples used horse chariots not only for hunting but also for warfare.

The designs of the bone piece and other evidence from Xiajiadian Upper Period cultural sites also underline the importance of dogs in the Eastern Hu's hunting lifestyle. A number of bronze vessels and weapons from the Xiajiadian Upper Period are adorned with dog designs (Fig. 21), and in many tombs from this period, dogs were found buried with the interred. This practice was prevalent in central China during the predynastic and dynastic eras, and—from his exami-

nation of the records of the descendants of the Eastern Hu, such as the Wuhuan—Jin Fengyi (1987) concludes that this was a funerary practice with a long history among the people of northeastern China as well.

So formidable were the Eastern Hu that various northern Chinese states adopted extraordinary tactics to defeat them. For example, during the Warring States era, when the Yen state that occupied northern Hebei was constantly suffering the raids of the northerners, the Yen general Qin Kai became a political hostage of the Eastern Hu, who held him in high esteem. After learning as much as he could about his captors, Qin Kai escaped back to Yen and led a massive campaign against the Eastern Hu, which forced them far north into Inner Mongolia. To ward off future incursions, the Yen subsequently built a section of the Great Wall that began north of modern-day Zhangjiakou in Hebei and extended east across portions of Inner Mongolia and Liaoning and Jilin provinces. The strategy of building a defensive wall was, however, only marginally effective in checking Eastern Hu political power in northern China. In fact, it was only at the hands of another formidable horseback-riding northern neighbor, the Xiongnu, that the Eastern Hu finally met their demise.

I N ACCOUNTS of the northern peoples in Chinese texts, there are references to a group of Hu called the Xiongnu. (The term, which appears relatively late in the ancient annals—during the late fourth century B.C.—is a derogatory Chinese appellation, something akin to "slave bastard.") Until recently, much of what was known about these northerners was taken from *Shiji* [Records of the Historian], the famous work of the Han historian Sima Qian (145 to 90 B.C.). The greater part of his accounts of the Xiongnu concerns their political history from the Western Zhou to the mid-Western Han eras (circa twelfth to second centuries B.C.; *Shiji juan* ["chapter"] 110). Sima Qian's text depicts a pastoral nomadic people wandering in search of grazing lands for their herds, which were mainly horses, cows, and sheep. He relates that the Xiongnu had no walled cities and did not engage in agriculture, and he tells us that because the men were trained from an early age to hunt on horseback with bow and arrow, they were formidable warriors.

In the last century, historians have struggled to go beyond Sima Qian's brief statements about the Xiongnu by studying their material culture through archaeological survey and exploration. The earliest excavations were carried out from 1896 to 1902 in the Lake Baikal area of southern Siberia by Russian archaeologists. In 1912, the accidental discovery of an ancient tomb in the northern regions of Mongolia by a gold prospector from Russia aroused the interest of that country's archaeologists, who subsequently conducted a series of excavations at this location, called the Noin-ulan site. Among the cultural remains uncovered were Chinese fabrics and a Chinese bronze mirror.

In 1924 and 1925, the Russian archaeologist Captain P.K. Kozloff excavated Noin-ulan and uncovered four small and eight large tombs. In excavations carried out over the next 2 years, a Chinese lacquer cup was retrieved from one of the tombs (Tomb #5); an inscription of sixty-nine Chinese characters on the cup includes the date of 2 B.C. Many other discoveries of Xiongnu remains have been made in Mongolia and in the Lake Baikal area since 1949—most of these sites date from the Qin dynasty to the Eastern Han era (221 B.C. to about A.D. 50).

The archaeological search for remains of the Xiongnu within the People's Republic of China began more recently. A few sites were excavated as early as the 1950s, but more important discoveries, made in the last several decades, have afforded specialists the opportunity to reconsider the material culture of the people

Figure 15. Bronze dagger with a curved blade and a ram's head pommel. Late Shang dynasty, circa fourteenth to eleventh centuries B.C. Unearthed at Balinzuo Banner, north of Chifeng. Length 37 cm; maximum width 4.3 cm. Collection of Balinzuo Banner Museum.

Figure 16 *(opposite)*. Bronze helmet with semicircular openings in the front and back. Xiajiadian Upper Period, eleventh to fourth centuries B.C. Unearthed in 1963 at Nanshangen site, Ningcheng County, south of Chifeng. Height 24 cm; width at base 20.3 cm. Collection of Chifeng Municipal Museum.

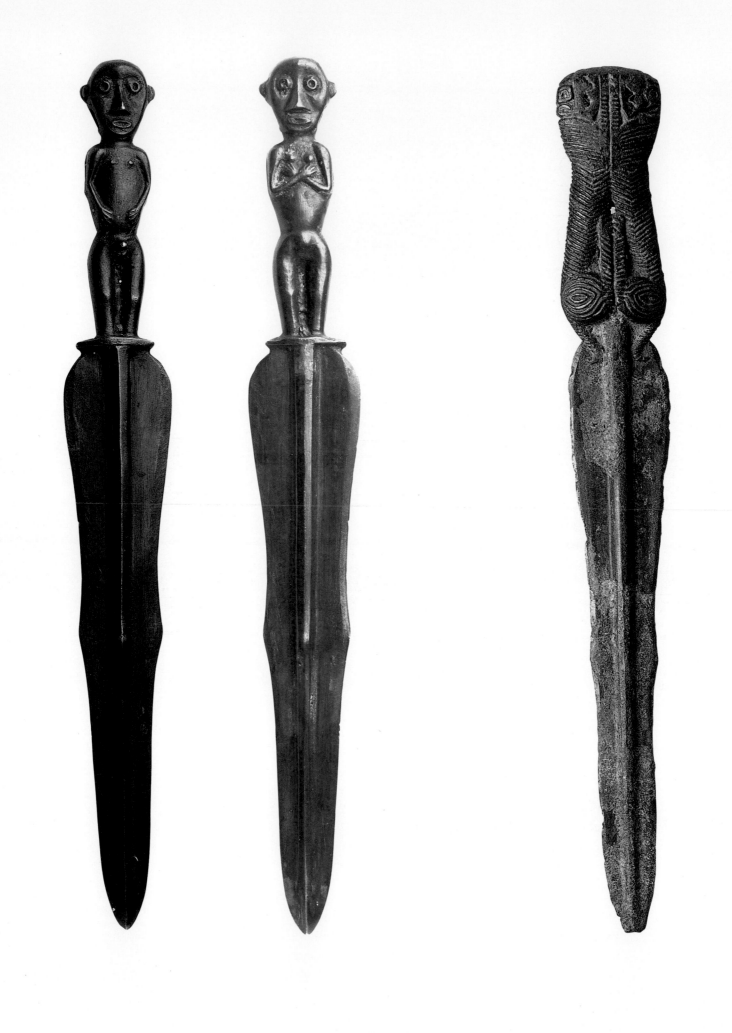

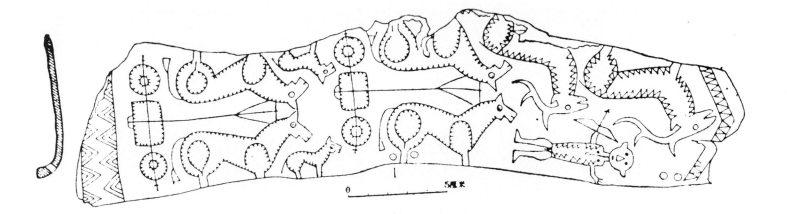

who inhabited China's northwestern frontier prior to the Qin and Han dynasties. The discoveries have prompted specialists to reconsider the histories of these peoples and to speculate about the origins of Xiongnu culture in general. This work in turn sheds light on the origins and interrelationships of all of the bronze-age peoples who inhabited the great Eurasian steppe in the several millennia preceding the birth of Christ.

Chinese archaeologists' work in the last several decades has given Tian Guangjin and Guo Suxin (1992) the confidence to challenge the conventional notion that the bronze culture of the Ordos was derived from cultures found elsewhere on the Eurasian steppe. Tian and Guo believe that the Ordos bronze culture originated directly from northern China and that it followed an independent course of development.

According to Sima Qian's account, the founding ancestor of the Xiongnu, Chunwei, was a descendant of the Xia people who fled to the northwest after the defeat of the last Xia emperor. Although many scholars discount this legend, Zhou Heng (1980) outlines the impact that the bronze-age cultures of the Xia and Shang dynasties had upon northern China. Archaeological discoveries of the past few decades have pointed to cultural contact and exchange between central China and the people of northern Shaanxi province and the Ordos during the Xia and Shang dynasties.

At the crux of the discussion of the origin of ancient cultures of the Ordos are the discoveries made at the Zhukaigou site, in the vicinity of Yijinhuoluo Banner City in Yikezhao League. As mentioned in Chapter 1, the Zhukaigou was a bronze-age culture that lasted from the late predynastic era through the Xia and into the early Shang dynastic periods (from about the twenty-fourth to the fifteenth centuries B.C.). Small bronze artifacts began appearing at the Zhukaigou site as early as the mid-Xia dynastic era, and by early Shang times, the people of

Figure 17 *(opposite, left and center)*. Bronze "Yin/Yang" (male/female) short sword. Xiajiadian Upper Period, eleventh to fourth centuries B.C. Unearthed in 1958 at Nanshangen site, Ningcheng County, south of Chifeng. Length 31.7 cm; maximum width of blade 4.2 cm. Collection of Inner Mongolia Museum, Huhehaote.
The lute-shaped blade bears a central ridge. The figure of a nude man with his hands on his belly adorns one side of the hilt *(left)*; the reverse bears a nude woman with arms crossed over her breasts. The legs of both figures are bowed.

Figure 18 *(opposite, right)*. Bronze short sword. Xiajiadian Upper Period, eleventh to fourth centuries B.C. Unearthed in 1963 at Nanshangen site, Ningcheng County, south of Chifeng. Length 34 cm; maximum width 4.2 cm. Collection of Chifeng Municipal Museum.
The sword and hilt are cast in a single piece; the hilt, which is hollow, depicts a pair of outward-facing couchant tigers.

Figure 19 *(this page)*. Bone slip decorated with a hunting scene. Xiajiadian Upper Period, eleventh to fourth centuries B.C. Retrieved from Tomb #102, Nanshangen site, Ningcheng County, south of Chifeng. Length 34 cm. From An Zhimin and Zheng Naiwu, 1981.
The piece is etched with two dogs standing between a pair of two-horse chariots *(at left)* and a man hunting deer with bow and arrow. There are holes on the lower (extant) edge of the piece.

Figure 20. Small bronze ornament of a human face. Xiajiadian Upper Period, eleventh to fourth centuries B.C. Retrieved in 1992 from Xiaheishigou site, Ningcheng County, south of Chifeng. Courtesy of Inner Mongolia Institute of Archaeology.

Zhukaigou already had a certain control of bronze metallurgy. This is well illustrated by the discoveries from Tomb #1040. Although a bronze dagger from this tomb is fundamentally comparable to daggers retrieved from early Shang dynastic city sites (Fig. 22, top), there is also a bronze knife (Fig. 22, bottom) characteristic of one found at the Xia dynastic city site of Erlitou (Yang Guozhong and Liu Zhongfu, 1983) as well as many pieces retrieved from the late Shang city site of Yinxu (Liu Yiman, 1993). These kinds of knives continued to be crafted in the Ordos from the Zhou through the Han eras (Fig. 23).

By the late Shang period the dragon and bird iconography of traditional China's Xia and Shang dynasties was well incorporated into the bronze knives made by the peoples of the Ordos. A good example is a late Shang-era short sword with a bell pommel (Fig. 24), retrieved from Yijinhuoluo Banner in the Ordos (this piece resembles short swords found together with late Shang bronze vessels at the Baode site in Shanxi province). The hilt of the Yijinhuoluo sword is decorated with a snake-scale design; Tian Guangjin and Guo Suxin (1986) maintain that the design links this piece with the legendary dragon of the Xia, which was traditionally depicted as having the body of a snake.

Remarkable evidence of Hu culture in the Ordos during the Warring States era has come from the Aluchaideng site, which was surveyed and excavated in 1972 and 1973. Most of the tombs at the site, located in the Maowusu Desert approximately 40 kilometers (25 miles) southeast of Hangjin Banner City, have been destroyed by shifting sands. The archaeological surveys of the spring of 1973 determined that the vast quantities of cultural materials retrieved at the site originally came from two of these tombs.

The majority of the several hundred artifacts retrieved from Aluchaideng are gold pieces, and among these is a crown in two parts (Fig. 25) with a rather

Figure 21. *(opposite)*. Bronze halberd. Xiajiadian Upper Period, eleventh to fourth centuries B.C. Unearthed in 1958 from Nanshangen site, Ningcheng County, south of Chifeng. Length 24 cm; width 10.3 cm. Collection of Inner Mongolia Museum, Huhehaote.

The two sides of the shaft socket *(detail this page)* are decorated with the design of four dogs.

complex design. The top of the crown is thick gold hammered into a skullcap and decorated in bas relief with four wolves struggling with four rams. Mounted on the apex of the cap is an eagle with extended wings, its body sculpted with gold strips, and its head made with turquoise inlay. Gold wires threaded through the turquoise headpiece connect it to the body so that the eagle's head swayed from side to side as the wearer of the crown moved; the same technique was used to give mobility to the bird's tail.

The bottom portion of the crown is a headband made up of three semicircular cast pieces that detach from each other (Fig. 25). Two of these pieces stack to form one side of the headband: small gold posts along the rim of the bottom piece attach it to the band above. These half bands are adorned with a string design; at one end of the top band is a crouching tiger with bared teeth, and below this, on the bottom band, is a reclining ram with large horns. The third semicircular piece latches to the lower of the other two sections to form the other half of the headband. It is also decorated with a string design; where it meets the animal design on the other band, it has an image of a kneeling horse, its head facing down.

Four belt ornaments, of which two were intact, were unearthed at Aluchaideng; each of these cast gold plates weighs approximately 220 grams (8 ounces). The decoration on these pieces (Fig. 26) is an overview of an ox whose body is being attacked on both sides by four tigers—the horns of the ox penetrate the ears of two of the tigers; this image is surrounded by a string design border. There are small holes at the corners of these ornaments that exhibit wear due to rubbing, indicating that the pieces were probably attached to hooks on a belt (similar corner holes are present in gold belt plates uncovered from the tombs at another Ordos location, the Xigoupan site in Zhungeer Banner).

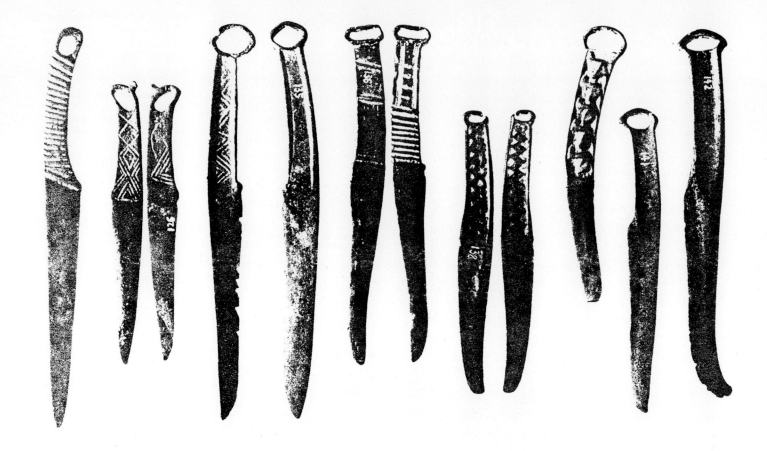

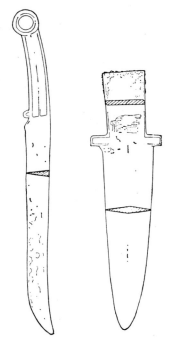

Figure 22. Bronze dagger and knife. Zhukaigou, early Shang era (circa fifteenth century B.C.). Retrieved from Tomb #1040, Zhukaigou site, Yikezhao League, southeast of Dongsheng. From Tian Guangjin, 1988.

Figure 23. Bronze knives *(top)*. Hu peoples, Western Zhou era (eleventh century to 771 B.C.). Retrieved in the Yikezhao League in the Ordos. From Tian Guangjin and Guo Suxin, 1986.

A pair of ornamental plates from the Xigoupan site in the Ordos (Fig. 27) are quite similar to the Aluchaideng belt piece. On the basis of an epigraphical analysis of the inscriptions in Chinese on the back of these pieces, Tian Guangjin and Guo Suxin (1980) conclude that they date from the late Warring States era.

Other ornamental objects from Aluchaideng and sites directly to the east, in Zhungeer Banner, give us a view of the artistic images of the pastoral nomadic Hu people who inhabited the Ordos during the Warring States era (Figs. 28-30). Several bronze chariot post finials have been retrieved (Figs. 31-33), and their purpose is verified by Chinese records stating that the Xiongnu used a horse chariot for warfare (the texts refer to this vehicle as the "chariot of the Hu people"). The Xiongnu even had a factory for the production of chariots in the area of modern-day Zhangye County in Gansu province (Lin Gan, 1977).

In all, these discoveries indicate that, in the millennia before the birth of Christ, the northeastern region of the Ordos was an important center for the pastoral nomadic peoples of Inner Mongolia. By the time of the Warring States era (403 to 221 B.C.), the tribes of this region had developed a rich and powerful society. The historical accounts of the Chinese states that struggled against the Hu peoples during the Warring States era are useful in appraising the newest archaeological remains from the Ordos. For example, the accounts of the activities of the Zhao state's King Wuling provide clues to the origins and uses of the golden headdress and belt ornaments from Aluchaideng.

In 307 B.C., in an attempt to defeat his northern adversaries, King Wuling ordered his militia to officially adopt the clothing of the Hu people. This outfit, which had slits in the front and back and did not have the cumbersome long flowing sleeves of traditional Chinese garb, improved mobility on horseback. King

Wuling also had his forces abandon the chariot warfare and weapons customarily used in China and adopt archery on horseback.

As a result of these measures and the Zhao general Li Mu's conquests in the mid-third century B.C., the Zhao solidified their hegemony over northern China, including such critical areas as northern Shaanxi and Shanxi provinces as well as the region south of the northern bend of the Yellow River—the Ordos area. The Zhao then built another section of the Great Wall north of the Yellow River; the new barrier extended from modern-day Linhe in Inner Mongolia as far east as Zhangjiakou in northern Hebei province.

Among the groups King Wuling of the Zhao attacked were people called the *Linhu* (an abbreviation, according to Ma Changshou [1962], designating certain Hu people who called themselves the Tanlin). By the time of the Warring States era, the Linhu had become a powerful nomadic group in the Ordos. Tian Guangjin and Guo Suxin (1986) have determined that the recent archaeological discoveries of the northeastern Ordos coincide with Chinese records of the Linhu, and they conclude that the Aluchaideng tombs must have belonged to tribal chieftains of the Linhu. The gold headdress found at Aluchaideng can be identified in Chinese records as the *huguan*, the Hu chieftain's traditional crown; and the belt ornaments may have adorned the *hudai*, the traditional belt of the Hu chieftain.

At the turn of the twentieth century, Wang Guowei studied old records of such objects and noted that the Hu crown and belt, which were worn by chieftains, became well known in Chinese history after they fell into the hands of the Zhao's king, Wuling. Wang explains that the crown was worn by a chieftain who had achieved military fame, and that the belt—referred to in Chinese as the *guoluodai*—differed from traditional Chinese belts in that it had decorations, often of gold (Wang Guowei, 1959).

The Xiongnu tribal confederation, which was most powerful from 209 to 128 B.C. during the reigns of its first three leaders, was established by Maodun, the eldest son of a chieftain named Touman. Sima Qian tells us that, in an attempt to install another of his sons by a different concubine as heir to his throne, Touman had sent the young Maodun to be a political hostage of the Yuezhi, who occupied the territory west of the Xiongnu (in the area between Dunhuang in the west and the Qilian mountains in modern-day Gansu). However, when Maodun escaped from the Yuezhi, Touman was impressed by his daring and made him an army commander. With the respect Maodun gained for his skill in horseback archery, he was able to assassinate his father and install himself as the new chieftain.

Maodun then began a series of military campaigns. He attacked and conquered the Eastern Hu confederation and retook the Ordos area south of the Yellow River, which had been claimed for the Qin dynasty by the famous general Meng Tian in 214 B.C. He forcefully incorporated a series of smaller tribal confederations to his north into his new empire, and he defeated the Yuezhi to the west and expelled them far into central Asia. Maodun also took control of some twenty-six states in central Asia. These successes added considerably to the military might and economic integrity of the Xiongnu confederation.

After his victories, Maodun moved his center of operations from the Yin mountains in Inner Mongolia north into what is now Mongolia. Ma Changshou (1962) maintains that this capital was located somewhere in the vicinity of modern-day Kosho-Tsaidam-nor. Wu En (1990) concludes that Maodun's capital was probably not a city proper but instead a large encampment of yurts.

The Xiongnu's policy toward those they conquered was primarily one of enslavement and exploitation. From nomadic groups, they brought under subservience many hundreds of thousands of horseback warriors and acquired vast herds of horses, cows, sheep, and camels. From such groups as the Eastern Hu and various central Asian states that engaged in agriculture, the Xiongnu acquired

Figure 24. Short sword with a bell pommel. Hu peoples, late Shang era (circa thirteenth to twelfth centuries B.C.). Retrieved from Yijinhuoluo Banner in the Ordos. Length 22 cm; maximum width 5.2 cm. Collection of Inner Mongolia Museum, Huhehaote.

The sword's blade is triangular and has a central ridge line that ends in a nipple-like protrusion at the base of the curved hilt. The circular loop below the bell pommel was perhaps used to attach the sword to a belt.

agricultural goods and animal feed for their herds. The new empire also benefited by capturing skilled craftsmen and architectural laborers: as Wu En (1990) points out, the discovery of a number of Han architectural elements in Mongolia gives us reason to believe that many of the enslaved laborers were Chinese.

In the case of some products, the Xiongnu acquired what they needed from central Asian states. For example, although the Han dynasty had established barter relations with the Xiongnu empire, during the reign of the emperor Wendi (179 to 157 B.C.) central China tried to prevent export of the raw ores that could be used by the Xiongnu to make iron weapons. As a consequence, the northerners turned to the central Asian countries south of the Taklamakan Desert to obtain the iron weapons that they needed.

Maodun's successor Laoshang carried on campaigns against the Yuezhi and, in 162 and 161 B.C., succeeded in forcing them into the northern reaches of Afghanistan. V.I. Sarianidi (1980) believes that the burial remains uncovered from 1969 to 1971 by a Soviet-Afghan archaeological team at Tillya-tepe (Golden Hill) near Shibergan in northwestern Afghanistan are the graves of these early Yuezhi.

From the start, the Western Han dynasty's policies in dealing with the Xiongnu empire put them at a grave disadvantage. The Xiongnu confederation had become very strong under Maodun's reign, when central China was in the midst of popular rebellions to overthrow the Qin dynasty, and the Xiongnu had taken advantage of the internal disorder to capture such areas as the northern section of modern-day Hebei and the northeast part of Shanxi.

In the winter of 200 B.C., when the founder of the Han dynasty, Liu Bang, was finally in a position stable enough to allow him to respond to these incursions, he led an attack on the Xiongnu in Shanxi. But Maodun sent some 40,000 of his finest cavalry and surrounded Liu Bang and his army at Baideng Mountain; after 7 days the Chinese forces were cut off from their outside reinforcements. By offering official gifts to the Xiongnu, the Chinese were able to end the standoff and negotiate a peace agreement. This agreement stipulated that the Chinese maintain marital ties with the Xiongnu and give annual tribute of silks, wine, rice, and other foodstuffs. The Han dynasty followed this policy off and on in dealing with the Xiongnu for the next 60 to 70 years.

In 1953 and 1954, Chinese archaeologists unearthed several architectural tiles from a tomb dating to the Western Han era (206 B.C. to A.D. 25) at the Zhaowan site, in the suburbs outside modern-day Baotou in Inner Mongolia. On one of these tiles (Fig. 34), molded in relief, is the four-character inscription "Conjugal amity with the Shanyu," which commemorates marital ties with the Xiongnu (shanyu being the name for the Xiongnu confederate chieftain).

In 1981, He Lin retrieved another such tile from a Han tomb at Zhaowan. Many scholars date this tile to several decades before the birth of Christ, when the Han had renewed peace with the Xiongnu by marrying the imperial concubine Wang Zhaojun to a Xiongnu chieftain named Huhanye. He Lin (1981) argues, however, that the tile dates instead to the era of the Han emperor Wendi. He Lin explains that in 177 B.C., Wendi was determined to mount an offensive against the Xiongnu but could not muster the support he needed from the Han nobility and ministers. In the hopes of averting greater losses on the northern frontier, Wendi stepped up tribute and extended marital ties with the Xiongnu.

Based upon a Han-era rectangular brick with a related inscription and other comparable tiles unearthed from Han tombs in the 1953-1954 and 1981 excavations, He Lin (1981) concludes that the tile found in 1981 was part of Wendi's elaborate gestures to appease the Xiongnu. In further support of this dating, He argues that there was little need for Han tiles commemorating the union of Wang Zhaojun and Huhanye because by the time of that marriage the Xiongnu had been under Han authority for several decades and posed no immediate military threat.

Figure 25. Gold headdress. Hu peoples, Warring States era (403 to 221 B.C.). Unearthed in 1973 from Aluchaideng site, 40 km southeast of Hangjin Banner City, Yikezhao League, in the Ordos. Maximum height of skullcap 7.1 cm; weight 191.5 grams. Diameter of headband 16.5 cm; weight 1020.2 grams. Collection of Inner Mongolia Museum, Huhehaote. Photograph by Kong Qun.

The skull cap is thick hammered gold decorated in bas relief with four wolves attacking four rams. The head of the eagle atop the cap is formed of two pieces of turquoise, and the head

and tail are attached to the body with gold wires, making them movable. The bird ornament and the bas relief designs on the cap compose a scene of an eagle circling and gazing down on wolves devouring their prey.

The lower part of the headdress consists of three semicircular gold pieces, two of which stack to form what was probably the front of the headband (attachment points are shown in the drawing at left). All three bands are adorned with braided string design, and each features an animal (a couchant ram, a horse, and a crouching tiger with bared teeth) at one end.

Figure 26. One of four cast gold plaques. Hu peoples, Warring States era (403 to 221 B.C.). Retrieved in 1973 from Aluchaideng site, 40 km southeast of Hangjin Banner City, Yikezhao League, in the Ordos. Length 12.7 cm; width 7.4 cm; weight 220.6 grams. Collection of Inner Mongolia Museum, Huhehaote.

An ox, its four limbs outstretched, struggles with four fierce tigers biting at its neck and belly. The ox stubbornly resists the attack and has thrust its horns into the ears of the tigers biting its neck. The piece is bordered with string design; the holes in each corner were perhaps used to attach the plaque to a belt.

Figure 27. One of a pair of cast gold plaques. Hu peoples, Warring States era (403 to 221 B.C.). Unearthed in 1979 from Tomb #2, Xigoupan site, Zhungeer Banner, Yikezhao League, in the Ordos. Length 13 cm; width 10 cm; weight 292.5 grams. Collection of Ordos Museum, Dongsheng.

A tiger with front paws outstretched is biting into the hind leg of a wild boar; the boar in turn is biting the tiger's hind leg, which is twisted upward. The piece is bordered with string design, and gold loops on the back probably attached it to a belt or other clothing. Traces of coarse hemp cloth were found on the back of this piece and its companion.

The influence of Chinese culture among the Xiongnu of the early Han era is well illustrated by the discoveries made in 1980 at Tomb #4 of the Xigoupan site in Zhungeer Banner in the Ordos. The skeletal remains appear to be those of a woman, and a complete headdress with necklaces and earrings (Fig. 35) was found positioned at the interred's head. At waist level, a gold belt ornament (Fig. 36) featuring a reclining ram in high relief was retrieved, and a total of forty-two openwork stone ornaments (Fig. 37) were found at the sides of the body.

In his excavation report, Tian Guangjin (1986) dates Xigoupan's Tomb #4 to the early Western Han dynastic era. He notes that the gold belt buckle and beaded necklaces are consistent with similar artifacts from the Warring States era found in the northeastern Ordos. However, he also points out that the openwork jade earrings, which have dragon and tiger designs, are quite comparable to Chinese jade pieces that date from the Spring and Autumn era (722 to 481 B.C.). Tian believes that the best example of the influence of central China is the design of a dancing woman on two of the stone ornaments (Fig. 38, left): it is very similar to the image on a mid-Han-era jade piece recovered from the Dabaotai Tomb north of Beijing (Fig. 38, right).

The Han policy of maintaining peaceful relations with the Xiongnu empire through marriage and tribute proved not only taxing to the Chinese but also frustratingly ineffective, because the Xiongnu continued to raid areas of Gansu, Shaanxi, Hebei, and Inner Mongolia. During these incursions, the Xiongnu seized property and killed or enslaved the local populace: Lin Gan (1979) estimates that some 10,000 Chinese died every year as a result of these raids.

By the time of the reign of the emperor Wudi (140 to 87 B.C.), the Han government could no longer endure the damages and insults being dealt them by the Xiongnu. In 129 B.C. Wudi and his generals began a series of military as-

Figure 28 *(left)*. Silver tiger's head ornaments. Hu peoples, Warring States era (403 to 221 B.C.). Retrieved in 1973 from Aluchaideng site, 40 km southeast of Hangjin Banner City, Yikezhao League, in the Ordos. Height of each piece 2.8 cm; width 4 cm. Collection of Inner Mongolia Museum, Huhehaote.

Figure 29 *(right)*. Gold hedgehog ornaments. Hu peoples, Warring States era (403 to 221 B.C.). Retrieved in 1973 from Aluchaideng site, 40 km southeast of Hangjin Banner City, Yikezhao League, in the Ordos. Height of each piece 1.9 cm; length 4.5 cm; weight 8.2 grams. Collection of Inner Mongolia Museum, Huhehaote.

These figures, two of ten recovered, are constructed of pressed gold sheet and are hollow. The hedgehog's snout is extended, and its legs are positioned as though it were climbing.

Pair of bronze plaques of tigers struggling with camels. Xiongnu, Western Han era (206 B.C. to A.D. 25). Length of each plaque 12.5 cm; maximum width 7 cm. Collection of Balinzuo Banner Museum.

saults; the Xiongnu suffered severe defeats and were forced to flee into the far north. In 104 B.C., the Han also initiated military actions in the west and brought Xiongnu territory in central Asia under their control.

Around 60 B.C., the integrity of the Xiongnu empire was further damaged by internal succession disputes, in which five different leaders claimed the right to the throne. This ended 3 years later with the split of the confederation into the Northern and Southern Xiongnu. The Northern Xiongnu retreated to the north to strengthen their forces; but in 36 B.C., the Han moved against them and killed their leader, Zhizhi.

The leader of the Southern Xiongnu, Huhanye, had meanwhile fled south and submitted his people to the Han for protection from Zhizhi's group. Subsequently, after almost a hundred years of struggle against the Xiongnu, the Han negotiated a truce: in 33 B.C., Huhanye presented himself to the Han court, pledging his allegiance to the emperor Yuandi. The Han in turn gave him many gifts and bestowed upon him the concubine Wang Zhaojun in marriage. Thus began another extended period of peace between the Xiongnu and the Han dynasty—a peace that lasted some 40 years.

The story of Wang Zhaojun's trek into the far north with Huhanye was a popular subject in Chinese classical literature, painting, and ceramics. Although the route that the procession took is not detailed in written records, Lin Gan (1979) believes that it must have passed through the Ordos across the northern bend of the Yellow River to the area of modern-day Baotou City and then into Mongolia. Traditional depictions, such as the Song dynasty artist Gong Suran's painting *Mingfei Chusaitu* [The revered concubine crosses the frontier], portray Wang Zhaojun riding a horse and clutching a traditional Chinese *pipa*, a balloon-shaped guitar (Fig. 39).

Figure 30. Two small bronze figurines of deer. Hu peoples, Warring States era (403 to 221 B.C.). Unearthed in 1950 from Waertugou site, Zhungeer Banner, Yikezhao League, in the Ordos. The standing figure of a buck is missing his antlers. Height 4.9 cm; length 6.7 cm. The reclining figure is a doe. Height 4.2 cm; length 6.7 cm. Collection of Inner Mongolia Museum, Huhehaote.

Figure 31 *(above)*. Bronze *Suan'ni* chariot finial. Hu peoples, Warring States era (403 to 221 B.C.). Unearthed in 1962 at Shujigou site, Zhungeer Banner, Yikezhao League, in the Ordos. Length 15.5 cm; height 7.8 cm. Collection of Inner Mongolia Museum, Huhehaote.

The figure of a *Suan'ni* (a mythic ferocious beast akin to a lion) perches at the end of the post socket, which is flared with a slight upward curve and has holes on either side that were perhaps used to fix the ornament to the post. The four feet of the beast are drawn together, giving the impression that it is about to pounce.

The tomb of Wang Zhaojun has yet to be located by archaeologists, but as Wang Longgeng (1981) explains, Chinese legend places it in the Baotou area. Some archaeologists believe that Chinese-style structural ruins uncovered by Russian archaeologists in Siberia in 1941 are the remains of the palace where the descendants of Wang Zhaojun resided (Wu En, 1990). One point is clear: Chinese cultural relics such as the lacquer cup and silk fabrics found in the 1920s at Noin-ulan date from the era after the peace accord between the Han and Xiongnu was sealed by Wang Zhaojun's marriage to Huhanye.

The final breakup of the Xiongnu state occurred during the Eastern Han dynasty (A.D. 25 to 220). Internal dissension over succession rights had in A.D. 47 once again forced a split into southern and northern contingents. Although the southern half pledged their allegiance to the Han court, disgruntled members of this group kept defecting to the north. The Han dealt with this problem by positioning forces at the northern frontier so as to cut off the flow of manpower and resources. They adopted the same policy to deal with the northern group's incursion to the west into central Asia, and these embargo tactics took their toll on the northern Xiongnu.

The northern Xiongnu were also under attack from some of the tribal groups that their empire had subjugated in the past. In A.D. 78 the Xianbei mounted an offensive against the northern Xiongnu and killed their king. When the brothers of this king then began to struggle with each other for succession to the throne, the southern Xiongnu joined forces with the Han in a series of campaigns against them. By A.D. 91, the northern Xiongnu were thoroughly routed, and what was left of their tribes fled west. Those groups that remained came under the suzerainty of the Xianbei, who now occupied the old Xiongnu lands.

The Xiongnu empire, which had persisted for almost 300 years, was the first

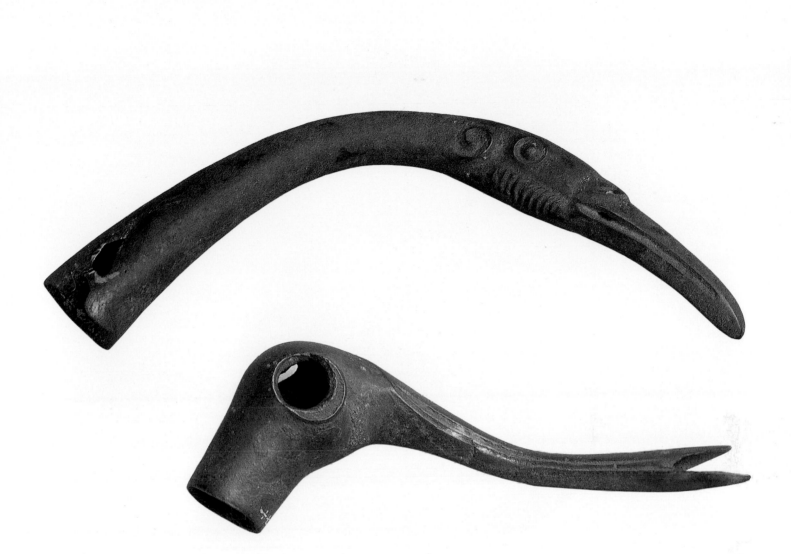

Figure 32. Two bronze chariot finials in the shape of long-billed cranes. Hu peoples, Warring States era (403 to 221 B.C.). Unearthed in 1962 at Shujigou site, Zhungeer Banner, Yikezhao League, in the Ordos. Lengths 24 cm *(top)* and 17.5 cm. Collection of Inner Mongolia Museum, Huhehaote.

Figure 33. Bronze ram's head chariot finial. Hu
peoples, Warring States era (403 to 221 B.C.).
Unearthed in 1974 at Yulongtai site, Zhungeer
Banner, Yikezhao League, in the Ordos. Length
20 cm; height 10.5 cm. Collection of Inner
Mongolia Museum, Huhehaote.

The neck of the ram extends to become the
socket for the chariot post; four holes in the
socket were probably used to attach the finial to
the post. The piece has abrasion on the under-
side. This finial compares closely to one retrieved
in the 1960s in the suburbs of Xian City, Shaanxi
province, which has an inscription dating to the
21st year of Qin Shi Huang's reign (i.e., 226
B.C.).

Figure 34. Portion of a gray pottery architectural tile. Western Han dynasty, 206 B.C. to A.D. 25. Retrieved from tomb at Zhaowan site in the suburbs of Baotou. Diameter 15.5 cm. Collection of Inner Mongolia Museum, Huhehaote.

The tile was originally tubular; this fragment, from one end, is damaged on the bottom. Four *lishu* (clerical script) characters molded in relief read "Conjugal amity with the Shanyu" and commemorate Chinese marital ties with the Xiongnu (*shanyu* being the name for the Xiongnu confederate chieftain).

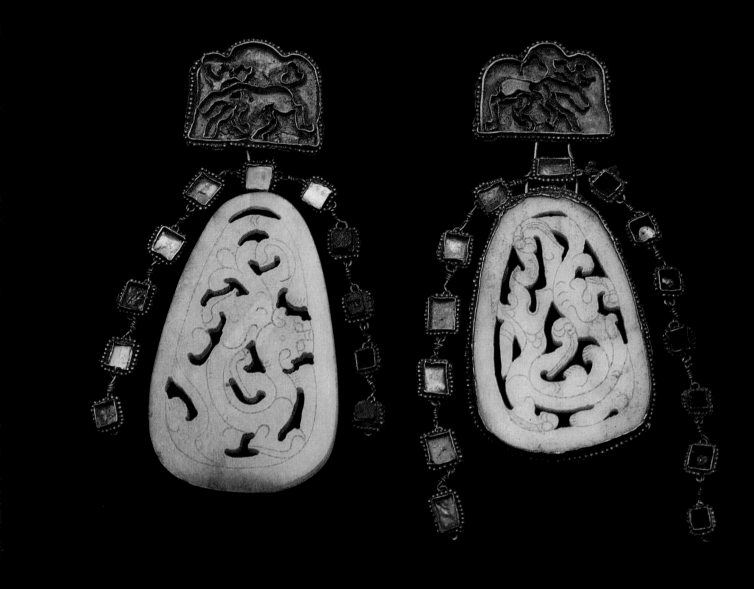

Figure 35. Earrings from the headdress of a
Xiongnu noblewoman, circa fourth to second
centuries B.C. Unearthed in 1979 from Tomb #4
Xigoupan site, Zhungeer Banner, Yikezhao
League, in the Ordos. Collection of Inner
Mongolia Museum, Huhehaote.

    The headdress *(right)* is constructed of
hammered and decorated gold strips and mother
of pearl inlaid in gold and was complete with
necklaces of quartz, agate, amber, and *liuli* (glass-
glaze) strung beads as well as earrings. The earrings feature large openwork jade pendants set in
gold rims attached to gold plaques that feature
relief designs of deer.

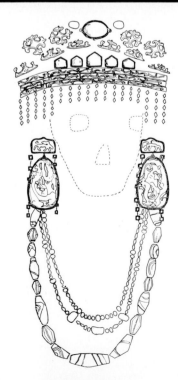

Figure 36 *(above)*. Gold reclining ram belt ornaments. Hu peoples, circa fourth to second centuries B.C. Unearthed in 1979 from Tomb #4, Xigoupan site, Zhungeer Banner, Yikezhao League, in the Ordos. Length 11.7 cm; width 7 cm; height 6 cm. Collection of Ordos Museum, Dongsheng.

The ornaments are made of hammered gold sheets laid over an iron core.

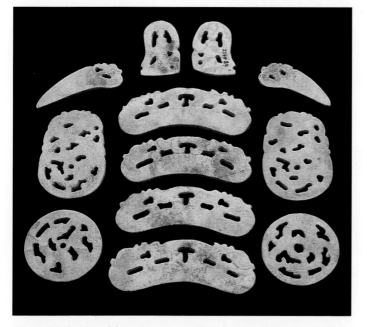

Figure 37. Twelve of forty-two openwork stone ornaments. Hu peoples, circa fourth to second centuries B.C.. Unearthed in 1979 from Tomb #4, Xigoupan site, Zhungeer Banner, Yikezhao League, in the Ordos. Collection of Ordos Museum, Dongsheng.

The pieces, which are carved from white sandstone, are incised with designs of dancers (see Fig. 38), several varieties of dragons, and dragons and tigers.

Figure 38. Design of two of the openwork stone ornaments shown in Figure 37 *(left;* height 5.5 cm), compared with the design of a jade openwork ornament from the Dabaotai tomb, north of Beijing, which dates to the mid-Western Han (second to first centuries B.C.). From Tian Guangjin and Guo Suxin, 1986.

of its kind on the Eurasian steppe, and its various features were characteristic of many empires to follow, up until the time of the Mongols. Even after the collapse of the confederation, the descendants of its members continued to appear in the annals of Chinese history for another 200 years. Although there is a great deal of contention over the matter, some scholars still believe that the Xiongnu who fled into western Asia were the ancestors of the Huns headed by Attila who invaded Europe in the fifth century A.D.

Figure 39. *Mingfei Chusaitu* [The revered concubine crosses the frontier], by Gong Suran. Ink on paper. Courtesy of Osaka Municipal Museum of Art (Abe Collection).

The Song artist Gong Suran, a Daoist priestess from Zhenyuan in modern-day Guangxi province, was active in the late twelfth century A.D. Her painting depicts the trek of the concubine Wang Zhaojun *(detail at left)* into Mongolia for her marriage to the Xiongnu king Huhanye in 33 B.C.; the betrothal was arranged as part of a peace accord between the Western Han court and the Xiongnu.

The colophon on the painting is that of the imperial commissioner to Gaozong, emperor of the Southern Song dynasty from 1127 to 1162 A.D.

3

The Xianbei and the Wuhuan

WHEN MAODUN established the Xiongnu tribal confederation in 209 B.C., among his first victims were the Eastern Hu. In defeat, many of the Eastern Hu affiliate tribes—such as the Wuhuan, the Eastern Xianbei, and the Tuoba Xianbei—were forced to flee north: the Wuhuan withdrew to the area north of the Xilamulun River, which is some 200 kilometers (125 miles) north of modern-day Chifeng City in Inner Mongolia, and the Xianbei retreated into the Greater Xinganling mountain range, northeast of the Wuhuan's new position. The Wuhuan and the Xianbei subsequently suffered a great deal under Xiongnu domination, and during the 400 years of the Han dynasty, the Chinese often used the enmity of these groups in its attempts to conquer the Xiongnu empire.

The Wuhuan are mentioned earlier than the Xianbei in the annals of Chinese history. During the Warring States era, when they were part of the Eastern Hu tribal confederation, the Wuhuan lived along the Laoha River in southeastern Inner Mongolia and in areas of modern-day western Liaoning province. Given the suitable terrain of this area, they were able to establish a thriving agricultural society.

In 119 B.C., after the Han dynasty had defeated the Xiongnu, it took steps to prevent their further incursions into northeastern China. The Han emperor relocated the Wuhuan to five prefectures in northern Hebei and Liaoning provinces, south of the Great Wall of that era. The Han court also established a "Commandant to Govern the Wuhuan," whose purpose was to strictly supervise any contacts between the Wuhuan and the Xiongnu along the northern frontier. To further ensure the goodwill of the Wuhuan, its chieftain was invited to make yearly trips to the Han court in Changan, which was in the vicinity of modern-day Xian in Shaanxi province.

After the final division of the Xiongnu Empire in A.D. 49, the Han emperor

Opposite: Leg of large bronze tray. Detail of Figure 43.

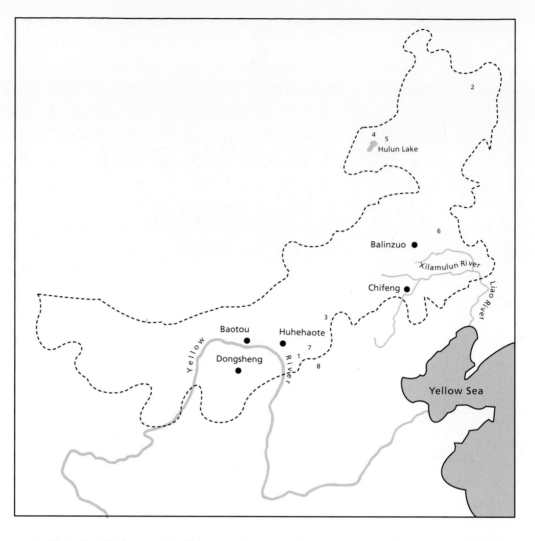

enfeoffed the Wuhuan chieftains and again relocated their populations, this time to ten prefectures along the northern frontier, from western Liaoning province in the east to the area around the northern bend of the Yellow River, north of the Ordos, in the west. Unfortunately, this strategy for securing China's northern frontier was not as effective during the Eastern Han era as it had been earlier. From the latter part of the first century A.D., the Wuhuan constantly rebelled, and by the second century, when internal political conflicts were tearing the Eastern Han dynasty apart, the Wuhuan were particularly unruly. But in 206, the tenure of the Wuhuan as a cohesive political power in the north was effectively ended by Cao Cao (who established the Wei state about 15 years later, after the collapse of the Eastern Han dynasty).

The discovery and excavation of an Eastern Han tomb at Xindianzi Commune southeast of Helingeer County in Inner Mongolia between 1971 and 1973 has given us a glimpse of the historical relations between the Han and Wuhuan. The tomb, which is some 95 kilometers (60 miles) south of the capital of Huhehaote, is approximately 20 meters (65 feet) long; it consists of a corridor that leads into three chambers, each about 4 meters (13 feet) high and built with light gray colored tiles. The walls are painted with frescoes, and—although the tomb was robbed in ancient times—a variety of artifacts were left in place. Based upon these remains and inscriptions, the excavators date this tomb to between A.D. 140 and 200 (Inner Mongolia Cultural Relics Team, 1974).

Although Han records do not specifically identify the person interred at the Helingeer tomb, specialists have deduced from the frescoes that he at one time held the position of "Commandant to Govern the Wuhuan" (Inner Mongolia Cultural Relics Team, 1974). For example, on one of the corridor walls, there is a fresco of the Ningcheng City garrison where this commandant was stationed. A

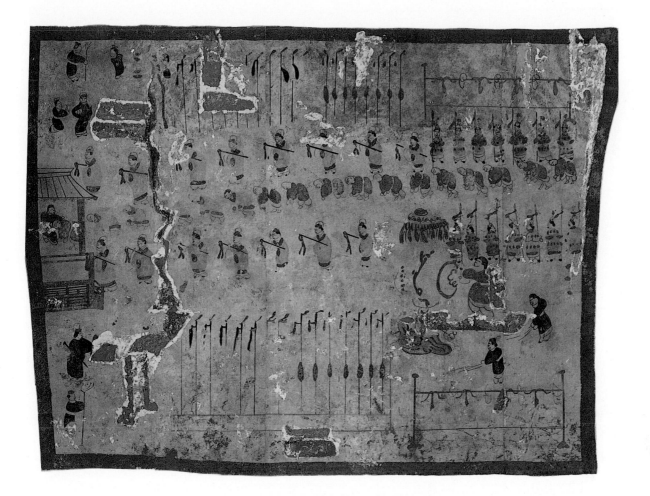

detail of this fresco (Fig. 40) shows a ceremonial procession of Wuhuan entering the garrison with heads bowed to show their respect for the commandant. They are surrounded by Chinese soldiers in armor holding spears; below the lower file of soldiers is a man beating a drum. The Wuhuan are depicted as having shaved heads and wearing the red-colored clothing of the Hu people.

Aғтеʀ тне ғаʟʟ of the Han dynasty in about 220, northern China entered a period of political disunion that lasted for several centuries, until the Tuoba Xianbei established the Northern Wei dynasty in 386. In the midst of this extended era of social disorder and turmoil, confederations of pastoral nomadic warrior tribes worked with the Chinese in establishing a series of sedentary states with cities and bureaucratic functions, the aim of which was to secure the hegemony of north China. Although the states were usually short-lived and unsuccessful, these joint ventures led not only to the cultural diversity but also to the centralization of power that characterized the later Tang dynasty (618 to 907).

Records of one of these confederations of warrior tribes, the Xianbei, appear comparatively late in Chinese texts, but several discoveries in the last 30 years have improved our understanding of the earliest history of these peoples. One of the most remarkable finds is the Gaxian cave site, which is on the eastern side of a long ravine called the Gaxiangou in the northern Greater Xinganling mountains in the far northeastern part of Inner Mongolia.

The cave, which is 25 meters (80 feet) above ground level in the side of a steep granite mountain over 500 meters (1600 feet) high, is impressively large.

Figure 40. Detail of a fresco from an Eastern Han tomb located 40 km southeast of Helingeer County Seat and excavated between 1971 and 1973. Photograph by Kong Qun.

The tomb dates from between A.D. 140 and 200. The fresco, which was on the wall of the corridor leading from the front to the central chamber of the tomb, shows the Ningcheng City garrison where the deceased acted as commandant during his career. Wuhuan are entering the garrison in ceremonial procession, their heads bowed to show respect. They are surrounded by Chinese soldiers in armor and holding spears; below the lower file of soldiers is a man beating a drum. The Wuhuan are shown as having shaved heads and wearing the red-colored clothing of the Hu people.

Figure 41. Gaxian cave, located on the eastern side of a long ravine called the Gaxiangou; northern Greater Xinganling mountains, far northeastern Inner Mongolia. The cave's triangular entrance *(left)* is 25 meters above ground level on a steep granite mountain 500 meters high. Photograph by Kong Qun.

    An inscription of over 200 Chinese characters *(above)* is carved at eye level in the rock face just inside the entrance; it bears a date of 443 A.D. and is signed by Li Chang, who with Fu Nou was sent in that year by the Northern Wei emperor Tuoba Dao to investigate reports of a mountain cave purported to be the Tuoba Xianbei ancestral cave. The text describes an ancestral worship ceremony carried out at the cave and describes how in ancient times the Xianbei ancestors had migrated south.

Figure 42. Large bronze pot with two ring handles. Xianbei, circa third century A.D. Unearthed in 1983 at Shangdu County, Wulanchabu League. Height 32 cm; diameter at mouth 14 cm, at belly 38 cm; weight 7.5 kg. Collection of Cultural Relics Work Station of Wulanchabu League. A two-character inscription in lesser seal script *(xiaozhuan; left)* etched beneath the neck of the piece reads *dayuan* ("all-encompassing Heaven"), referring to the fact that the piece was used as a ritual vessel in obeisance to Heaven.

Figure 43. Large bronze plate or tray with three bear feet. Xianbei, circa third century A.D. Unearthed in 1983 at Shangdu County, Wulanchabu League. Height 8 cm; diameter 46.7 cm; weight 6 kg. Collection of Cultural Relics Work Station of Wulanchabu League.

The outside rim of the tray is decorated with three sets of curling cloud design made with the *pingtuo* applique technique, in which the design is laid down in gold wire and then polished to bring the wire into relief. The bear feet *(see also page 66)* were cast in molds and welded to the plate. Round and peach-shaped gemstones were originally inlaid into the bear figures but are now lost. Trace of gold leaf indicate that the piece was gilded.

Several comparable trays exist, including one in the collection of the Handan City Museum, Hebei province, and another housed in the Palace Museum in Beijing. The gilding and gemstone inlays are relatively better preserved on the Beijing piece, which was retrieved from Shaanxi province; it bears an inscription indicating that it was manufactured in Sichuan province in 45 A.D. Given the fact that this was the era when the Xiongnu confederation was torn with internal strife, it is possible that the tray from Sichuan was manufactured as a gift for the Wuhuan and Xianbei, who were at that time being encouraged to attack the weakened Xiongnu by the Eastern Han court.

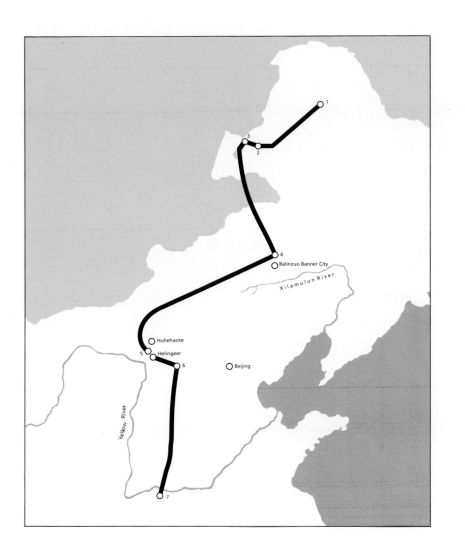

Figure 44: Map of Xianbei migrations, Eastern Han era (A.D. 25 to 220). After Su Bai, 1977. *1*, Gaxian Cave site, Elunhchun Autonomous Banner, Hulunbeier League; *2*, Wangong site, Xinba Erhuzuo Banner; *3*, Zhalainuoer site, Manzhouli City, Hulunbeier League; *4*, Nanyangjiayingzi site; *5*, Shengle city site, Helingeer County, Huhehaote Municipal District; *6*, Pingcheng city site (first Northern Wei dynasty capital), Datong city, Shaanxi province; *7*, Luoyang site (second Northern Wei dynasty capital), Henan province.

The triangular entrance (Fig. 41) is approximately 12 meters high and 20 meters wide at its base (40 by 65 feet), and the four adjoining chambers in the interior together measure 120 meters north to south by 27 meters (about 400 by 90 feet). The ceiling rises over 20 meters (65 feet) at its highest point.

In 1980, on the fourth survey expedition to the cave, archaeologists discovered an area above eye level near the cave entrance where the natural stone had been worked. After brushing the rock face clean, they found a Chinese inscription of over 200 characters carved into the surface (Fig. 41).

The Tuoba Xianbei have a legend that their distant ancestors emerged from a "sacred cave." And the historical records of their dynasty, the Northern Wei, also contain references to a cave. According to the Northern Wei histories *(Weishu)*, in A.D. 443, representatives of a small northeastern tribe, the Wuluohou, sought an audience with the Wei emperor Tuoba Dao to inform him that, in an area northwest of his country, there was a cave where the local populace worshiped Xianbei ancestors. Upon hearing this, Tuoba Dao ordered his ministers Fu Nou and Li Chang to travel to the cave and conduct ceremonies to honor Heaven and Earth and the Xianbei ancestral forebears *(Weishu, juan* ["chapters"] 100, 108a). The inscription from the Gaxian cave is in basic agreement with these Wei dynastic records—it dates from 443 and is signed by Li Chang. In fact, the inscription records the great ancestral worship ceremony carried out at the cave and describes how the Xianbei ancestors had migrated south.

The Gaxian cave description of the Tuoba Xianbei rituals can be studied in conjunction with a pair of extraordinary Xianbei bronze ritual vessels uncovered in 1983 in Shangdu County in Wulanchabu League (northeast of Huhehaote) among a hoard of artifacts found some 20 centimeters (8 inches) below ground level. One of the bronzes is a large flat-bottomed pot with heavy ring-shaped

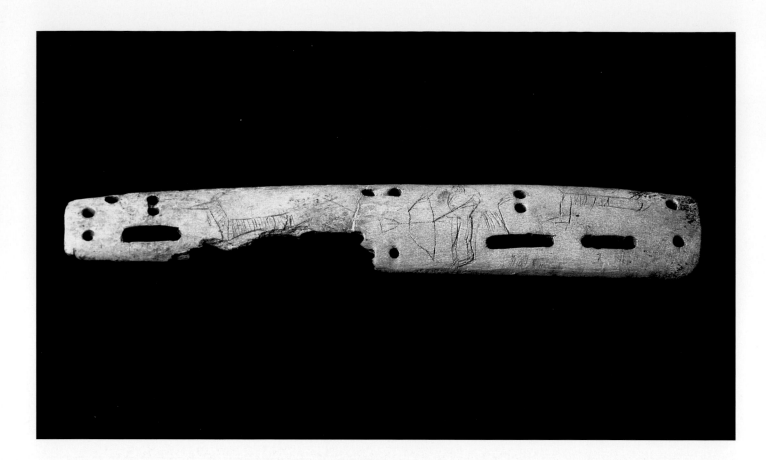

Figure 45. Narrow bone plaque etched with the scene of a man hunting a deer with bow and arrow. Xianbei, Eastern Han era (A.D. 25 to 220). Unearthed in 1960 from Zhalainuoer site, Manzhouli City area, Hulunbeier League. Length 14.9 cm; width 2.5 cm. Collection of Inner Mongolia Museum, Huhehaote.

In all there are sixteen rectangular or circular holes in the piece, which is broken along the edge with three rectangular holes (it appears that there was a fourth rectangular hole along this edge). The rectangular holes were perhaps used to attach the piece to another object, such as a sword sheath, but the distribution of the round holes suggests that they represented notations in some kind of tally system.

handles (Fig. 42). The neck of the vessel bears a two-character inscription that means "all-encompassing Heaven." On top of this pot was a large bronze tray (Fig. 43), the feet of which are cast into the shape of a kneeling bear with mouth agape and front paws extended.

Chen Tangdong (1991) concludes that the Shangdu County hoard must date to sometime between the late second and the fourth century A.D. After the death of the Tuoba chieftain Tanshihuai in A.D. 181, the tribal confederation that he had built dissolved, and various Tuoba tribes migrated into Wulanchabu League. In 258, the Tuoba chieftain Liwei formed another confederation and determined to place a capital city for his new state in the Helingeer County area. Su Bai (1977) suggests that this move was an attempt to centralize the state in a fertile area and to convert the livelihood of the Tuoba from pastoral nomadism to agriculture. After the move to the Helingeer area, Liwei held a ritual obeisance ceremony to Heaven, Earth, and the Tuoba ancestors. On the basis of the topography around the Shangdu site, which appears amenable to farming but borders on extensive grasslands suitable only for pastoral nomadism, Chen (1991) suggests that the Shangdu bronze vessels found there were buried in another ritual obeisance ceremony, one carried out by Liwei prior to leaving the steppe for the Helingeer area.

The Shangdu County hoard and the Gaxian cave have given specialists insight into legends about the cultural origins of the Xianbei. For instance, Lu Sixian (1989) believes that the bear design of the feet of the Shangdu bronze tray fits with Tuoba Xianbei legends that they were descended from the Yellow Emperor. Traditional accounts describe the Yellow Emperor as among those who founded Chinese civilization during the third millennium B.C. He taught his northern confederate tribes to be fierce like the *Pi* bear *(Ursus arctos)* so that

74

they could fight against his enemy, Zhuyou, in a battle that occurred in what is now northern Hebei province. Because his forces were victorious in this battle, the Yellow Emperor's clan came to be known by the surname of "Bear" (*Youxiongshi*).

The *Weishu* also states that the Xianbei were descended from one of the sons of the Yellow Emperor, Changyi, who was enfeoffed with land in the north. The histories recount that, in this region, earth was called *tuo,* and a ruler was a *ba;* hence the Xianbei surname became *Tuoba,* or "rulers of the northern land" *(Weishu, juan* 1). The bear is a cave-dwelling animal, and so its presence on a vessel used in Xianbei ancestor worship (Fig. 43) is consistent with the Xianbei legend of ancestors emerging from a sacred cave. The bears on the bronze tray are shown kneeling, and this human posture suggests that they represent the Pi bear (in some ancient records, the Pi is also called the *Renxiong,* or "bear with humanlike features").

The "Tianhui" chapter of the Warring States era text, the *Yizhoushu* [History of the Zhou dynasty], identifies the totem of the Eastern Hu as the Pi bear, indicating that the legend of the Yellow Emperor as ancestor of the Tuoba Xianbei had become part of their lore at least as early as the Eastern Zhou era (770 to 256 B.C.), when these people were members of the Eastern Hu tribal confederation (Zhu Youzeng, 1971). The model for the bear feet of the Shangdu bronze tray may trace back to the Spring and Autumn era rulers of the Qi state, Duke Xiang and his son Duke Huan (697 to 643 B.C.). Qi bronze vessels carry inscriptions that are among the earliest extant Chinese records of the famed Yellow Emperor, and one of these bronzes has three feet shaped like bears (Xu Zhongshu, 1933). Duke Huan was constantly battling the Shanrong peoples on his country's borders, and it is possible that these people became aware of his ritual vessels and

Figure 46 *(left).* One of a pair of gold-gilded bronze ornaments. Xianbei, Eastern Han era (A.D. 25 to 220). Unearthed in 1960 from Zhalainuoer site, Manzhouli City area, Hulunbeier League. Length 10.4 cm; width 6.5 cm. Collection of Inner Mongolia Museum, Huhehaote.

The ornaments have oval holes along the short ends that may have been used to affix them to a belt. The design of a rampant winged horse *(drawing right)* with a long horn-like snout is cast in relief. This beast is described in the Northern Wei histories *(Weishu)* as having guided the early Xianbei chieftain Jifen and his tribes in their migration south.

Gold ornamental plaque of a kneeling horse with a smaller horse on its back. Xianbei, Eastern Han to Western Jin eras (second to fourth centuries). Unearthed in 1984 in Keerqin Zuoyizhong Banner, Zhelimu League. Length 6.6 cm; width 5.6 cm; weight 41.7 grams. Collection of Zhelimu League Museum.

Comparable bronze ornaments have been uncovered in Qinghai Province in an Eastern Han era tomb at Huzhu prefecture and at a site in Hainan prefecture (Xu Xinguo, 1981).

Figure 47 *(opposite)*. Cast gold pendant of a kneeling horse. Xianbei, Eastern Han to Western Jin eras (second to third centuries). Unearthed in 1984 from Liujiazi site, Keerqin Zuoyizhong Banner, Zhelimu League. Length 8 cm; width 4.9 cm; weight 91.1 grams. Collection of Zhelimu League Museum.

adopted their design features. As Qin Weibo (1988) points out, one prevalent view among scholars is that the Shanrong peoples later became known as the Xianbei.

Both the Wuhuan and the Xianbei derived their name from a sacred mountain. Lin Gan (1989) places the sacred Wuhuan mountain northwest of Alukeermi Banner City in Inner Mongolia. He believes that the "Great Xianbei Mountain" of the Tuoba Xianbei was located in the vicinity of the Gaxian cave site at Alihe Township in the Elunchun Autonomous Banner of Hulunbeier League.

After their stay in the area of the Gaxian cave, the Xianbei began a migration that eventually led them to the Ordos. Su Bai (1977) has used archaeological discoveries to map the course of the migration (Fig. 44). The Xianbei chieftain Tuiyin apparently moved his people south from the Gaxian cave site to a "great marsh," and Su Bai interprets this to mean the Hulun Lake area in northwestern Hulunbeier League, where several important early Xianbei finds (such as the Zhalainuoer and Wangong sites) have been made. However, not all scholars agree with Su Bai. Qin Weibo (1988), for instance, argues that the Hulun Lake area can in no way be called a marshland; he instead identifies marshy areas in northwestern Jilin and northeastern Liaoning provinces as the probable destination of the Xianbei migrations. As evidence, Qin points to archaeological sites in these areas that date to early Xianbei times.

Regardless of this controversy, artifacts found at early Xianbei sites confirm that these people emerged from the cultural milieu of the Eastern Hu of north China. A good example, from the Zhalainuoer site just north of Hulun Lake, is a bone slip (a narrow plaque) etched with the scene of a man hunting a deer with bow and arrow (Fig. 45); An Zhimin and Zhen Naiwu (1981) point out that it is comparable to a bone piece decorated almost 1,000 years earlier (Fig. 19) that

was retrieved from the Eastern Hu Nanshangen site.

Two other artifacts that seem to tie the Xianbei to the Hu are a pair of gold-gilded bronze plaques (one is shown in Fig. 46) retrieved from the Zhalainuoer site. The design on the pieces is of a rampant winged horse with a long hornlike snout. Pieces with a similar motif have been recovered at early Xianbei sites such as Laoheshencun in Jilin province's Yushu County. After an extensive analysis, Chen Sixian (1984) concludes that these plaques were belt ornaments like those decorating the so-called *guoluodai* belts of the Hu peoples during the Warring States era (Figs. 26, 27). Chen is intrigued because the earliest mentions of the term "Xianbei" in pre-Qin records refer to a supernatural beast commonly depicted on the belt ornaments of the Eastern Hu; in other words, the term may have originally referred to the flying beast and only later have become the name of a people.

The Xianbei beast is described in the *Weishu* (*juan* 1) as having guided the chieftain Jifen and his tribes in their migration south, into southeastern Inner Mongolia, and then west, to the Ordos, after the fall of the Xiongnu Empire around A.D. 90. A coin found at the Nanyangjiayingzi site, in modern-day Balinzuo Banner, suggests to Su Bai (1977) that one part of Jifen's journey was a move south, to the area directly north of the Xilamulun River near Balinzuo Banner City. Su Bai deduces that the Xianbei lived in this area during the late Eastern Han dynastic era (i.e., in the late second century A.D.).

In 1984 a set of tombs was unearthed approximately 200 kilometers (125 miles) east of Balinzuo Banner City at the Liujiazi site, and a variety of Xianbei gold and silver ornaments dating from the Eastern Han dynastic era were retrieved. One cast gold pendant, which has two gold chains attached to rings on its upper corners, is in the shape of a kneeling horse, its head inclined down (Fig. 47). The image is reminiscent of the kneeling horse on the headband of the Xiongnu gold crown uncovered in the Ordos (Fig. 25) and lends credence to the notion that, after the breakup of the Xiongnu Empire, the Xianbei subsumed the Xiongnu people who remained in the Xilamulun River area and were subsequently influenced by their culture.

By the time of the Western Jin dynasty (A.D. 265 to 317), the Xianbei peoples were spread across northern China, from northern Hebei and Shanxi provinces all the way to the area south of the Daqing Mountains in Inner Mongolia. A 1956 excavation at the Xiaobazitan site in Liangcheng County, Wulanchabu League, yielded a number of Xianbei artifacts dating from this era, among them an openwork gold ornamental plaque with an abstract design of four animals (Fig. 48). Su Bai (1977) notes that, although the workmanship of this piece is characteristically Xiongnu, the design seems to be distinctly Xianbei. Chen Tangdong and Lu Sixian (1992) believe that the four-animal design fits with Chinese legends of a supernatural beast that lived among the northern Di people in the area where the descendants of the Yellow Emperor resided.

On the reverse of the Xiaobazitan four-animal ornament is a three-character inscription in Chinese that reads "Yituo's gold" (the transliteration of the name as "Yituo" is according to Mongolian Studies Center of the Inner Mongolia University, Huhehaote, 1977; many scholars read it as "Yiyi"). As mentioned earlier, in 258, the Tuoba chieftain Liwei had formed a Xianbei tribal confederation and established its capital in Helingeer County. Thirty-seven years later, his youngest son, Tuoba Luguan, reestablished Liwei's confederation and placed the Liangcheng area of Wulanchabu League under the command of his brother Yituo. Yituo helped Sima Teng, the Western Jin governor of Bingzhou (in modern-day northern Shanxi province), fight off the attacks of a man named Liu Yuan, a Xiongnu by descent who was determined to reunite the Xiongnu Empire. For Yituo's services, the Western Jin enfeoffed him and bestowed golden seals upon him.

Figure 48 *(opposite)*. Openwork gold ornamental plaque with an abstract design of four animals. Xianbei, third to fourth centuries A.D. Unearthed in 1956 from Xiaobeizitan site, Liangcheng County, Huhehaote Municipal District. Length 10 cm; width 7 cm; weight 91.4 grams. Collection of Inner Mongolia Museum, Huhehaote.

A three-character inscription on the back of the piece reads "Yituo's gold," referring to the son of the Xianbei chieftain Liwei. Yituo worked with his brother Tuoba Luguan to reestablish the Tuoba tribal confederation's hegemony over north China after 295 A.D.

Figure 49. Gold *(top)* and silver seals with antelope handles. Xianbei, Western Jin era (265 to 316). Unearthed in 1956 from Xiaobeizitan site, Liangcheng County, Huhehaote Municipal District. Gold seal: height 2.7 cm; face 2.2 cm square. Silver seal: height 2.6 cm; face 2.1 cm square. Collection of Inner Mongolia Museum, Huhehaote.

The gold seal reads "[Seal of the] Righteous Xianbei Marquis Loyal to the Jin"; the silver seal reads "[Seal of the] Xianbei Commandant and Brigadier General of the Jin." The seals were given to the Xianbei for their aid to the Western Jin in repelling attacks led by a descendant of the Xiongnu determined to reunite the Xiongnu empire.

The excavators of the Liangcheng Xiaobazitan site found a gold and a silver seal with antelope-shaped handles (Fig. 49) together with the inscribed four-animal design ornament. When the seals were deciphered, they were found to corroborate the ancient records of Yituo. The gold seal reads "[Seal of the] Righteous Xianbei Marquis Loyal to the Jin," and the silver seal reads "[Seal of the] Xianbei Commandant and Brigadier General of the Jin."

A third gold seal was also retrieved from Xiaobazitan; it reads "[Seal of the] Righteous Wuhuan Marquis Loyal to the Jin." The existence of such a seal is comprehensible when one recalls the intertribal rivalry of the time. The Wuhuan, like the Xianbei, were old enemies of the Xiongnu and, to improve their relations with the Western Jin, were willing to fight against any who tried to reestablish a Xiongnu state in the north. However, the Xianbei wished to keep strict controls on the Wuhuan. In fact, one of the first things that Yituo did when given his command by his brother was to divide and conquer the Wuhuan. He forcibly relocated the pastoral nomadic Wuhuan tribes of Bingzhou to the north, into Inner Mongolia, and then set out on military campaigns to subdue other Wuhuan groups. In a word, that a Wuhuan seal would have fallen into the hands of the Xianbei leader Yituo is consistent with his historical activities.

After Tuoba Luguan's death, his descendants made a series of attempts to concentrate the Xianbei confederate hegemony. This was the era in which northern China was suffering from great military struggles and social upheaval, and many tribal chieftains had gathered together coalitions of ethnically diverse northern tribes and launched campaigns of conquest. Most significant of these was the sacking and burning of the Western Jin capital at Luoyang in Henan province in A.D. 311 by the Xiongnu leader Liu Yuan and his sons. This event resulted in two rather short-lived states called the Former and Later Zhao.

In the middle of the fourth century, the ethnically diverse forces of one of the northern chieftains, Fujian, swept across north China, and a state called the Former Qin was founded. Needless to say, like the earlier attempts at conquest, this campaign resulted in vast carnage and caused great misery. The Former Qin relocated the Xianbei tribes to Shandong province in eastern China, forcing them to engage in agriculture; officials were posted to keep strict control over their activities. Meanwhile the Former Qin relocated the current Xianbei chieftain Tuoba Gui to their capital Changan in modern-day Shaanxi and made the tribal people in Shandong pay taxes to the Former Qin court as well as tribute to Tuoba Gui.

In the late fourth century, after a failed campaign to conquer southern China, the Former Qin collapsed. At that time Tuoba Gui was intent upon establishing a new Chinese-style state for the Xianbei and not the tribal confederation of his forebears. From his experiences in Changan, he had become aware of the importance of having a capital city and of maintaining an active bureaucracy based upon a rational method of selecting officials. After proclaiming himself the King of Wei in 386, he set out on a series of military conquests of northern China, and in 398, moved to his new capital Pingcheng, which was located at modern-day Datong City in northern Shaanxi. Pingcheng was to remain the capital of the Northern Wei dynasty for the next hundred years.

Remains of ancient Pingcheng have been identified at Datong and in the surrounding area. Su Bai (1977) explains that artifacts from the Northern Wei era retrieved northeast of the Datong Train Station indicate that this was the location of the Pingcheng imperial palaces or its offices. A Northern Wei pounded-earth wall has been uncovered north of the train station, and two Northern Wei residences have been found south of Datong. Pingcheng appears to have been designed in the fashion of other capitals of the day, such as Changan and Luoyang. Moreover, the fact that the palace parks are in the southern part of the imperial city indicates that the layout of Pingcheng was also in imitation of that of the

Figure 50 (overleaf). A pair of pottery tomb guardian figures. Xianbei, Northern Wei era (386 to 534). Unearthed from a tomb near Daxue Road, Huhehaote. Heights 39 and 43.5 cm. Collection of Inner Mongolia Museum, Huhehaote.

The heads and hands of these pieces are removable. The figures wear helmets and high boots and are clad in half-length tunics with round collars. Their facial features are grotesquely exaggerated and threatening; their hands are in martial positions.

original capital of a contemporary Xianbei state that the Tuoba had conquered, the Yen's city of Ye, located in the southernmost part of modern-day Hebei.

After his conquest of the north, Tuoba Gui relocated great numbers of peasants, craftsmen, and Chinese patricians from the northeast to Pingcheng to boost the economy of the capital (this kind of relocation was practiced by the Tuoba throughout the Northern Wei dynasty). When the agricultural production of the area proved insufficient to sustain the large population at Pingcheng, major transport roads were built to bring taxes from the northeast.

To keep the pastoral nomadic groups from acting as militarily autonomous agents, Tuoba Gui restricted their wanderings to the Pingcheng geographical domain. He centralized the military by creating an elite imperial guard of the sons of the tribal chieftains, and he solidified his ties with these chieftains through marriage, thus creating a ruling class of Xianbei tribal compatriots. By taking members of powerful Chinese families as hostage, the Xianbei were able to staff the civil administration at Pingcheng; Chinese dissidents often filled civil positions.

Xianbei society underwent many changes during the period when Pingcheng was the capital city. Tuoba Gui's successors worked on centralizing the power of the emperor by building a corps of civil servants. At the same time, Xianbei warriors were sent on campaigns to conquer western China and vast areas of central Asia. A system of military garrisons was established, and Xianbei warriors were made garrison officials. However, when the military actions ceased, the prestige of Xianbei military officials waned in Northern Wei society. The inevitable result was a conflict between the central court and the military.

In the course of its development, the civil official class of the Northern Wei had adopted the high culture of China; its members now wished to distance themselves from their Xianbei origins. This trend culminated in 493, when the Northern Wei emperor Xiaowendi rebuilt the ancient southern capital of Luoyang, which had been sacked and burned in 311. In addition to moving the government away from the steppe to Luoyang in 494, Xiaowendi also issued edicts outlawing the use of the Xianbei language and dress at court and forcing the Xianbei to adopt Chinese surnames.

The influence of Chinese culture on the official class at Pingcheng is illustrated by a Northern Wei tomb unearthed in 1975 near Daxue Road in modern-day Huhehaote. All the artifacts retrieved from the tomb, which contained a man and a woman, are pottery (Figs. 50, 51). Guo Suxin (1977) concludes that in construction the tomb compares closely to those built in central China in the Luoyang area from the Three Kingdoms era through the Western Jin (220 to 317). Guo also finds it similar to the tomb of Sima Jinlong, a descendant of the Jin royal family who served under the Northern Wei and was stationed at Pingcheng. She notes that figurines of a musical troupe with a central dancer (Fig. 51) found in the tomb near Daxue Road compare closely to objects from Sima Jinlong's tomb, which is dated to 484.

Xiaowendi's relocation of the capital south to Luoyang took its toll on the integrity of the Northern Wei state. As the northern frontier became impoverished, Xianbei garrison chieftains were virtually excluded from the power and prestige of the central court. They in turn vented their frustration on the local populace, which only worsened matters. At the same time, the Northern Wei official class became thoroughly corrupt. The economic strain was intensified by Xiaowendi's massive campaign to conquer southern China. After a hundred years in power, the Northern Wei found itself in the throes of civil war: in 524 an insurrection of the Xianbei military leaders (the Six Garrisons Rebellion) began, and the Northern Wei dynasty fell 10 years later.

In the Eastern and Western Wei states that followed, Xianbei heritage was

Figure 51 *(pages 84 and 85)*. Eight pottery figurines of a musical troupe with dancer. Xianbei, Northern Wei era (386 to 534). Unearthed from a tomb near Daxue Road, Huhehaote. Heights range from 15.5 to 19.8 cm. Collection of Inner Mongolia Museum, Huhehaote.

The figures are wearing hats and floor-length, narrow-sleeved robes and are standing, crouching, or kneeling. The dancer's arms are outstetched; the musicians display various positions related to blowing or plucking instruments.

revivified. However, fundamental changes in the general makeup of the population had come about through the turmoil of the rebellions, and Chinese and non-Chinese groups had been brought into the sphere of the central state. Two of the military leaders of the centuries following the Northern Wei era, Yang Zhong and Li Yuan, were quite aware of the importance of a strong military under a central state undivided by ethnic differences. The lessons they learned during their lifetimes were passed on to their descendants, who established the Sui and the Tang dynasties (581 to 907).

4

The Qidan and the Liao Dynasty

THE QIDAN (Khitan) were hunting and pastoral people who originated from eastern Inner Mongolia. Their name first appears in the Chinese records of the Northern Wei dynasty (A.D. 386 to 534), and these and other texts maintain that the Qidan were a branch of the Xianbei people and thus had roots in the Eastern Hu tribal confederation. At the beginning of the third century B.C., when the Eastern Hu confederation was destroyed by the Xiongnu, the Qidan may have been among the tribes that retreated into northeastern Inner Mongolia.

There are many ideas regarding the forebears of the Qidan people. One theory, which appears relatively objective given the prehistory of the Xianbei, is that the Qidan originated from the Yuwen tribe of the Eastern Xianbei, who were descended from groups that participated in the Eastern Hu confederation, and that the Qidan were made up of Xiongnu and Xianbei tribes.

This theory is consistent with Chinese records, which state that after the breakup of the Xiongnu Empire in the Eastern Han era, the Xianbei subsumed the Xiongnu people that had been left behind in the Xilamulun River area. Archaeological evidence also supports this theory of the Qidan's origins: as Zhang Bozhong (1984) points out, in the last 10 years archaeologists have found remains of what they call the Shegen culture type in the Zhelimu League area, and they believe that these finds represent the Eastern Xianbei tribes from the time of the Eastern Han through the Three Kingdoms. They conclude from their discoveries that the Qidan were originally part of the cultural matrix of the Eastern Xianbei tribal confederation.

Textual accounts of Qidan prehistory cover some 500 years, from the mid-fourth century until their establishment of the Liao dynasty in 907. The first phase of this prehistory was the era of the Ancient Eight Tribes, from 344 to 628, when the Qidan wandered nomadically along the banks of the Xilamulun and

Opposite: Detail of bronze candelabra (see page 101).

Archaeological sites of the Liao dynasty.

1. Upper Capital, Lindongzhen, Balinzuo Banner, Chifeng Municipal District.

2. Zuzhou, Sifangzi, Balinzuo Banner, Chifeng Municipal District.

3. Tomb #1, Dayingzi Village, Chifeng Municipal District.

4. Tomb, Keerqin Youyizhong Banner, Xingan League.

5. Tomb, Erlinchang, Tongliao County, Zhelimu League.

6. Sifangcheng, Balinzuo Banner, Chifeng Municipal District.

7. Tomb, Guojiatun, Tuquan County, Xingan League.

8. Liao site, Keerqin Zuoyizhong Banner, Zhelimu League.

9. Hadayingge Commune, Balinzuo Banner, Chifeng Municipal District.

10. Chenguo Gongzhu tomb, Qinglongshanzhen, Naiman Banner, Zhelimu League.

11. Tomb #6, Wanzishan, Chahaer Youyiqian Banner, Wulanchabu League.

12. Tomb, Lingzidonggou, Guangdegong, Wengniute Banner, Chifeng Municipal District.

13. Tomb, Jiefangyingzi, Wengniute Banner, Chifeng Municipal District.

14. Tomb, Bayanerdeng Sumu, Balinyou Banner, Chifeng Municipal District.

15. Fengshuishan, Balinzuo Banner, Chifeng Municipal District.

16. Liao site, Zhungeer Banner, Yikezhao League.

17. *Baita* ("White Pagoda"), Baita Village, Huhehaote Municipal District.

18. Middle Capital, south of Ningcheng County City, Chifeng Municipal District.

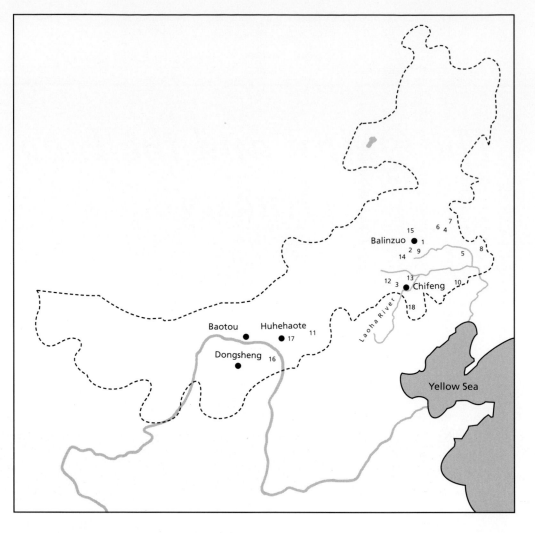

Laoha rivers north of modern-day Chifeng. During this era, the Qidan grew from two to eight tribes and were at one time or another under the suzerainty of the Northern Wei, the Northern Qi (550 to 577), the Tujue Empire, the Gaoli State, and the Chinese Sui dynasty (581 to 618). In Northern Wei times, the eight tribes paid tribute independently and had separate barter markets with the court; but at about the time of the Sui dynasty, there began to be a certain loose degree of alliance between them.

A second period of Qidan predynastic history was the era of the Dahe confederation, from 628 to 730, when the Qidan were under the jurisdiction of the Tang dynasty. During the time of the Dahe confederation, which was the first long-lasting tribal alliance in Qidan history, a council composed of the leaders of the eight tribes made all major military decisions, without exception, and was the most powerful entity in the confederation. The leader of the confederation itself had no authority to make decisions on his own, and if he became presumptuous would quickly meet with censure and in some cases assassination. Nor could individual tribes act independently, except in cases concerning internal tribal affairs.

The final period of Qidan predynastic history, the time of the Yaonian confederation, lasted from 730 to 907. The era began when the last of the Dahe leaders was assassinated, and the Yaonian clan took over in a bloody coup. Order was restored when a new confederate leader was installed by Yali (Yali was an ancestor of the Yelu tribe, whose members were appointed to high positions in charge of the Qidan cavalry).

During the 170 years of the Yaonian confederation, the Qidan continued to practice hunting and animal husbandry but also gradually developed handicrafts and agriculture. Furthermore, cities with permanent buildings began to appear on the Qidan grasslands.

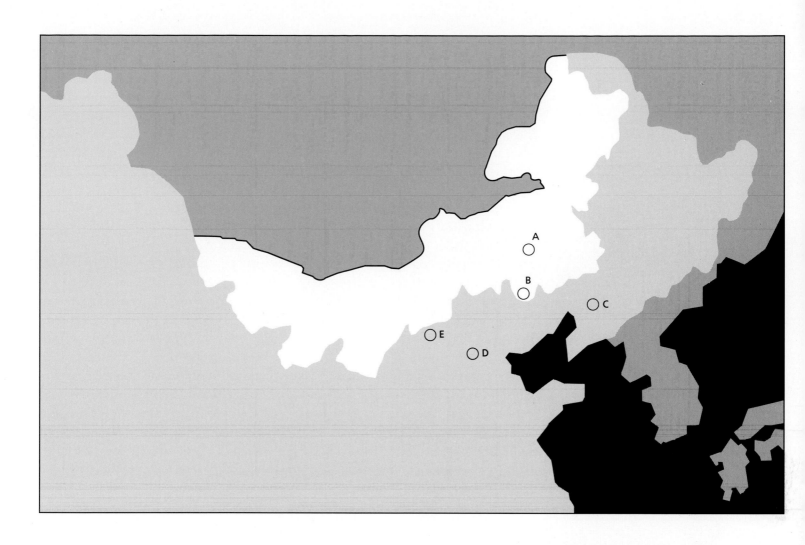

In the final years of the Tang dynasty, regional military commissioners began to set up their own separate regimes in defiance of the court, and uprisings of the peasants further weakened the state. At the same time, the great non-Chinese confederate empires of the northern frontier also declined, one after another.

In 901, the new chief of the Yaonian confederation, Yelu Abaoji, seized the opportunity to begin campaigns of conquest. He subsequently defeated the Nüzhen (Jurchen) to his east, the Xi people to the west, and the Shiwei to the north; he also overran the northern parts of modern-day Hebei and Shanxi provinces and many other Tang prefectures to the south.

At a tribal ceremonial meeting, Yelu Abaoji used the prestige he had gained with his victories to usurp power from the eight tribes, executing their chieftains. In 916, he formally established a state, thereby pioneering a border dynasty in northern China (the dynasty name alternated between Qidan and Liao until 1066, when it henceforth became the Liao dynasty).

Yelu Abaoji turned his attention to the east in 926, to eliminate any danger to his flank before attacking Chinese territories to the south. He quickly conquered the Bohai state, which had been established during the seventh century by the Mohe people in what is nowadays China's northeastern peninsula. Yelu Abaoji died that same year, but as a consequence of his conquests, the whole area of northeastern China had fallen to the Qidan.

Ten years later, under the leadership of Yelu Deguang, the Qidan invaded north China. After destroying the Later Tang dynasty, they aided a warlord in establishing the Later Jin in China, making him into a Qidan puppet. With the acquiescence of the Later Jin, the Qidan then formally obtained control of sixteen prefectures from northern Hebei and Shanxi provinces, which included the Beijing and Datong areas. As a consequence, central China was exposed to the north and

Figure 52. Map of five capital cities of the Liao dynasty (907 to 1125). The principal capitals were *A*, Shangjing, the Upper Capital, north of Chifeng, Balinzuo Banner, and *B*, Zhongjing, the Middle Capital, south of Chifeng, Ningcheng County, in an area that borders on northern Hebei and western Liaoning provinces. The Liao also established the auxiliary capitals of *C*, Dongjing, the Eastern Capital, near present-day Liaoyang City, central Liaoning province; *D*, Nanjing, the Southern Capital, at present-day Beijing; and *E*, Xijing, the Western Capital, at present-day Datong, northern Shanxi province. Courtesy of Inner Mongolia Museum, Huhehaote.

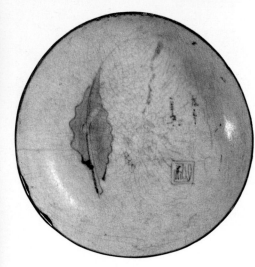

Figure 53 *(top)*. Stone structure, north-western section of Zuzhou site, Balinzuo Banner. Liao dynasty, circa tenth century. Photograph by Li Jingtai.

The building is made of seven giant slabs of granite, each almost 60 cm thick, and is 6.7 meters wide, 4.8 meters long, and 3.5 meters high. It was originally surrounded on all sides by a wall. The structure appears to be a temple erected by the Qidan in the traditions of their Xianbei forebears.

Figure 54 *(bottom)*. Small blue and white porcelain plate. Liao dynasty, circa eleventh century. Courtesy of Singapore Art Museum, University of Singapore.

A design of a leaf is drawn in outline technique with a blue wash. The inscription reads "Made to be used for offerings on ceremonial occasions during the Taiping reign-year era [i.e., 1021 to 1031]." This blue and white piece may have been made in southern China by the Northern Song dynasty and offered by them in tribute to Liao leaders for use at Zuzhou's "Wood-Leaf Mountain" during traditional spring and autumn ancestral worship ceremonies.

without defensible borders, and Qidan horsemen could conveniently make southern incursions to seize property and capture people.

In 960 the Northern Song dynasty was established, with its capital at modern-day Kaifeng in Henan province. One of the first priorities of the Northern Song was to regain hegemony over the sixteen northern prefectures the Qidan had acquired during the Later Jin. To this end, they sent their troops on offensives twice in 986 but met with defeat. After these Chinese campaigns the Qidan decided to retaliate; in 1004 they mounted a massive campaign to take the Song capital. When they reached the area of modern-day Puyang City in northern Henan, they pressured the Northern Song into signing the humiliating Shanyuan Treaty, which stipulated that tribute of 200,000 bolts of silk and 100,000 taels of silver (a tael equals about 38 grams; 100,000 taels is roughly 8,400 pounds) be delivered annually to the Qidan (the tribute amounts were raised in 1042 to 300,000 bolts of silk and 200,000 taels of silver).

The Qidan thus established a formidable empire covering a vast territory of diverse peoples. At the height of their power, the borders of the empire reached the Sea of Japan in the east, central Asia in the west, the Yellow Sea to the south, and southern Siberia in the north. The territorial administrative organization of the state included 6 major districts; 56 prefectures, military prefectures, and prefectural towns; 209 counties; 52 tribal groups; and about 60 vassal states.

To govern this empire, Yelu Abaoji and the Liao rulers that succeeded him carried out a series of political reforms. Even though Yelu Abaoji had executed the leaders of the eight Qidan tribes, the problem of these groups' long tradition of relative autonomy remained. To address this and to centralize authority in the hands of the emperor, Yelu Abaoji divided and dispersed the tribes. He also established a "Palace Guard," a personal army composed of some 2,000 elite warriors drawn from the various tribes (Karl A. Wittfogel and Feng Chiasheng, 1949). As Lin Gan (1989) notes, the Qidan were using the same methods that their predecessors, the Xianbei emperors of the Northern Wei, had employed in establishing their sedentary state.

The Qidan rulers also innovated beyond the Northern Wei policies. Instead of trying to conglomerate the divergent cultures of the pastoral nomadic groups with those of the sedentary agricultural peoples—a tactic that had led inevitably to the downfall of the Northern Wei—the Qidan divided the administrative apparatus of their government into a northern and a southern part. The northern pastoral nomadic groups were governed by officials from the Qidan nobility; Chinese and Bohai people in the south were governed by Chinese landlords as well as Qidan nobility, using the traditional county-prefecture administrative system. This intelligent and well-thought-out scheme, which was responsive to different economic and cultural circumstances, successfully maintained Qidan rule in north China for some 200 years.

After its conquests, the Qidan state fully exploited the assets and manpower at its disposal. There is no question that the principal resources of the Qidan's economy were their constituent pastoral animal-raising groups: these not only provided horses and other animals but also contributed to the military might of the state. However, it is also evident that, as early as the time of Yelu Abaoji's grandfather, the Qidan had developed an interest in agriculture.

With their conquest of north China, and particularly the rich lands of the former Bohai state, the Qidan became well aware of the wealth that could be added to their state through agricultural production. Like the Xianbei, they relocated farmer populations to the Balinzuo Banner area north of modern-day Chifeng to enhance agricultural output. They also moved many craftsmen—metal workers, ceramicists, blacksmiths, printers, and fabric workers—to this area. Chinese who had been captured or had defected to the Qidan helped to design and build cities, palaces, temples, and other structures for the new state.

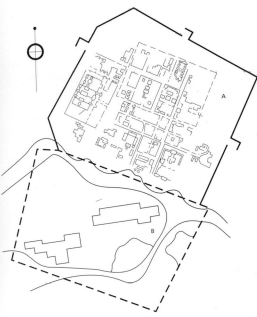

Figure 55. Site of Liao Upper Capital, north of Chifeng, Balinzuo Banner *(left)* and city plan: *A,* Imperial City. Excavations of the Imperial City since the 1960s have revealed the palace remains of the Qidan rulers as well as a variety of ancient offices, temples, shrines, and residences; *B,* Han City. Surveys of the Han City in the south of the Liao Upper Capital has revealed a variety of marketplaces, workshops, residences, and an official posthouse for receiving diplomatic envoys from foreign states. Photograph courtesy of Jin Yongtian; city plan courtesy of Balinzuo Museum.

Since the establishment of the People's Republic of China, archaeological survey and exploration have revealed numerous Qidan sites, including cities, administrative centers, graveyards, tombs, mausoleums, stone inscriptions, wall paintings, ceramic kilns, and Buddhist pagodas and temples. These sites and the cultural remains they have yielded are critical in scrutinizing the often vague and disparaging Chinese historical accounts of the Qidan. In addition they afford us glimpses of hitherto unknown aspects of Qidan culture.

In the last several decades, almost 200 cities established by the Qidan have been uncovered within Inner Mongolia, including Shangjing (the Upper Capital), one of five capital cities built to oversee the empire (Fig. 52). Located north of Chifeng near Lindong in Balinzuo Banner, the Upper Capital was the first of the five administrative centers to be constructed, and it remained the central Liao capital for more than 200 years, until shortly before the fall of the dynasty.

There is reason to believe that the Qidan built this city in the Balinzuo Banner area not only because this was the birthplace of Yelu Abaoji's most immediate ancestors but also because they believed that this country was their ancestral homeland. Zuzhou, another Qidan city located very near the Upper Capital, seems to further connect the Balinzuo Banner area with the Qidan's distant past.

According to medieval records, Yelu Abaoji and his imperial consort were enshrined in a precipitous mountain ravine several kilometers to the northwest of a city called Zuzhou. (The word *Zuzhou* literally means "Ancestral District," and the mountain directly behind this city was sometimes referred to as *Zushan* or "Ancestral Mountain.") In the 1930s, Japanese archaeologists excavated the remains of a city near the Upper Capital and determined that its organization and structure fundamentally coincide with the medieval records of Zuzhou (Zhang Songbo and Feng Lei, 1991).

Zuzhou faced southeast and was basically rectangular in shape; it was sur-

rounded by a wall about 1,800 meters (6,000 feet) long. Based on the various temple remains found there and Zuzhou's structural similarities to the nearby Upper Capital, Zhang and Feng (1991) believe that it was one of the cities that Yelu Abaoji built in the early years of his reign as a center for Qidan ancestral worship.

Of particular interest is a large intact stone structure in the northwestern section of the Zuzhou site (Fig. 53). This rectangular one-room building with a flat roof is made of seven giant slabs of granite, each almost 60 centimeters (2 feet) thick. The building is 6.7 meters wide, 4.8 meters long, and 3.5 meters high (22 by 16 by 11 feet). The building was surrounded on all sides by a wall, and there were no other structures in its immediate vicinity. Chen Yongzhi (1991) concludes that the structure was erected between 901 and 912, prior to the construction of the Upper Capital.

The stone structure is not like ancestral temples of central China's Tang dynasty, as are worship sites uncovered in other parts of Zuzhou and in the nearby mountains. Zhang and Feng (1991) make a convincing argument that the stone room was used by the Yelu clan rulers to pay obeisance to distant Xianbei ancestors. The Yelu and other Qidan tribes believed that they were descended from the Xianbei, who worshipped an ancestral mountain. The discovery of the Gaxian cave and its inscription are evidence that the Xianbei used a natural cave as an ancestral worship temple. Zhang and Feng point out that, when the Xianbei moved south into the area of modern-day western Liaoning province in the first century A.D., they chose a mountain in this new area as an alternate ancestral mountain and built a stone room as a temple in commemoration of the Gaxian cave. In a word, the Zuzhou site's stone structure appears to be a temple erected by the Qidan in the traditions of their Xianbei forebears.

Zushan, the "Ancestral Mountain" directly behind Zuzhou, was also called "Wood-leaf Mountain" *(Muyeshan)*, and this may have bearing on the origins of a

Figure 58. Fresco, mid-Liao dynasty (circa eleventh century). From the western corridor wall of Tomb #1, unearthed in 1978, at the Beisanjia Village site, Aohan Banner, Chifeng Municipal District. Photograph courtesy of Inner Mongolia Museum, Huhehaote.

The painting depicts a Qidan man leading a horse by the reins with one hand and holding a short staff in the other; the man stands 153 cm high. Another man behind the horse appears to be beating a drum.

Figure 59. Reconstruction of the basic Qidan horse gear, including *a*, pommel, *b*, fender, *c*, cantle, *d*, skirt, *e*, crouper, i.e., straps under horse's tail, *f*, latigoes, i.e., straps hanging from saddle, *g*, stirrup, *h*, breast collar, *i*, tassle, *j*, breast plate, and *k*, bit. Courtesy of Inner Mongolia Museum, Huhehaote.

(opposite)

Figure 60. Designs of ornaments for horse saddle fittings. Early Liao dynasty, tenth century. Based on artifacts retrieved in 1954 from a husband and wife burial (Tomb #1) at Dayingzi Village, near Chifeng, dated to 959. Ornaments in collection of Inner Mongolia Museum, Huhehaote.

a. Chrysanthemum surrounded by three deer kneeling in cropped grass. Gilded silver ornament, length 9.2 cm.

b. Deer kneeling in cropped grass. Gilded silver bridle ornaments, rectangular 4.5 by 2.6 cm; tablet-shaped 5 by 2 cm.

c. Honeysuckle design. Gilded silver bridle buckle, 6.6 by 2.6 cm.

d. Dragons on three sides and two mirror-image dragons playing with a pearl. Gilded bronze ornament, 9.4 by 9.2 cm.

e. Dragons. Gilded bronze ornaments, octagonal 5.4 by 2.4 cm; tablet-shaped 5.4 by 2.2 cm.

blue and white porcelain plate currently housed in a Singapore museum. The plate (Fig. 54) bears an underglaze inscription that reads "[vessel] made to be used for offerings on ceremonial occasions during the Taiping reign-year era" (Taiping was a Liao dynasty period that lasted from 1021 to 1031). Beside the inscription is the design of a single leaf drawn in an outline technique with a blue wash.

There is good reason to believe that this blue and white piece was made in southern China by the Northern Song dynasty, and that it was offered in tribute for use by Liao leaders at Zuzhou's "Wood-leaf Mountain" during traditional spring and autumn ancestral worship ceremonies. The existence of this piece, moreover, challenges the assumption that Chinese blue and white porcelain was first manufactured during the Yuan dynasty, more than 250 years later.

In contrast to Zuzhou, the nearby Upper Capital was a very large complex (Fig. 55) with an outside perimeter of approximately 14 kilometers (7 miles). The northern part of the Upper Capital, the Qidan Imperial City, was basically rectangular, and the pounded-earth walls that surrounded it were 6 to 10 meters (19 to 33 feet) high and 12 to 16 meters (40 to 50 feet) wide at the base (Fig. 56). In the inner part of the Imperial City were the Qidan imperial palaces, and a wide road leading south from these palaces was lined with the offices, temples, shrines, and residences of the Qidan.

Although the cultural strata of the Imperial City are now approximately 3 meters (10 feet) below ground level, various remains are scattered at the surface: in the southeastern sector, there is a stone statue approximately 4 meters (14 feet) high (Fig. 57).

The southern part of the Upper Capital, called the Han City, was also rectangular and surrounded by walls. Within the Han City, scattered along the east- to west-running roads, were a variety of structures—marketplaces, workshops, and residences. There was an official posthouse for receiving diplomatic envoys from the Song dynasty and Xixia state and a hostel for travelling Uighur merchants. Because no structures in the Han City can be identified with the ruling Qidan, Li Yiyou (1964) concludes that this southern part of the Upper Capital was the home of the Qidan's subject population of Chinese (or Han) and other non-Qidan peoples.

The Upper Capital had been designed for the Qidan by their Chinese officials Kang Muoji and Han Tinghui and built between 918 and 925 by a labor force composed primarily of Chinese and people of the conquered Bohai state. Wei Changyou (1988) believes that prior to building the Imperial City, some initial construction must have been carried out in the southern Han City to accommodate the farmers and craftsmen who were being relocated to the area.

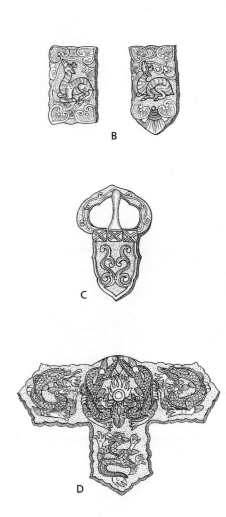

Remains from within the Upper Capital and surrounding area and from other Qidan sites show that in early Liao times, these people stayed close to their ancient equestrian traditions (Fig. 58) and spent much of their time on horseback, either hunting or practicing military maneuvers (the Qidan were famous for their skilled mounted archery warfare and complex, coordinated attacks during battle). Government policy decisions were rarely made at the capitals. Instead, throughout the year, the Qidan emperor and his entourage of nobility and officials hunted and made touring inspections of various territories. These trips, which often lasted for months, no doubt served to sustain the vitality of the Qidan cavalry, particularly the Palace Guard forces directly under the command of the emperor.

Qidan horse-gear has been retrieved from a great many excavations, one of the most impressive of which is the Qidan husband and wife Tomb #1 near Chifeng at Dayingzi Village, which was discovered in 1953 after it was exposed during a summer rainstorm. The tomb is one of the oldest of the Liao burials excavated within Inner Mongolia to date: the tomb inscription dates the burial to 959. Although there is disagreement regarding the identity of the occupants of the tomb, it is clear that the man was a high official in the Liao government. The woman is without question his consort. On the basis of the tomb inscription and relevant records, Jin Yufu (1956) concludes that the interred male was Xiao Quli, who was married to Zhigu, the daughter of the founder of the Liao dynasty, Yelu Abaoji.

Many horse harnesses and fittings were among the over 2,000 artifacts retrieved from this tomb. All are of exquisite workmanship and high-quality materials; they are considered some of the finest Qidan horse-gear yet recovered. As Zheng Shaozong (1956) explains, these pieces have helped clarify many questions about the makeup of the Qidan horse dress (a reconstruction of the basic fittings is shown in Fig. 59). Zheng concludes that the designs (Fig. 60) and workmanship of these artifacts, which are typical of the Tang and Five Kingdoms cultural eras (A.D. 618 through 960), reflect the great cultural exchange occurring then between the Qidan and central China. The deer designs (Fig. 60, a and b) are characteristically Qidan, but the paired dragons playing with a pearl (Fig. 60, e) are classically Chinese. Given the fact that a great many Chinese craftsmen were captured when the Later Jin ceded sixteen northern prefectures to the Qidan, there is reason to believe that the Tomb #1 horse-gear was made by Chinese craftsmen expressly for the Qidan high official interred there.

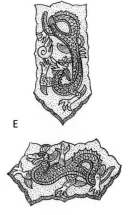

THE QIDAN EXPLOITATION of Chinese craftsmen has bearing on the complex problem of the provenance of ceramics uncovered in Qidan cultural sites. We know that ceramic pieces were given in tribute to the Qidan state by the Chinese during the Five Kingdoms and Song

Figure 62. Pottery cockscomb pot with light green glaze. Liao dynasty, 907 to 1125. Retrieved in 1978 from Liao tomb at Erlinchang, Tongliao County, Zhelimu League. Height 24.5 cm; diameter of mouth 5 cm. Collection of Inner Mongolia Museum, Huhehaote.

This pot has a lid and two strap holes on the top lip. It is decorated with incised curling grass patterns.

eras, and it is thus not surprising that many of the ceramic artifacts found at Qidan sites are thoroughly consistent in form and workmanship with traditional Chinese products. As discussed above, the blue and white "Taiping" plate with the inscription referring to ceremonial offerings (Fig. 54) was quite possibly a piece offered in tribute to the Liao dynasty by the Northern Song in the early eleventh century. Chen Wanli (1956) has analyzed the incidence of Yue porcelains in early Liao tombs. He explains that the Wuyue state, which was situated in Zhejiang province during the Five Kingdoms era, sent tribute to the Liao dynasty on ten separate occasions, and that this tribute included porcelains.

It is also evident that other ceramic pieces were made in imitation of Qidan objects. The best examples are the so-called cockscomb pots (*jiguanhu*) or horse-stirrup pots (*madenghu*) that have been found at Tomb #1 and at other Qidan sites. The form of these pottery and porcelain vessels has its origin in the satchel-like containers made of leather in which the early Qidan peoples carried liquids, such as water, milk products, and wine. The oldest examples of the ceramic cockscomb pot closely imitated the features of the leather vessels—the knotted buttons and the hole for attachment of a carrying strap. Many of these early pieces, such as those found at Tomb #1, had large bellies.

An interesting variant of the early cockscomb pot was retrieved in 1981 from a Liao tomb in the Xingan League's Keergin Youyizhong Banner. This large-bellied pot (Fig. 61) has a dark green glaze with a reddish body, and its neck is adorned with a dragon whose tail extends down the side of the vessel. The piece is quite comparable to a cockscomb pot retrieved from the Liao-era Guangdegong tomb at Wengniute Banner City in the mid-1960s. Xiang Chunsong (1989) finds the Guangdegong cockscombs to be relatively primitive in form, materials, and workmanship, and he concludes that they were fired at a low temperature. He notes

Figure 61 *(opposite)*. Pottery cockscomb pot with dark green glaze and red-colored body. Early Liao dynasty (tenth century). Unearthed in 1981 from tomb in Keerqin Youyizhong Banner, Xingan League. Height 28.5 cm; diameter of mouth 4 cm; maximum width of body 18 cm. Collection of Inner Mongolia Museum, Huhehaote.

The pot has a large belly; its top is adorned with a dragon whose tail extends down the side of the vessel.

Figure 63 *(above)*. White porcelain glazed dish. Early Liao dynasty, tenth century. Retrieved in 1954 from a husband and wife burial (Tomb #1) at Dayingzi Village, near Chifeng, dated to 959. Height 5 cm; diameter at lip 22.3 cm, of footring 8.8 cm. Collection of Inner Mongolia Museum, Huhehaote.

The piece has a gold rim on its lip and footring. In the center of the footring is the character *guan* ("official"), indicating that the piece was made in official kilns for special use by the Qidan imperial family and officials.

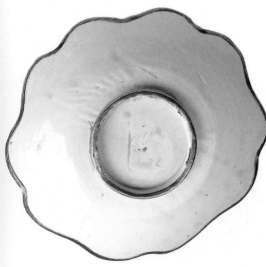

that these pieces are in turn similar to other early cockscomb pots retrieved from the Chifeng area.

With time, the design of the cockscomb pot changed: the body became flatter, and a second strap hole was placed at the top; in addition, the mouth was often covered with a lid. A cockscomb of this later type, with a pottery body and a green glaze (Fig. 62), was unearthed from a Liao-era tomb at Erlinchang in Tongliao County, Zhelimu League. Based on his analysis of this and other artifacts retrieved from the tomb, Zhang Bozhong (1985) concludes that the person interred was a Liao official or nobleman who lived in the late tenth to early eleventh centuries.

Several porcelain pieces retrieved from Tomb #1 at Dayingzi Village have stimulated investigation of the history of the Qidan ceramics industry. These pieces have the character *guan* ("official") inscribed on the bottom, indicating that they were made in official kilns for special use by the Qidan imperial family and officials. One of these pieces is a white porcelain dish with a gold band rimming its lip and footring (Fig. 63). The discovery of this dish in the 1950s set archaeologists searching for the Liao official kilns.

Several important Liao ceramic kiln sites have been uncovered at the Upper Capital and at sites near modern-day Chifeng and Beijing. The Gangwa site near Chifeng has yielded shards with the *guan* character (Feng Yongqian, 1984). It is clear that during the Liao dynasty great amounts of high-quality ceramics were being manufactured at these kilns—no doubt by craftsmen captured from the sixteen northern prefectures.

The fine products produced at these kilns followed in the artistic traditions of the ceramics of the Tang and Five Kingdoms eras. A Liao-era inkstone unearthed at Sifangcheng in Balinzuo Banner (Fig. 64) is an example of the variety

Figure 64. *Sancai* ("tricolor") pottery inkstone in two parts. Liao dynasty, 907 to 1125. Unearthed at Sifangcheng, Balinzuo Banner, north of Chifeng. Height 8 cm; diameter of inkstone 21.7 cm, of laver 23 cm. Collection of Inner Mongolia Museum, Huhehaote.

This artifact has two separate pieces; when assembled, the top serves as the inkstone and the reverse as a basin for washing brushes. The inkstone has a flower petal shape; at its edge is a trapezoidal area for grinding ink; the top and sides of this piece are decorated with a peony pattern in relief and glazed with yellow, white, and green. The laver has a yellow glaze; the rest of this component is unglazed. An ink inscription in Qidan script is discernible (although illegible) on the outside of the laver.

Figure 65 *(opposite)*. Green-glazed vase. Liao dynasty, 907 to 1125. Unearthed in 1952 from Liao tomb at Guojiatun, Tuquan County, Xingan League. Height 37 cm; diameter of mouth 10.2 cm, of base 6.9 cm. Collection of Inner Mongolia Museum, Huhehaote.

The top of the vase is a petal-shaped cup affixed to a phoenix head. Two sets of peony and flower-and-leaf designs are incised on the belly.

Page 101: Bronze candelabra. Liao dynasty, 907 to 1125. Retrieved at the Liao Upper Capital. Height 29 cm. Collection of Balinzuo Banner Museum.

The candelabra was cast in bronze in nine parts, assembled with dowels, and then riveted together. The three-legged base is in a tea-leaf shape and is topped by an openwork sphere. Above this is a flat lotus leaf incised with a sea or water pattern; a dragon erupts from the water and coils up around the shaft. At the top is a maid-servant with her hair in a bun, wearing a long robe with a small collar and gathered waist; she is kneeling on a lotus throne with upraised petals and holding a dish containing the candle socket.

of tricolor *(sancai)* glazed ceramics produced at Liao-era kilns. This unusual and innovative piece has two separate components; when these are put together, the top of the object serves as the inkstone, and the reverse as a laver for washing brushes.

Although many ceramics produced at Liao kilns are classically Chinese in shape and proportion, some show the influence of northern and western cultures. A fine green-glazed vase (Fig. 65) found in a Liao tomb at Guojiatun in Tuquan County, Xingan League, in 1952 is a case in point. The mouth of the vase is a petal-shaped cup atop a phoenix head. Li Wenxin and Zhu Zifang (1962) note that vessels of this design can be seen in wall paintings from Gaochang in central Asia, and that many similar pieces (referred to as the "vases of the Hu [people]") date from the Tang dynasty. Li and Zhu believe that the appearance of this form in Liao ceramics shows the cultural influence of the central Asian states of the Turks and the Uighurs.

Another example of foreign influences on the Liao was unearthed at Keerqin Zuoyizhong Banner in Zhelimu League. It is a tricolor glazed ewer in the shape of a beast with a dragon's head and a fish's body and tail (Fig. 66); the ewer's circular foot is false—the piece's bottom is actually flat.

The ewer's Capricornus shape can be traced to Indian legends of a super-natural beast. Xia Nai (1976) maintains that the beast originally had the body of a ram and the tail of a fish and represented the twelfth house of the zodiac (i.e., Capricorn) in Babylonian astrology. It was later used in India and, around the sixth to seventh century A.D., came across the Silk Road to China. Cui Rui (1983) notes that it was called the "Mojialuo Fish King" (i.e., a whale) by some Chinese; others thought it derived its shape from a fish, an elephant, and a crocodile.

The appearance of Capricornus coincided with the transmission of the Bud-

Figure 66. *Sancai* ("tricolor") glazed Capricornus. Liao dynasty, 907 to 1126. Unearthed at Keerqin Zuoyizhong Banner, Zhelimu League. Height 21.5 cm; length 30 cm. Collection of Zhelimu League Museum.

The horned head is extended upward, and there are rectangular openings at the mouth and neck; the beast has wings at the center of its body. There is a handle between the wings and the tail, and the belly rests on two layers of upward-facing lotuses. The piece has a false circular foot—the bottom is flat.

dhist religion to China, and the beast was believed to have magical powers that could ward off disaster and evil and guarantee peace. Bai Junpo (1984) studied a similar artifact uncovered at Ningcheng County in 1981; he suggests that such pieces may have been funerary ware with symbolic significance comparable to that of tomb guardian figurines.

Bronze signature seals retrieved in Balinzuo Banner may also reflect foreign influences upon the Qidan. The seals are incised with Chinese characters, Qidan characters, and pictorial images and were used by workshops, business establishments, and individuals. Some were colophon seals used by literati on their collections of calligraphy and paintings. The knobs of several of the seals are human figures; on the center of the forehead of one of these (Fig. 67) is a circle—a mark unusual in cultural relics of the Far East. The forehead mark is reminiscent of those on Buddhist images and may be an example of the influence of Indian culture on the Qidan.

Like their predecessors, the Qidan originally lived in yurts. Chinese records of the yurt date back to the Han dynasty, when the dwelling of such peoples as the Xiongnu and Wusun was called a *qionglu*. Based on an analysis of these texts and extant objects, Michael V. Kriukov and Vadim P. Kurylev (1989) conclude that the *qionglu* had a rounded arched roof, was covered with felt, and had a frame made from willow branches. They found that the fully collapsible yurt could be traced back to the Northern Wei era.

Even when the Qidan adopted a sedentary Chinese model of rulership and began building cities, they actively maintained their steppe traditions. In the Upper Capital, for example, there were areas in the Imperial City where no structures were erected, to allow room for members of the Qidan ruling class to pitch their yurts. A gray pottery funerary urn found in 1973 in the vicinity of the

Hadayingge Commune in Balinzuo Banner gives us a look at the Qidan yurt.

The Hadayingge urn (Fig. 68), which is approximately 25 centimeters (10 inches) high, is in the shape of a yurt with a single piece door and two windows; at the apex of the urn, there is a round lid imitating the dome cap that covers the roof window in the traditional yurt. The outside of the yurt urn is etched with designs of deer that are comparable to Liao-era images of these animals carved on rocks in the mountains of Keshiketeng Banner north of the Xilamulun River. Deer often appear in pottery decoration and frescoes from the Liao era (Zhao Guodong, 1992); they were important prey of Qidan hunts in the spring and autumn—the Zuzhou area just north of the Upper Capital was famous as the autumn deer hunting grounds of Yelu Abaoji.

Jing Yongtian (1984) concludes that the yurt urn has the rich flavor of the Qidan's pastoral nomadic heritage and also fits with records of these people's early funerary practices, in which the deceased were cremated. During their pre-history, the Qidan's principal method of burial was to take the deceased's corpse up into the mountains and leave it in the trees for about 3 years, when relatives would return to collect and burn the bones and bury the ashes (Tian Guanglin and Zhang Jianhua, 1992).

According to Tian and Zhang (1992), such recent discoveries as the Wusitu tomb in Tongliao County in southeastern Inner Mongolia coincide with records of these early Qidan burial practices. In the Wusitu tomb, the cremated remains of the deceased were found mixed with birch ashes and covered with several strips of birch bark. Tian and Zhang conclude that this cremation burial shows the impact of the Buddhist religion upon northerners such as the Qidan beginning in the Northern Wei era. On the basis of other tomb discoveries, they believe that despite the influences of central China and many

Figure 67. One of eleven bronze signature seals. Liao dynasty, 907 to 1125. Collected in the Han City section of the Liao Upper Capital. Height 5.9 cm. Collection of Balinzuo Banner Museum.

The knob of the seal is cast in the shape of a Qidan man who holds his hands palm to palm in a traditional position to practice *Qigong* (Daoist breathing exercises). There is a ring on the center of his forehead.

The seal face *(right)* bears the character *Yong* ("everlasting").

Figure 68. Gray pottery funerary urn. Liao dynasty, 907 to 1125. Uncovered in 1973 near Hadayingge Commune, Balinzuo Banner. Height 25 cm; diameter at base 31 cm. Courtesy of Balinzuo Banner Museum.

The urn is in the shape of a yurt with a single door and two side windows; a round lid imitates the dome cap that covers the roof window in a traditional yurt. The outside is etched with designs of deer.

other cultures upon the Qidan funerary practices, the basic method of cremation followed by burial was still prevalent in the late years of the Liao dynasty.

The import of the discovery of the yurt-shaped Qidan burial urn comes into focus when one examines the structure of Liao dynasty tombs. Xiang Chunsong (1979, 1989) studied two tombs in Wengniute Banner north of Chifeng—an early Liao-era tomb discovered in the late 1960s at Guangdegong and a mid-Liao-era tomb unearthed at Jiefangyinzi Commune in 1970. At the apex of the cone-shaped ceiling of each tomb, there is a rounded hole, and the Jiefangyinzi tomb has a stone slab over this hole: the tombs are in effect large versions of the yurt-shaped burial urn, with its dome hole capped with a round lid. Li Yiyou (1991) concludes that, whether round or octagonal, the tomb of a Qidan official or nobleman was given the domed ceiling of a yurt to reflect an important facet of his way of life.

Various other features of Qidan burial practices are also quite ancient. In over thirty different Qidan tombs, a gold, silver, or gilded bronze burial mask has been found placed over the deceased's face, and in some the body was wrapped in wire mesh. Both funerary masks and body mesh wrapping were found in two rich discoveries of the 1980s. The first, a Qidan woman's grave (Fig. 69), is Tomb #6 at Wanzishan in Chahaer Youyiqian Banner, north of Huhehaote, which was unearthed in 1981. The second is the Chenguo Gongzhu husband and wife burial excavated in 1985 in Naiman Banner in Zhelimu League in southeastern Inner Mongolia.

Tian and Zhang (1992) studied several Liao burials and found that the funerary masks appear to reflect the facial features, age, and sex of the interred. One of the largest Qidan funerary masks uncovered to date (Fig. 70) was found at Naiman Banner in Zhelimu League. It is roughly 26 centimeters (10 inches) in diameter and made of gilded bronze sheets. The face has curved eyebrows over closed eyes, the bridge of the nose is somewhat flat, and the cheekbones and mouth denote a faint smile. The body on which this spectacular piece was found was wrapped in a mesh of gold and silver wire.

Clues to the origins of the Qidan funerary mask can be found in two tombs from an earlier time—Tombs #2 and #45 from the Zhoujiadi site in Aohan Banner east of Chifeng. The artifacts uncovered at this site, which were excavated in the 1970s, date to the Xiajiadian Upper Period, and the burials have been identified as belonging to the Eastern Hu of the Warring States era (403 to 221 B.C.).

The head and face of the interred of Tomb #2 was found covered with a mask composed of bronze and turquoise pieces attached to a hemp cloth; a giant shell covered the face of Tomb #45's interred. An Lu (1985) believes that these discoveries show that the Qidan's custom of using funerary masks was passed down from their Eastern Hu ancestors. Unlike the metal mesh body suits, which first appear in Qidan burials from the mid-Liao era and seem to have been derived from the traditional jade burial suits of the Chinese (Tian and Zhang, 1992), funerary masks have been found in the early Liao burials (An, 1985). The use of the masks seems to have roots in the very ancient cultural traditions of the north.

Although a few scholars believe that the Qidan's funerary mask was intended to preserve the interred, many others think the mask is a product of shamanistic religious beliefs. An Lu (1985) notes that one interpretation of the Chinese character for "ghost" in Shang-dynasty oracle bone inscriptions is that it is a pictograph of something being placed on the face of the deceased; he maintains that the mask was a shamanistic technique employed to aid the deceased in travelling from the world of the living to the world of the dead.

Li Yiyou (1991) maintains that, during the Liao dynasty, Qidan shamanistic beliefs had become merged with Buddhist beliefs. A hammered gold statue of a female spirit (Fig. 71) unearthed at Naiman Banner gives evidence of this synthesis. The figure is seated cross-legged on a triple lotus flower throne, and her palms are pressed together in an *angali* mudra gesture; she is surrounded by two coiled dragons, and a triple nimbus is at her back. Although the iconography of the piece is clearly Buddhist, the face of the spirit figure is quite comparable to that of Qidan funerary masks.

The back of this small piece bears a pin that would allow it to be mounted on a hat. An intact silver funerary crown found at the Chenguo Gongzhu tomb has a similar ornament at its apex (Inner Mongolia Institute of Archaeology, 1993).

There is no doubt that, during the Liao dynasty, the Qidan were profoundly influenced by the funerary practices of central China, particularly after they had subsumed the populations of the sixteen northern prefectures. The Qidan began to use differing tomb constructions to denote status, and they adopted other Chinese burial features, such as wooden coffins and coffin bases and tomb frescoes, stele, and guardians. The influence of Tang-era practices is most readily discernible in Qidan burials, although a number of Song traits began to appear in the middle Liao dynasty.

For example, the tomb at Guangdegong yielded a wooden coffin (Fig. 72), a rare find in a Qidan tomb. The coffin is 275 centimeters (9 feet) long and measures 160 centimeters (over 5 feet) at its highest point; it has three separate components and is decorated with inlaid wood in a *xumizuo* pattern, a feature of Buddhist iconography. The V-shaped casket cover has an entwined peony design, and the casket's sides are painted with the Daoist deities of the four cardinal points: the green dragon, the white tiger, the vermillion bird,

Figure 69. The interred of Tomb #6, a Qidan woman's grave, uncovered in 1981 at Wanzishan, Chahaer Youyiqian Banner, Wulanchabu League, north of Huhehaote. Mid- to late-Liao dynasty, circa eleventh or twelfth century. Photograph courtesy of Inner Mongolia Museum, Huhehaote.

The deceased was interred without a coffin; instead the body was laid on a platform constructed of bricks with the head facing north. The head originally rested on a wooden pillow 15 cm high by 40 cm long. The body was dressed in many layers of silk clothing and encased in bronze wire mesh; the face was covered with a gold-gilded bronze funerary mask.

Figure 70 *(opposite)*. Gold-gilded bronze funerary mask. Liao dynasty, 907 to 1125. Found in Naiman Banner, Zhelimu League. Length 26.5 cm; width 25.7 cm. Collection of Zhelimu League Museum.

The mask is made of bronze sheets, which were assembled and then gilded. This is one of the largest Qidan funerary masks found in Inner Mongolia to date.

Figure 71 *(above)*. Gold statue of a Qidan *Apsaras* (female spirit). Liao dynasty, 907 to 1125. Found in Naiman Banner, Zhelimu League. Height 11.2 cm; weight 94.2 grams. Collection of Zhelimu League Museum.

The piece is made from hammered gold. The spirit figure is wearing a crown and is seated cross-legged on a triple lotus flower throne; her hands are pressed together in an *angali* mudra gesture. She is surrounded by two coiled dragons, and a triple nimbus is at her back. A pin on the back of the piece suggests that it was a hat ornament.

and the tortoise with a snake. The best preserved painting is the dragon (Fig. 72); this dynamic beast has a crest, an open mouth, and four-taloned feet and is riding on a billowing cloud.

With this coffin were two pieces of wooden funerary furniture, which Xiang Chunsong (1989) finds comparable to pieces uncovered at the nearby Jiefangyinzi Liao tomb in Wengniute Banner. The small chair and small low table (Fig. 73) were found near the coffin and were probably intended for use in making funerary offerings. Xiang (1979, 1989) attributes the use of these pieces to the influence of Song funerary practices on the Qidan.

Another example of the influence of Chinese funerary habits on the Qidan are the wooden doors to a burial chamber (Fig. 74) that were unearthed from a Liao tomb at Baiyanerdeng sumu in Balinyou Banner north of Chifeng. Painted on one side of these pieces are the traditional door guardians Shenlu and Yulu, brothers renowned for their ability to catch and overpower evil spirits, which they then bound with rushes and threw to tigers to eat. The obverse of the doors shows the legendary generals Qin Shubao and Hu Jingde, who were employed by the Tang emperor Taizong to guard his sleep from being disturbed by demons; the generals' images later came into common use to ward off ghosts. These were Daoist beliefs.

The use of tomb guardians is typically Chinese and is a practice that even the Qidan's predecessors, the Xianbei, adopted. But there is reason to believe that the Qidan also integrated the concept of door guardians into their more traditional cremation burials. This is illustrated by a small gilded bronze plate (Fig. 75) unearthed at Fengshuishan in Balinzuo Banner. The pegs protruding at top and bottom of one side of this item show that it is a door, one of a pair perhaps attached to a funerary urn. The images depicted in relief on either side of this piece are comparable to the tomb guardians painted on the wooden doors from Baiyanerdeng.

Figure 72. Painted wooden coffin *(right)*. Early Liao dynasty, tenth century. Unearthed in 1965 from a tomb at Lingzidonggou, Guangdegong, Wengniute Banner, north of Chifeng. Overall length 275 cm; height at highest point 160 cm. Collection of Chifeng Municipal Museum.

The piece is composed of three parts: the casket, the casket base, and the four-legged pedestal. The base has inlaid *xumizuo* patterns (the term is derived from Sanskrit; the design is the equivalent of the "Diamond Throne" of Buddhist iconography). The casket cover is painted with a design of entwined peonies. The Daoist deities of the four cardinal points—the green dragon *(above)*, the white tiger, the vermillion bird, and the tortoise with snake—are painted on the sides of the casket. There were originally two small doors on the large end of the casket; these were painted with two maidservants, one raising a toiletry case and the other holding a mirror.

Figure 73. Funerary table and chair. Liao dynasty, 907 to 1125. Unearthed in 1970 from a tomb at Jiefangyingzi, Wengniute Banner, north of Chifeng. Table height 22.8 cm; length 68 cm; width 32.2 cm. Chair height 50 cm; length 41 cm; width 40 cm. Collection of Chifeng Municipal Museum.

The table's legs have a cloud-design shape. The top consists of two boards laid in a rectangular frame raised slightly above the boards; the boards are attached to the frame with bamboo nails. The chair's seat is two small boards set into a frame; a panel between the front legs bears an openwork *xumizuo* design. These pieces of furniture were probably used for making funerary offerings.

Like the Xianbei, the Qidan left behind some remarkable Buddhist monuments. In the Upper Capital area, there are stone grottoes and many shrines. Inscriptions on funerary urns have aided archaeologists in locating the remains of shrines mentioned in ancient records as being in the Upper Capital region (Jing Yongtian, 1988).

Most prominent among Liao Buddhist monuments are the massive pagodas that can be found throughout Inner Mongolia. An example is the Daming Pagoda at the site of the Middle Capital, south of Chifeng in Ningcheng County (Fig. 76), which was constructed after 1007. A flying Buddha sculpture adorning one of the pagoda's upper walls (Fig. 76) is comparable to a small jade figurine (Fig. 77) collected from Zhungeer Banner in Yikezhao League in the northeastern Ordos. A number of Liao-era cities have been found directly northeast of Zhungeer Banner, in the Huhehaote, Tuoketuo, and Helingeer areas (Mongolian Studies Center of the Inner Mongolia University, Huhehaote, 1977). A jade figurine of a flying Buddha has also been retrieved from the Jiefangyinzi Liao tomb in Wengniute Banner (Xiang Chunsong, 1979).

One of the most remarkable Liao monuments is the Wanbu Huayanjing Pagoda, also known as the "White Pagoda" *(Baita;* Fig. 78), which is outside of present-day Huhehaote. It is an impressive 36 meters (118 feet) high, has seven stories, and is octagonal—its foundation has the shape of a lotus flower. Gu Juying (1979) infers that it was built to house Buddhist sutras. The only remains today are the inscriptions on its walls written in several languages, including Chinese, Mongolian, Tibetan, and Qidan script, and dating as far back as 1172. There are records showing that the pagoda was repaired in 1167 during the Jin dynasty, when it was renamed Damingshi (Li Zuozhi, 1977); however, the date of its construction is not known, although Gu believes it was built during the late Liao dynasty.

When repair work on the White Pagoda was undertaken in 1983, a number of architectural ornaments were uncovered in the vicinity from approximately 20 centimeters (8 inches) below ground level. Among these was a large gray pottery dragon head (Fig. 78). Although the original use of this piece is uncertain, it may have adorned the end of an upper eave of the pagoda. There is some speculation that it was taken down during the repair work of 1167.

One other matter of great interest in the study of Liao cultural remains is the Qidan writing system. The Qidan did not originally have a writing system but instead sent messages using incised pieces of wood (a practice that was also used by the Xianbei during their predynastic era). During Yelu Abaoji's time, Chinese officials aided him in creating several thousand characters, which became known as the Qidan Greater Script *(Qidan dazi)*. In the year of Yelu Abaoji's death (926), another kind of Qidan writing, called the Qidan Lesser Script *(Qidan xiaozi)*, was invented. Qidan writing continued to be used through the mid-thirteenth century.

In the 1930s, samples of Qidan writing were discovered on the tomb stele of several Qidan emperors. Since the establishment of the People's Republic of China, Qidan writing has been found on various metal objects and on other tomb stelae, some of which have inscriptions in Chinese as well as Qidan script (Fig. 79), and several objects with Qidan writing have been found in the Balinzuo Banner area. Because the grammar of the Qidan language is completely different from that of Chinese, it has been quite difficult to decipher these inscriptions, but Wang Weixiang (1988) reports that specialists can now recognize more than 370 characters of the Qidan Lesser Script.

In the year before the fall of the Liao dynasty, a descendant of its royal family, Yelu Dashi, led a contingent of Qidan north across the steppeland, through what

Figure 74. A pair of wooden painted funerary doors.
Liao dynasty, 907 to 1125. Unearthed from a tomb at
Baiyanerdeng, Balinyou Banner, north of Chifeng.
Height of each piece 124.6 cm; width 53 cm. Collection
of Chifeng Municipal Museum.

The figures painted on the outer sides of the doors
(this page) are the traditional door guardians Shenlu and
Yulu, brothers renowned for their ability to overpower
evil spirits. On the inside *(opposite)* are portraits of the
legendary generals Qin Shubao and Hu Jingde, who
were employed by the Tang emperor Taizong to keep his
sleep from being disturbed by demons.

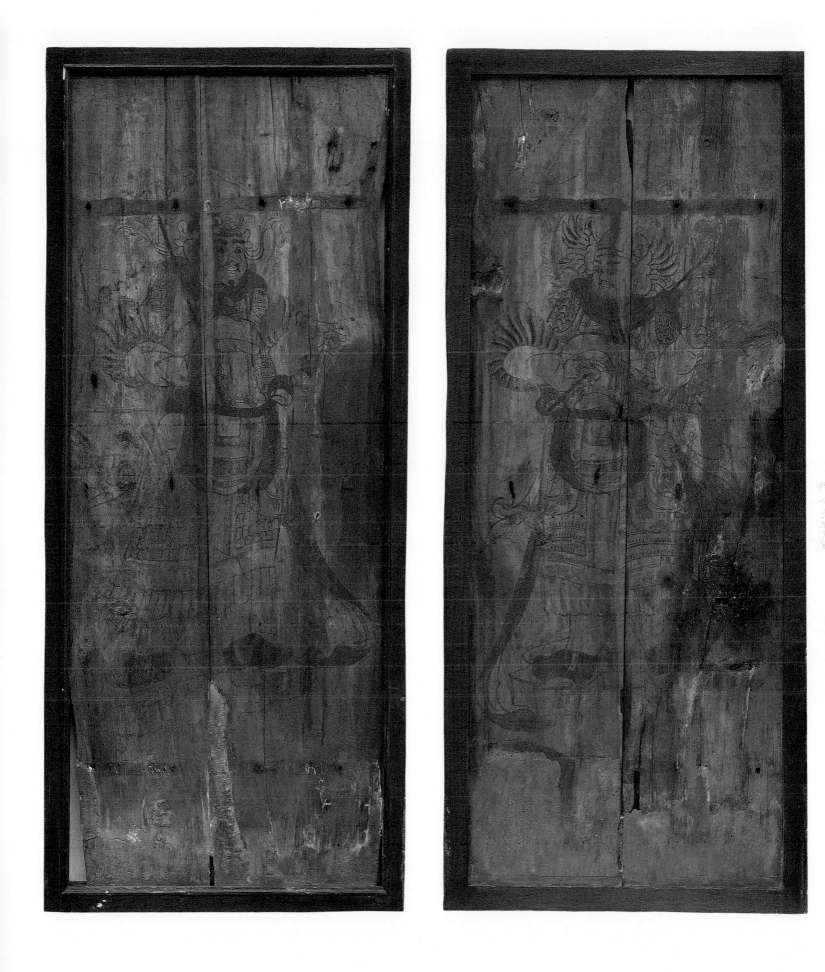

Figure 75 *(right)*. Small gold-gilded bronze funerary door. Liao dynasty, 907 to 1125. Unearthed at Fengshuishan, Balinzuo Banner, north of Chifeng. Height 15.5 cm; width 6 cm. Collection of the Balinzuo Banner Museum.

This door, probably for a cremation urn, has a long peg at the top of one side and a short peg at the bottom. The outer side is decorated in relief with a goblin-like door guardian with a terrifying expression standing on top of a beast and holding a sword in his right hand. The inside of the door is decorated with a majestic figure completely clad in armor and holding a sword in front of him at waist level with both hands. These images are comparable to the guardian figures on the wooden doors shown in Figure 74.

Figure 76 *(below)*. Daming Pagoda, constructed after 1007 at the site of the Liao Middle Capital, south of Chifeng, Ningcheng County. On the upper portion of a wall *(bottom)*, there is an image of a flying Buddha figure molded in relief. Photograph by P. Dematté.

is now Wulanchabu League in Inner Mongolia, and conquered various peoples along the northern Tianshan mountains in central Asia. The Western Liao state that he established had a great influence on the political and economic developments of central Asia during the twelfth century.

In studying the takeover of central Asia by the Qidan, it is important to keep in mind that, as early as the time of Yelu Abaoji, the founder of the Liao, many of the countries and peoples of this region were under the control of the Liao state. Vast quantities of tribute were sent to the Liao court from central Asia, and there was also a great deal of trade, which contributed to East/West cultural exchange (Zhang You, 1991).

These facts are important to the study of artifacts retrieved from Liao era sites. A number of Islamic glass artifacts have been retrieved (Ma Wenkuan, 1992), and Zhang You (1991) believes that many jade, agate, and amber pieces retrieved from Liao sites came from central Asia.

A jade plaque (Fig. 80) discovered at the Liao Upper Capital is intriguing in this regard. The piece was recovered from the Han City, where Chinese and other non-Qidan groups resided. There are holes on its four corners, indicating that it was an ornament, perhaps made to adorn a belt. Carved in relief on the little plaque is the image of a man sitting cross-legged and playing a drum; ribbons draped over his arms flutter out behind him.

This type of drum, a *yao* ("waist") drum, was also called the "Slender-Waist Drum" in Song dynastic records. It is mentioned in ancient texts as one of the principal drums of the traditional Liao musical ensemble. Liao music and dance were heavily influenced by the traditions of central China during the Tang and Later Jin dynasties (618 to 947; Tian Guanglin and Wang Jingzhi, 1988). James C.Y. Watt (1990) dates a comparable piece, one of a set of ten objects, to the

Tang dynasty and maintains that it comes from central Asia.

In the twelfth century, the political integrity of the Liao dynasty began to collapse, in large measure because many of the subject peoples could no longer tolerate the abuse and suffering that the often coldhearted Qidan nobility inflicted upon them (this was true as much for the pastoral nomadic groups as for the sedentary agricultural peoples). The Qidan had been ruthlessly exploitive in support of their lavish lifestyle, and there were many popular uprisings against them.

The enmity that the Nüzhen (Jurchen) people felt for the Qidan was especially strong. In his work *Songmuo Wenji* [Records of experience on the pine-forest plain], the Song official Hong Hao (1088 to 1155) indicates that the Qidan nobility used Nüzhen virgins as "comfort women," placing them in special houses of prostitution. Toward the end of the Liao dynasty, they even began indiscriminately to take Nüzhen women from the upper classes for this purpose without inquiring as to their marital status (Luc Kwanten, 1979). It was at the hands of the Nüzhen that the Liao dynasty finally fell in 1125.

Figure 77. Jade figurine of a flying boy. Liao dynasty, 907 to 1125. Collected in Zhungeer Banner, Yikezhao League. Length 8.5 cm; width 4.6 cm. Collection of Ordos Museum, Dongsheng City.

The boy holds flower petals in his upturned, outstretched hands. One of his bare feet is twisted around to the front, and the sole is visible. The jade is of high quality, probably from the Khotan area in central Asia.

Figure 78. Wanbu Huayanjing Pagoda or *Baita* ("White Pagoda"), outside of Huhehaote, probably built during the late Liao dynasty (twelfth century). Height 36 meters. Photograph by Kong Qun.

The pagoda has seven stories; it is octagonal in shape, and its foundation has the shape of a lotus flower. The dragon head architectural ornament *(top;* collection of Inner Mongolia Museum, Huhehaote) was uncovered in 1983 near the pagoda and 20 cm below ground level; this sculpture, which is 56 cm high and 55 cm long, may have adorned an upper eave of the pagoda and been taken down in 1167, when the building was repaired by the Jin Dynasty.

Figure 80. Jade plaque. Liao dynasty, 907 to 1125. Retrieved from the Upper Capital, Balinzuo Banner, north of Chifeng. Length 5 cm; width 4.5 cm; thickness 0.6 cm. Collection of Balinzuo Banner Museum.

The design is of a man with a bald head sitting cross-legged and wearing a performer's costume with narrow cuffs and a small collar. Ribbons are draped over the arms of the figure and flutter behind him. He holds a narrow-waisted drum between his knees, and his arms are raised in the act of beating the instrument. The four holes on the corners of the piece indicate that it was attached to a belt.

Figure 79. Tomb stelae in Chinese *(top)* and in Qidan Greater Script of Yelu Xiwen, dating from the late Liao dynasty (eleventh or twelfth century). Unearthed in 1987 in Balinzuo Banner, north of Chifeng. Photographs courtesy of Jin Yongtian.

5

North China during the Pre-Mongol Era

IN THE CENTURIES prior to the Mongol conquest, China was divided into separate northern and southern states whose historical developments were inextricably intertwined. One of the northern states was the Liao dynasty of the Qidan (Chapter 4); another was the Xia state (1032 to 1226). The Xia, which is referred to in Chinese records as the *Xixia* (or "Xia State in the West"), was established by the Dangxiang and extended over large portions of western Inner Mongolia, Ningxia, Gansu, and Qinghai.

Study of the Xia state is difficult and complex because there is no official history of these people. In the past, scholars have relied upon more recent Chinese chronicles or the records of contemporaneous states, which contain brief accounts of the Xia that primarily concern their political and economic relations with the state in question. Archaeological exploration and survey has therefore come to be an important supplement to our understanding of the ancient Xia.

The Dangxiang, or as they are referred to in eighth-century Turkic inscriptions, the Tangut (Talat Tekin, 1968), were one of the Qiang tribal groups that since antiquity had occupied the high plateaus of what is now northwestern China's Qinghai province and Tibet (some scholars believe that the Qiang, who were known to the Chinese as the Western Qiang, were the ancestors of the Tibetan people). According to the Liao histories, the Dangxiang were descendants of the Sanmiao tribes, who originally lived south of the Yangzi River in modern-day Hunan and Zhejiang provinces. Because of their disobedient and rebellious behavior, sometime in the latter part of the third millennium B.C., the Sanmiao tribes were expelled by the Sage king Shun to an area near present-day Dunhuang in Gansu.

The earliest mention of the Dangxiang appears in Chinese records of the late sixth century A.D., around the beginning of the Tang dynasty. At that time, they were an unconfederated group of pastoral nomadic tribes inhabiting the grass-

Opposite: Plaque on *Jun*-ware censer. Detail of Figure 88. Photograph by Kong Qun.

Archaeological sites of north China in
the pre-Mongol era.

1. Xia imperial tombs, west of Yinchuan
   City, Ningxia province.
2. Mingai Village, Yijinhuoluo Banner,
   Yikezhao League.
3. Gaoyoufang, Linhe County,
   Bayannaoer League.
4. Heicheng city site, Ejina Banner,
   Alashan League.
5. Luchengzi, Ejina Banner, Alashan
   League.
6. *Baita* ("White Pagoda"), Baita Village,
   Huhehaote Municipal District.
7. Yenjialiang, Baotou Municipal District.
8. Tuoketuo County, Huhehaote
   Municipal District.
9. Tomb, Wutonghua, Wengniute
   Banner, Chifeng Municipal District.
10. Hajinggou Village, Dayingzi, Linxi
    County, Chifeng Municipal District.
11. Adulai Village, Baotou Municipal
    District.

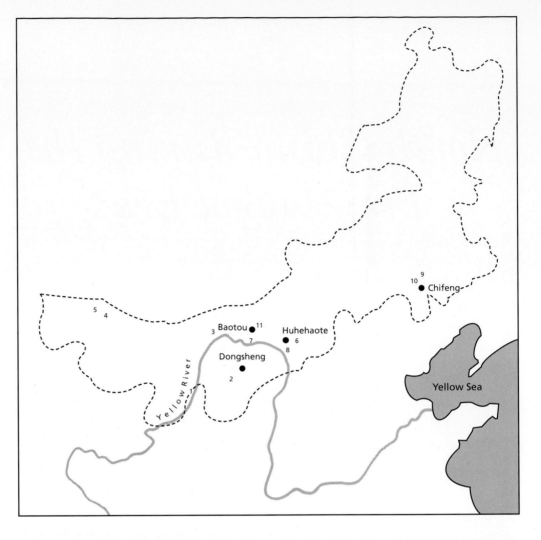

lands of southeastern Qinghai province. During the Tang era, their area of activity
expanded to include western Sichuan and southern Gansu provinces.

The most powerful of the Dangxiang tribes had the surname Tuoba, as did
the Xianbei rulers of the Northern Wei dynasty, and they maintained that they
were the descendants of the Xianbei. Although there is disagreement among scholars regarding this point, an extensive analysis of relevant firsthand sources by Wu
Tianchi (1982) provides justification for the Xia kings' claims of Xianbei origins.

Following internal conflicts (the An Lushan Rebellion) in the mid-eighth
century that necessitated movement of troops away from the border regions, the
Tang dynasty lost political control of China's western frontier. The Tibetan empire of that era then seized its opportunity and conquered Gansu province and
the Tarim Basin of Chinese central Asia. The Dangxiang had often collaborated
with the Tibetans in raids against the Tang dynasty, and many of them now sought
refuge from the Tang within the Tibetan empire.

To control and exploit the Dangxiang, the Tang relocated some of their
clans into areas of Shaanxi province, but this only strengthened the northerners'
will to resist. Furthermore, they began to trade with Chinese merchants in Shaanxi
and, despite Tang edicts against the sale of arms, were able to augment their
stores of weapons.

By the mid-ninth century, the Tibetan empire fell apart because of internal
strife. Toward the end of the century, the Dangxiang leader Tuoba Sigong aided
the Tang in putting down the Huang Chao Rebellion. For his help, the Tang
court enfeoffed him as the Duke of Xia at Xiazhou in southwestern Inner Mongolia
and bestowed upon him the Tang imperial surname, Li.

During the Five Kingdoms era (907 to 960) that followed the collapse of
the Tang dynasty, the Dangxiang tried to stay out of the warfare occurring in

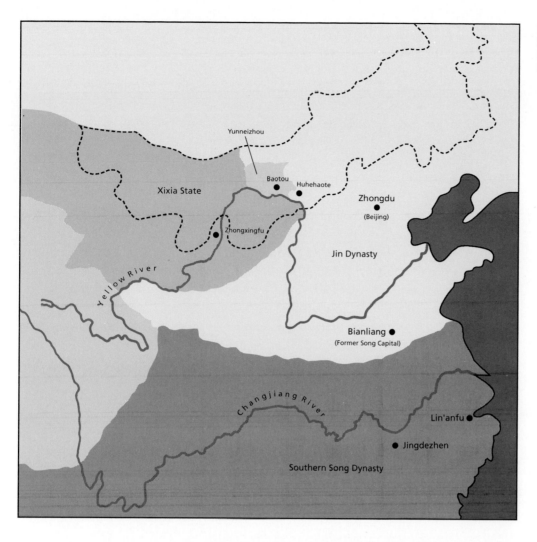

Boundaries of Jin, Xia, and Southern Song territories, twelfth century. Courtesy of Inner Mongolia Museum, Huhehaote.

central China but were nevertheless drawn into a major conflict with the Later Tang state (923 to 936). After a bitter standoff at Xiazhou that lasted 100 days, the Later Tang—who were having difficulty supplying their armies—ended up in retreat. The Dangxiang benefitted from this terrible conflict by gaining possession of large quantities of weaponry that the Later Tang were forced to abandon.

The reconsolidation of China was accomplished by the Northern Song dynasty (960 to 1127). The Song strengthened their hegemony in the north after 979, when they conquered the Northern Han state, a victory in which the Dangxiang played a collaborative role. Although the Dangxiang leader then offered to recognize Song suzerainty over Xia lands, the northerners had had a change of heart by the time the Song envoy reached their court. They soon rose against the Song, and when they entered into alliance with the Liao dynasty, it became evident that the Song were up against more than they could handle (one of their primary difficulties in fighting the Dangxiang was a problem the Later Tang had experienced—how to maintain the flow of supplies to their armies during prolonged conflict in the north).

By the early years of the eleventh century, the Dangxiang leaders Li Jiqian (reigned 982 to 1004) and his successor Li Deming (reigned 1004 to 1031) had consolidated their military control of Ningxia and Inner Mongolia as well as Gansu province, a principal thoroughfare into central Asia to the west. In solidifying their hegemony over Gansu, the Dangxiang set themselves up as middleman in East/West trade relations. They took advantage of this unique position as early as 1007, when Li Deming established barter markets with the Northern Song. The subsequent influx of material goods considerably augmented the economic infrastructure of the Dangxiang.

Li Yuanhao, the son of Li Deming, assumed the throne in 1032 and estab-

Figure 81. Imprint of a bronze official seal in Xia writing. Xia state, eleventh century. Unearthed in 1958 in Yijinhuoluo Banner, Yikezhao League, in the Ordos. Seal height 3.2 cm; face 5.4 cm square. Collection of Inner Mongolia Museum, Huhehaote.

The seal face has two Xia characters that read *Shouling* ("leader"). Two lines of four Xia characters are etched on either side of the seal's knob handle; one line indicates that the piece dates from 1061, the other is perhaps the name of a Dangxiang (Tangut) leader.

Figure 82 *(opposite)*. Ceramic vase with brown glaze. Xia state, 1032 to 1226. Unearthed in 1956 in Yijinhuoluo Banner, Yikezhao League, in the Ordos. Height 34 cm; diameter of mouth 4.2 cm, of base 9.5 cm. Collection of Inner Mongolia Museum, Huhehaote.

The vase has incised designs of flowering Chinese crabapples set into linked-arc lozenges against a line-wave design background.

lished the Xia state, confidently declaring independence from the Song. This act of provocation led to war in 1039, and after a series of engagements, the Song were roundly defeated. In a peace settlement concluded in 1044, the Song recognized Li Yuanhao as "Lord of Xia" and agreed to pay the Xia annual allotments of silk and silver. Li Yuanhao changed his surname from Li to Weiming, and this appellation was used by all subsequent Xia kings (Dunnell, 1984).

The Xia capital was Xingqingfu, near modern-day Yinchuan City in Ningxia (the city was renamed Zhongxingfu by the early twelfth century; Dunnell, 1989). The capital was ravaged during the Mongol conquest, and it continued to decay in the succeeding centuries. However, nearby are tombs of the Xia kings, and as of the early 1970s, archaeologists had surveyed and excavated many of these, recovering associated remains.

The Xia imperial tombs are located 25 kilometers (15 miles) west of Yinchuan on the eastern slopes of the Helan Mountains. Nine tombs have been detected within an area running approximately 11 kilometers (7 miles) from north to south. Each tomb was apparently surrounded by a complete array of traditional structures, making it an imperial mausoleum covering a surface area of approximately 10,000 square meters (2.5 acres). Although most of the ancient structures associated with the three northernmost tombs are no longer extant, the complexes of the remaining six are fundamentally intact.

The interred of two of the tombs have been identified on the basis of unearthed remains and inscriptions: Tomb #2 is the mausoleum of the fifth Xia emperor, Renxiao (reigned 1140 to 1193), and Tomb #8 is said to be the final resting place of the eighth Xia ruler, Zunxiang (reigned 1211 to 1223). Scholars have different ideas about the identity of the emperors interred in the remaining tombs. As Li Fanwen (1984) explains, some believe Chinese records stating that the first rulers interred at these tombs were the Dangxiang monarchs Li Jiqian and Li Deming; this would make the last emperor buried Weiming Dewang (reigned 1223 to 1226), the ninth Xia emperor. Other scholars disagree, maintaining that the first emperor to be buried here was the founder of the Xia, Weiming Yuanhao (reigned 1032 to 1048); this theory maintains that the last emperor buried at the site was the seventh Xia emperor Weiming Anquan (reigned 1206 to 1211).

Analysis of the imperial tombs and surrounding structures has underscored the profound influence of Chinese culture upon Xia burials. Many of the Xia kings coveted Chinese cultural products: as we have mentioned, the Xia had established barter relations with the Northern Song in the early eleventh century. These commercial exchanges were carried on despite political and military clashes, and they played an important role in the development of Xia economy and culture. Although some features of the Xia tombs resemble those of Liao burials, in layout and structure, the mausoleums are fundamentally consistent with Tang-era imperial tombs and comparable to a Song-era tomb uncovered at Gongxian in Henan province (Zhong Kang, et al., 1978). Han Zhaomin and Li Zhiqing (1987) believe that the location for the Xia imperial tombs was clearly influenced by Tang/Song-era principles of geomancy.

In recent decades, archaeologists working in the Inner Mongolia Autonomous Region have uncovered a variety of Xia cultural sites and remains, many of which were located near the state's border. For example, Xia remains have been recovered near the northern bend of the Yellow River in the Ordos, a region of tremendous strategic importance to the Xia because it bordered in the eleventh century on the Liao and Song states and in the twelfth century on the lands of the Jin (Nüzhen) dynasty.

The Xia city sites in the Ordos have yielded various official seals. A Xia bronze official seal (Fig. 81) was recovered in 1958 at Mingai Village in the northeastern

Figure 83. Gold cup with salver. Xia state, 1032 to 1226. Uncovered in 1959 and 1960 at Gaoyoufang city site, Bayannaoer League. Height 5.2 cm; diameter at top 12.4 cm, at base 7.1 cm; weight 220.6 grams. Collection of Inner Mongolia Museum, Huhehaote.

The piece, made of hammered gold sheets, consists of a cup, a salver, and a base, all with lotus petal shaped edges. The exterior of the cup rim, the center and inner edge of the salver, and the outer edge of the base are incised with entwined grass and leaves design.

Ordos, near the border of modern-day Shanxi province. The piece is almost perfectly square and bears an intaglio two-character inscription in Xia folded seal script that reads *shouling,* or "leader." There are two lines of four Xia characters etched on either side of the seal's knob handle; one line indicates that the piece dates from 1061, during the reign of the Xia king Weiming Liangzuo (1049 to 1068). Shi Jinpo, et al. (1988) interpret the other line of characters to be the name of a Dangxiang leader. This is one of the earliest dated Xia official seals yet recovered.

A great many ancient ceramics have been retrieved from Xia sites in Ningxia, and Xia kilns for the manufacture of pottery and ceramic architectural components have been excavated at the Ganzijing site near the Xia imperial tombs (Dong Juan, 1978). Mingai Village has also yielded Xia ceramics, including a vase with an incised brown glaze and a decoration of Chinese flowering crab apples framed by linked-arc pattern lozenges (Fig. 82). Wu Tianchi (1982) calls this piece one of the finest products to come out of the Xia ceramic kiln industry.

In studying such a piece, it is crucial to keep in mind that Chinese culture's impact on the Xia extended to ceramics. There is good reason to believe that Chinese ceramics—especially those produced with high-quality materials and expert craftsmanship by imperial order at official kilns—commanded quite a high price at Xia barter markets. And it is understandable that Xia ceramic craftsmen would have emulated the Song's ceramic forms and designs, which are among the most technically and artistically sophisticated the world has known.

A case in point is the black glaze *yuhuchun* ("wine") vase uncovered in 1965 at the Weicheng site at Shizuishan in Ningxia; the piece stands approximately 26 centimeters (10 inches) high, and its dimensions and overall shape are comparable to Song-era ceramic *yuhuchun* vases. Wu Tianchi (1982) finds this vase and other ceramics retrieved from Weicheng to have a relatively thick and coarse body, and he infers that they date to the early years of the Xia ceramic industry.

Another ancient cultural site that has yielded important Xia relics is the Gaoyoufang city site in Linhe County, Bayannaoer League, south of the Langshan mountains, in the northernmost region of the Ordos. The city was basically square in shape and had gates at the north and south; it was surrounded by walls approximately 990 meters (3,200 feet) long and, judging from those still standing, at least 5 meters (16 feet) high and 7 to 8 meters (23 to 26 feet) wide at the base. The corners of the walls had towers, three of which are still discernible.

In 1959 and 1960, a variety of gold and silver artifacts were retrieved from the inside northeast corner of the Gaoyoufang site. One of these relics, a cup and salver on a base (Fig. 83), is constructed of hammered gold sheets; the cup and salver are in the shape of lotus blossoms, and the object is decorated with incised grass and leaf designs. The form of the gold cup is clearly Chinese: in shape, it is comparable to Tang silver pieces, and particularly to Song lacquer cupstands made to serve a strong black tea grown in southeastern China. The Xia nobility prized high-quality gold objects like this cup, and their emperors took steps to recruit craftsmen capable of producing such fine pieces.

Written records do not clearly identify the city located at the Gaoyoufang site. However, from the time of the founding of its state, the Gaoyoufang city would have been of strategic importance to the Xia's northern defenses. Moreover, as Chen Sixian and Zheng Long (1987) point out, this city was a center for Xia barter with its neighbors, the dynasties of the Liao (907 to 1125) and the Jin (1115 to 1234). Chen and Zheng infer that the city must have been in existence during the early eleventh century: it was located in what was called the Hetao plain, and it was from this area that the Xia launched troops to aid the Liao dynasty when it was under attack by the Jin (Nüzhen) in 1122.

In the early thirteenth century, one of the principal lines of attack during the Mongol conquest of the Xia passed through the Hetao plain. Because the Mongols easily penetrated this northern line of defense in their final assault on the Xia, Chen and Zheng (1987) infer that the Gaoyoufang city must have been destroyed long before 1227. Although the matter requires deeper study, it is possible that the Gaoyoufang city site is the remains of the Xia garrison called Wulahai. This garrison was captured by Genghis Khan in 1209 and may have been used by the Mongols as a staging base for their conquest of the Xia in 1226, as well as their campaigns against the Jin dynasty from 1211 on (Dunnell, 1992).

One of the most significant Xia sites surveyed and excavated in this century is Heicheng (i.e., Khara-khoto; Fig. 84), located in the far northwest of Inner Mongolia, on the edge of the Gobi Desert. The Ejina (Estingol) River, which emerges from the Qilian Mountains of Gansu province, flowed northwest of the Heicheng site in ancient times on its course into Juyanhai Lake. To the north of Heicheng is the Mongolian steppeland, to its west the opening of the Gansu Corridor leading into central Asia.

Heicheng was first explored by the Russian captain P.K. Kozloff, between 1908 and 1909. Sir Aurel Stein worked there beginning in 1914, and Sven Hedin excavated the site from 1934 to 1935. More recently, in 1983 and 1984, a team from the Inner Mongolia Institute of Archaeology carried out a thorough exploration of the site. Each group of surveyors gathered cultural remains, including bronze, iron, and wooden objects, paper manuscripts, coins and paper money, household utensils, fabrics, leather objects, ornaments, ceramics, and Buddhist relics.

The archaeologists studied a variety of structural remains and delineated the fundamental organization of the Heicheng site: it consists of a small inner city lodged in the northeast corner of a larger outer city. The inner complex coincides

Figure 84. Ruins of Heicheng, also called Khara-Khoto, in far northwestern Inner Mongolia, 25 km southeast of Dalai Hubu Township, Ejina Banner, Alashan League, on the edge of the Gobi desert. Photographs by Ta La; courtesy Inner Mongolia Museum, Huhehaote.

A garrison, now called the Inner City and lodged in the northeast corner of the site, was built by the Xia state (1032 to 1226). A larger city, Yijinailu, was built on top of the Xia city during the Yuan Dynasty (1279 to 1368). The various structures remaining include a gate to the Yuan city *(top, right)*, a circular tower fortification from the corner of the Yuan city walls *(bottom, left)*, and ruins of a Buddhist stupa within the Yuan city walls *(bottom, right)*.

with Chinese records of the Xia state's city of Heishuicheng. Stratigraphically superimposed over Heishuicheng is the outer metropolis, the Yuan-era city of Yijinailucheng, which was apparently built by the Mongols around 1286, some 60 years after they had conquered and destroyed the Xia state (Guo Zhizhong and Li Yiyou, 1987).

The perimeter of Heishuicheng, which is about 950 meters (3,100 feet) long, was originally marked by pounded-earth walls; five sections of the southern wall can still be detected—the longest runs about 63 meters (200 feet) . The walls of Yijinailucheng, the outer city (Fig. 84, b), are relatively well preserved and measure 421 meters (east to west) by 374 meters (1,400 by 1,200 feet); they are 12.5 meters (41 feet) thick at the base and originally stood almost 10 meters (30 feet) high. The fortifications of both cities indicate that they were military garrisons (Fig. 84, b and c).

Various Buddhist structures in the inner and outer cities (Fig. 84, d) have been explored by archaeologists, and many Buddhist figures (Fig. 85) and printed texts have been retrieved. The Buddhist religion was of tremendous political and cultural importance to the Xia state: its rulers saw the promotion of this doctrine as a crucial element in their relations with the Liao, Song, and Uighur states, where the religion had long been established. As Wu Tianchi (1982) explains, in the 40 years prior to the founding of the Xia state, the Xia court sent tribute envoys to the Northern Song with requests for sets of the Buddhist Tripitaka texts. And in the latter half of the eleventh century, the Xia court offered gold Buddhist statues and Buddhist scriptures to the Liao dynasty in tribute.

A number of Buddhist texts have been discovered in the ruins of Heicheng and in its surrounding area. In 1908, in a stupa outside the site, Kozloff uncovered a library of documents, most of which are Buddhist texts written in the Xia language, a complex script that used Chinese as its model. The Xia characters were developed between 1020 and 1030, and the language was disseminated during the reign of Weiming Yuanhao (1032 to 1048). In the Yuan dynasty (1279 to 1368), a massive edition of the Buddhist Tripitaka was published in the Xia language, and inscriptions found on stone pillars in Hebei indicate that the script continued to be used until at least as late as the early sixteenth century (Shi Jinbo, 1988).

Kozloff's finds include Xia-language translations of Chinese, Tibetan, and Sanskrit Buddhist texts (Wu Tianchi, 1982), and in some of these pieces there are phonetic marks written alongside the Xia text to aid the Tibetan reader (Shi Jinpo, 1989). After the fall of the Tibetan empire in the mid-ninth century, Tibetan groups had become a significant component of the Xia state's population. Tibetan clerics often held high positions with the Xia, and Tibetan Lamaism had a profound impact on Xia religious doctrines and practices (Wu Tianchi, 1982).

A Buddhist scripture written in the Xia language (Fig. 86) was discovered in 1990, together with two painted clay Bodhisattva statues and a colored silk painting, at the ruins of two temples at Luchengzi, about 20 kilometers (12 miles) west of the Heicheng site. The scriptures are printed on yellow or earth-colored linen paper; one sheet bears a woodblock illustration. The texts appear to be discussions of such Buddhist practices as confession rituals. As we know, the Chinese made major advances in the technology of printing during the Song dynasty, and there is reason to believe that many extant Xia-language publications, such as these scriptures, were produced by Chinese craftsmen.

Great quantities of Chinese ceramic shards and vessels were unearthed at Heicheng, and the discovery of Chinese blue and white porcelain there is particularly significant. To comprehend the historical significance of these and other finds of ceramics in Inner Mongolia, it is necessary to examine the political and economic interrelations of the Xia, Jin, and Southern Song states.

From the late tenth to the early twelfth centuries, the Xia bordered on the Northern Song to the south and southeast, and on the Liao state to the east and northeast. The Xia reached accord with the Northern Song in 1044. But the state's relations with the Liao continued to be problematic. Despite several early military clashes, the Xia state had from its inception made efforts to forge peaceful ties with the Liao dynasty through royal marriage alliances. However, when the Xia supported a rebellion of the Dangxiang peoples living inside Liao territory along the northeastern Xia border, east of the northern bend of the Yellow River, the Liao retaliated with a series of unsuccessful punitive campaigns against them. In the latter half of the eleventh century, the Xia made tremendous efforts to improve their political relations with the Liao, finally renewing the marriage alliance in the early twelfth century. They also sent troops to aid the Liao when the Jin conquest began.

THE ORIGIN of the founders of the Jin dynasty, the Nüzhen (or Jurchen), is a complex matter. The annals of Chinese history are not directly helpful: according to Song-era historians, the name *Nüzhen* did not appear until the Later Tang dynasty (923 to 936). Most modern scholars believe that these people descended from either the Sushen or Mohe, which were tribal groups that inhabited the forest areas of Manchuria south of the Amur River (now in the Russian Far East) during the fifth and sixth centuries A.D. Sun Jinyi, et al. (1987) discount the premise that the Mohe were the Nüzhen's ancestors; they maintain that the Nüzhen were clearly descended from the Sushen, a much older group mentioned in pre-Qin texts as existing in the late third millennium B.C., during the reign of the Sage king Shun.

With the fall of the Tang dynasty, the Liao had captured many of the peoples of the northeast, including the Nüzhen. During Liao overlordship, which was brutally repressive, the Nüzhen's component tribes struggled fiercely among themselves until one group, the Wanyan, achieved supremacy. Aguda, the leader of this tribe, began to rally the Nüzhen people in the late eleventh century, and after careful preparation, led a rebellion against the Liao in 1114. The uprising gained momentum, and the Liao suffered one defeat after another. Aguda then formally declared himself the emperor of a new northern state, which he called the Jin dynasty. By 1123, the Nüzhen forces had captured most of the Liao territories, including their southern capital at present-day Beijing.

As the Jin conquest of the Liao was in progress, the Northern Song saw a chance to regain the sixteen northern prefectures that had been Liao territory since the tenth century, and to liberate themselves from the necessity of making yearly tributary payments to the Liao. However, the Jin not only claimed hegemony over the Song's former territories but also maintained that they were to succeed to the Song's annual tribute.

Relations between the two groups quickly deteriorated when the Song failed to live up to the agreement that had been struck, and war ensued. The Song forces were badly defeated in Hebei and Shanxi provinces. A peace was declared in 1126, but hostilities broke out again, and in 1127 the Jin conquered the Northern Song capital of Bianjing, which was at modern-day Kaifeng in eastern Henan province. The Song emperors Huizong and Qinzong were taken captive, as were their wives and imperial relations. The Jin also looted the imperial storehouses and carried thousands of Northern Song treasures away to the north.

The capture of Bianjing meant the fall of the Northern Song dynasty; what remained of its government fled south and subsequently founded the Southern Song dynasty (1127 to 1279), with its capital of Lin'anfu at modern-day Hangzhou in Zhejiang province. A peace accord that the Jin and the Southern Song reached in 1141 left Hebei, Henan, Shanxi, and Shaanxi provinces in the hands of the Jin; the Song territory was then the lands south of the Huai River. But hostilities between the two dynasties continued until 1165, when the Longxing Peace Accord was signed.

The Jin's plundering of the Northern Song capital of Bianjing has bearing on the origins of imperial Chinese ceramic pieces found by archaeologists in northern China. For example, a white porcelain wide-shouldered vase (Fig. 87) was retrieved outside of Chifeng in Inner Mongolia; on the shoulder, written vertically in a rust-colored pigment, are the two characters *neifu,* or "Palace Repository." The term, which has a very long history in China and was used up until the Qing dynasty, does not in itself give a precise context for the piece, and there is disagreement among scholars as to whether this vase and others like it date to the Song or the later Yuan dynasty.

Other pieces of porcelain with similar imperial marks have been retrieved in the Beijing area (at the Houyingfang and Liangxiang sites), and vessels marked "Palace Repository" have been found in southern China, at Hangzhou in Zhejiang. These finds seem to link widely separated geographic locations—the Hangzhou area, the locus of the Southern Song capital, and Inner Mongolia and the Beijing area, which had become Jin territory with the fall of the Liao dynasty (the Jin rebuilt the Liao city at Beijing and relocated their capital there in 1153). The connection may be the Jin; the wide-shouldered palace repository vessel from southeastern Inner Mongolia may represent part of the loot brought north by the Jin after they sacked the Northern Song capital of Bianjing.

The interrelations of the Song and Jin are fundamental to the dating of other Chinese ceramics retrieved in Inner Mongolia in the last several decades. For example, 20 kilometers (12 miles) east of Huhehaote, near Baita Village, is

Figure 85 *(opposite).* Gilded bronze Sakyamuni statue. Xia state, 1032 to 1226. Unearthed in 1958 at Heicheng site, Ejina Banner, Alashan League. Height 39.5 cm. Collection of Inner Mongolia Museum, Huhehaote.

Figure 86. Cover sheet and fragments of two collections of scriptures from a Buddhist text in the Xia language. Xia state, 1032 to 1226. Discovered in 1990 at Luchengzi, Ejina Banner, Alashan League. Each page 13.2 by 7 cm. Collection of Inner Mongolia Museum, Huhehaote. Photograph by Kong Qun.

The text is printed on yellow or earth-colored linen paper; one sheet includes a woodblock illustration.

Figure 87 (opposite). Porcelain guan (wide-shouldered jar). Song/Yuan era, eleventh to fourteenth centuries. Retrieved outside of Chifeng, Hongshan District. Height 31.5 cm; diameter of mouth 5.3 cm, of base 14 cm. Collection of Chifeng Municipal Museum.

The character Neifu ("Palace Repository") is written on the jar's shoulder. Similarly marked pieces have been found at Zhongdu (Beijing), where the Jin dynasty (1115 to 1234) had its capital, and to the south, near Hangzhou in Zhejiang province, at the site of the Lin'anfu capital of the Southern Song (1127 to 1279). Such pieces may have originally been in the stores of the Northern Song palace at their capital of Bianliang, which was sacked in 1127 by the Jin.

the ancient city site of Fengzhou, which was established by the founder of the Liao dynasty, Yelu Abaoji (reigned 916 to 926), and occupied during the Jin and Yuan eras (Li Zuozhi, 1977). In the northwest corner of Fengzhou is the Wanbu Huayanjing or Baita Pagoda (Fig. 78), which was probably built during the late Liao era and repaired in 1167 by the Jin.

In 1970, two large black-glaze jars containing six Chinese porcelain artifacts were uncovered about a half kilometer (one-third mile) southeast of the pagoda. Also retrieved was the broken head of a green liuli glazed pottery Bodhisattva figure. Given the jars' proximity to the pagoda, specialists have concluded that the porcelains were not the possessions of ordinary people or local officials but instead were donated pieces belonging to the temple.

Among the artifacts retrieved from the jars was a lavender-blue glaze censer (Fig. 88) bearing a small rectangular plaque with a fifteen-character inscription in Chinese that reads "One censer made by the Lesser Song on the fifteenth day of the ninth month of the year Jiyou." (Jiyou was an ordinal term for a year in the Chinese Heaven-stem Earth-branch dating system of rotating 60-year cycles.) The censer was manufactured at the ancient Junzhou kilns, which were near modern-day Yuxian in Henan province.

Study of the censer's inscription suggests that it was made in 1129, shortly after the fall of the Northern Song dynasty. The Jin dynasty had conquered the Northern Song capital of Bianjing in 1127, and they took the area of western Henan where the Junzhou kilns were located in the spring of 1128. As early as 1126, when the Northern Song were negotiating with the Jin in an attempt to regain territory lost to the Liao and to halt heavy tribute payments to northerners, Song diplomatic emissaries were instructed to use the appellation "Great Jin dynasty" (Da Jinguo) as a term of respect when addressing the Jin leaders. Critical

to the dating of the censer is the fact that the inscription states that the piece was made by the "Lesser Song" *(Xiao Song)*—"Lesser" indicating respectful address to one's conquerors. The use of the term suggests that the censer was offered in tribute to the Jin by the conquered Chinese of western Henan. The piece must have been donated to the Wanbu Huayanjing temple by the Jin after they rebuilt the pagoda in 1167.

Proper titles were an important matter in the diplomatic negotiations of this era. Wu Tianchi (1982) notes that, when the Northern Song were negotiating the 1044 treaty with the Xia, the question of whether the Xia would be allowed to be called the "Great Xia" alongside the name "Great Song" was hotly debated. And when the Southern Song envoy Wei Qi went to the Jin court in 1165 to discuss the Longxing Peace Accord, the Jin insisted that the title "Great Song" be striken from the diplomatic documents, leaving only the name "Great Jin" (in the end, in the papers that sealed the treaty, both the Song and Jin retained the appellation "Great").

The Jin conquest and the new geopolitical configuration of northern China meant that the Xia were now virtually isolated from the Song dynasty and the barter market that they valued. According to medieval records, the Xia hoped to improve their situation by capturing lands to the south; as a first step, they crossed the Yellow River and attempted to occupy the Yunneizhou, an area that extended along the Jin/Xia national border from modern-day Wuyuan in the west to Baotou and Huhehaote in the east. But the Jin quickly took back this territory. In 1127 the Xia submitted diplomatic documents to the Jin claiming rights to all territories that the Northern Song had seized from them since 1068. The Jin promptly rejected the petition and suggested that the Xia seek compensation for their losses with the Song. The Yunneizhou area then fell firmly into the grip of the Jin dynasty.

One of the most remarkable discoveries of Chinese porcelain in Inner Mongolia in the last several decades was made in what was the Yunneizhou area, at the Yenjialiang site, located 1 kilometer (one-half mile) west of Machi Village south of Baotou City. In 1979, archaeologists surveyed and excavated a site about 600 meters (2,000 feet) south of Yenjialiang Village; according to Liu Huanzhen (1981), they found a number of porcelain shards scattered at the surface, as well as stratified cultural remains approximately 2 meters (6.5 feet) below the exposed face of the sloping terraced paddy fields. Coins of the Song and Jin dynasties were uncovered within the stratified remains, and an intact, high-quality blue and white jar (Fig. 89) was also retrieved from the site.

Blue and white pieces such as this jar are particularly interesting. The technique of underglaze painting with cobalt-bearing minerals, in which designs painted on the feldspathic porcelain body of a vessel appear fixed beneath a transparent glaze, was an important development in the history of ceramics. There are several opinions about the origins of this technique. Although many western scholars maintain that it was introduced to China from the Middle East, via the Mongols, sometime after the 1320s (Garner, 1954; Medley, 1974), Chinese specialists have presented arguments that the technique of underglaze painting and the use of cobalt were of autochthonous Chinese origin (Feng Xianming, 1973, 1980; Zhu Boqian, 1980).

Although there is lively discussion about the origin of the techniques involved in creating blue and white porcelain, there has been little debate about the timing of this technological development: porcelain specialists have long believed that all extant high-quality blue and white porcelain lacking reign-year dates or other marks offering a clue to their dating were manufactured during the Yuan dynasty (1279 to 1368).

However, in the 1970s, shards of blue and white porcelain vessels dating to

Figure 88 *(opposite)*. *Jun*-ware censer with lavender-blue glaze. Early Southern Song dynasty, 1127 to 1279. Unearthed in 1970 about 0.5 km from Wanbu Huayanjing Pagoda, outside Huhehaote. Height 42.7 cm; diameter of mouth 25.8 cm. Collection of Inner Mongolia Museum, Huhehaote. Photograph by Kong Qun.

Two rectangular lugs above the censer's rim are connected to the belly with animal-shaped handles. Around the neck are three *qilin* ("griffins") molded in relief. A small rectangular plaque *(see page 120)* on the neck bears a fifteen-character inscription in Chinese *kaishu* ("regular script") that reads "One censer made by the Lesser Song on the fifteenth day of the ninth month of the year Jiyou." The piece is supported by three small animal-design legs. Because of the thickness of the glaze, it has run across the surface during firing.

The censer was manufactured at the Junzhou kilns, near modern-day Yuxian in Henan province, in 1129, shortly after the fall of the Northern Song dynasty and the capture of western Henan; it was offered up to the Jin conquerors, who subsequently carried it north into Inner Mongolia. It was probably then donated to the Wanbu Huayanjing Pagoda by the Jin after they had refurbished the temple in 1167.

the Tang dynasty (618 to 907) were retrieved from sites in Zhejiang and Henan provinces (Gu Feng and Xu Liangyu, 1985; Yang Wenxian and Zhou Kun, 1985). These shards, and more recent finds from Inner Mongolia, suggest that pieces now labelled as Yuan products may actually date to the Song dynasty and even earlier. In short, we need to reexamine the attributions of unmarked high-quality Chinese blue and white porcelain now in collections in China and abroad.

Clues to the date of the Yenjialiang blue and white jar were provided by Liu Huanzhen's 1989 excavations at the site. In a stratum superimposed by a house foundation, he uncovered a shard from the lower portion of another large blue and white porcelain jar in association with a Jin Dading-era coin. Liu (1989) concludes that the house foundation dates from the Yuan era, and that the artifacts found below it are from an earlier time. Dading-era coins were last struck between 1178 and 1184, which suggests that the shard found with the coin beneath the foundation predates 1184. This is surprising, considering that the earliest blue and white is assumed to date to the Yuan, which began almost 100 years later, in 1279. How may we account for the presence of blue and white porcelain in the hands of the Jin dynasty prior to 1184?

Records of diplomatic efforts between the Song and Jin bear on this question. In ancient China, official gifts of wine and fruit were traditionally delivered on porcelain—the fruit on large plates and the wine in large jars. The Chinese were famous for their porcelain, and foreign countries coveted the containers as well as the products that they carried. In 1163, prior to the signing of the Song/Jin Longxing Peace Accord, a meeting was held at the Song court, and one of the items of business was to decide upon the quantity and kind of local southern products, such as wine, fruit, and silks, that would be sent as gifts with Wei Qi and other Song envoys being dispatched to the Jin court. The decision was made, and the envoys were underway when the Jin attacked Song territories in Jiangsu province.

The reigning Song emperor, Xiaozong, was enraged by this offensive in the midst of a peace mission and decided to have the diplomatic gifts that had been prepared for the Jin distributed instead to the Song army. But Wei Qi disagreed, arguing that if the Jin later resumed peace talks, he would be ill-equipped to conclude the negotiations, lacking the gifts crucial to the diplomatic protocol of the time.

High-quality porcelain such as blue and white required the use of expensive materials and the superior craftsmanship of potters at Song official kilns. Wei Qi had insisted that the gifts intended for the Jin be reserved for diplomatic purposes, for he knew that, if needed, they would be difficult to replicate at short notice (*Songshi* [Song dynastic history], *juan* ["chapter"] 385). On the inside of the rim of the large blue and white jar found at the Yenjialiang site is an X-mark written underneath the glaze, indicating that this jar was produced for special order, perhaps to be carried by a Song emissary like Wei Qi.

Another artifact retrieved in southeastern Inner Mongolia may have reached the area with a diplomatic envoy. In 1956, a large blue and white plate (Fig. 90) was discovered in Tuoketuo, which lies just inside what was Jin territory along the Jin/Xia national border. There is reason to believe that the plate is the kind used by Southern Song diplomats to deliver official gifts of fruit. Chinese missions from 1165 were probably furnished with many large blue and white porcelain pieces like the Yenjialiang jar and the Tuoketuo plate, tributeware to be presented to the Jin court.

Several other discoveries in Inner Mongolia suggest that blue and white porcelain was being manufactured during the Song dynasty, and that such artifacts found their way into the north, either as official gifts or through trade. For example, in 1988, a fine blue and white *yuhuchun* ("wine") vase (Fig. 91) was un-

Figure 89. Blue and white porcelain jar. Southern Song dynasty, 1127 to 1279. Retrieved in 1979 from Yenjialiang Village, south of Baotou. Height 29 cm; diameter of mouth 22 cm, of base 19 cm. Collection of Inner Mongolia Museum, Huhehaote.

The neck is decorated in underglaze blue with a flower-and-leaf design, the shoulder with pomegranate floral design, and the belly with entwined peonies; the foot has lotus-petal panels. A strip of curling grass pattern separates the entwined peonies and the lotus-petal panels. The inside rim bears an X-mark, the top of which is underneath the glaze.

The piece was probably made on special order to be offered to the court of the Jin dynasty (1115 to 1234) by envoys of the Southern Song; it may have held a product such as the famous yellow wine from Shaoxing in Zhejiang province. Jars such as this were manufactured at kilns in the Raozhou district of Jiangxi province, the site of the *Yutu* ("Royal Earth") porcelain industry that was established and run by the Song imperial eunuch Shao Chenzhang in the early twelfth century.

covered in a tomb in Wengniute Banner, north of Chifeng; the tomb also contained five bronze coins, the latest of which dates to between 1063 and 1093. In 1984 a hoard of ancient iron, bronze, and Chinese porcelain objects was found on a slope 300 meters (1,000 feet) northwest of Hajingou Village, Dayingzi Commune, northeast of Chifeng. Five blue and white stem cups (Fig. 92) were among the porcelains. With the Hajingou artifacts were fifty-five coins, the latest of which are Jin Dading coins, struck between 1178 and 1184.

As is the case with most hoards, the Hajingou artifacts may have been buried to avoid their being seized by an enemy; their owners may have hoped to return and recover their property at a later date. The chronological facts of the Hajingou hoard fit well with the notion that it was buried by the Jin fleeing the Mongol conquest. It has been suggested that the hoard was buried at the end of the Yuan era, but this interpretation is difficult to reconcile with the fact that the collection of artifacts contained Song and Jin coins that would have been 150 to 250 years old at that time, as well as with the general lack of evidence that Mongols valued Chinese ceramics.

After the Jin conquest, the Xia had to go through the Jin to obtain Chinese goods. They were aggressive in their attempts to establish trade with the Jin dynasty, and in 1141, the Jin emperor approved the Xia emperor Renxiao's proposal to establish barter markets. After the signing of the Longxing Peace Accord in 1165, Jin/Song trade relations flourished, giving the Jin significant entrepreneurial opportunities to offer Chinese merchandise in trade with the Xia.

One of the principal areas where the Jin and Xia engaged in extensive barter trade after 1165 was possibly Yunneizhou, where the Yenjialiang site is located. In 1980, a collection of more than 10,000 iron coins weighing more than 200 catties (260 pounds) was uncovered at Adulai Village outside of Baotou. He Lin (1981) analyzed the reign-year dates on the coins and found that 4 percent are of the Northern Song Xuanhe period (1119 to 1125), 8 percent are Xia Tiansheng (1149 to 1169; Fig. 93), and the remaining 88 percent are Xia Qianyou (1170 to 1190; Fig. 93). The presence of such a large hoard of Xia currency within Jin borders supports the notion that the Jin and Xia were engaged in extensive trade in the area. Further exploration is needed to determine whether or not Yenjialiang itself was the site of a medieval barter market.

Chinese blue and white may have found its way into Xia territory through diplomatic missions as well as trade. It would not have been easy for the Song to travel to the Xia after the Jin conquest; but Song histories do confirm that, in the early twelfth century, Song diplomatic emissaries, such as Xie Liang, arrived in the north, possibly bringing with them blue and white porcelain as official gifts *(Songshi, juan* 486). Indeed, Liu Huanzhen (1989) states that the blue and white shard from a large jar that he found in stratigraphic context at the Yenjialiang site closely resembles pieces uncovered at the Heicheng site in northwestern Inner Mongolia during excavations in 1983 and 1984.

The work of the Inner Mongolia Institute of Archaeology at the Heicheng site in 1983 and 1984 suggests that much of the blue and white porcelain found there in this century was manufactured during the Song dynastic period. The British ceramics specialist R. L. Hobson was one of the first to suspect that such was the case; in 1928, he tentatively identified blue and white shards from Heicheng as Song pieces (Stein, 1928). The Institute of Archaeology workers found some fifty blue and white shards from at least eleven vessels; a great many of these were unearthed within the Xia inner city. Li Yiyou (1988) identifies one blue and white porcelain cup (Fig. 94) from this group of objects as a Song product of the *Yutuyao* ("Royal Earth") kiln industry, which was administered by the Song imperial eunuch, Shao Chengzhang, and was under the jurisdiction of the Raozhou area, near modern-day Jingdezhen in Jiangxi province. During the Song dynasty, products of government or official kilns in the Raozhou area were called Yutuyao wares (Jiang Siqing, 1959).

The Heicheng discoveries challenge the prevalent assumption that all extant unmarked blue and white porcelains must be products of the Yuan dynasty. It is very difficult to imagine that the Mongols would have imported blue and white porcelain to their distant Yijinailucheng garrison. In contrast, the Xia valued Chinese ceramics and probably carried such wares to their garrison at that same site.

Many of the Heicheng blue and white porcelains were found in the northeast corner of the site, where Mongol and Xia cities are superimposed. It might be argued that the artifacts from the two eras were somehow mingled through time or in excavation, and that the finds thought to be Xia are Yuan after all. However, in the Yuan era, this quarter was the location of the houses of common people; very little blue and white has been found in the part of the city where the Mongol officials resided. The Mongols prized gold and silver objects but did not esteem ceramics.

The consensus of opinion of those conducting the 1983 and 1984 surveys of Heicheng is that the Yuan-era people residing at Yijinailucheng merely used the things that had been left behind by the Xia in their retreat from the Mongols in 1226, and that these resources included some blue and white. The Xia's hasty exodus may explain Sven Hedin's 1934 and 1935 discoveries of assemblages of blue and white shards in association with tenth- to twelfth-century coins at two house sites (K801 and K802) south of Heicheng. The Xia may have smashed vessels they could not carry away, to prevent these treasures from falling into the hands of the Mongol invaders.

There is reason to believe that the large blue and white presentation plate (Fig. 90) found at Tuoketuo in southeastern Inner Mongolia was manufactured

Figure 90 *(opposite)*. Blue and white porcelain plate. Southern Song dynasty, 1127 to 1279. Retrieved at the Tuoketuo train station, south of Huhehaote. Height 7.3 cm; diameter of plate 40 cm, of footring 23.6 cm. Collection of Inner Mongolia Museum, Huhehaote.

In the petal-shaped central design, mandarin ducks frolic in a lotus pond. This area is surrounded by six *ruyi yun* ("scepter-shaped") panels in an ocean-wave background; set in the panels are other mandarin ducks, deer, white crane, and lotus flowers. Along the petal-shaped rim are cloud-and-water and whorl patterns. The reverse of the plate, from the footring to the rim, is decorated with entwined peony and bowstring patterns.

Like the jar in Figure 89, this plate may have been made on special order for use in presenting fruit as a diplomatic gift. Plates such as this were manufactured at Hutian, a *Yutu* kiln of the Raozhou district of Jiangxi province.

at the Hutian kiln, one of the Yutuyao official kilns under Raozhou jurisdiction in the Southern Song era. During archaeological explorations in 1972, a shard from another large blue and white plate was retrieved at the kiln site; it compares closely in material, dimensions, and designs to the more complete plate retrieved at Tuoketuo.

The explorations of the Hutian kiln site have aided specialists attempting to date such Chinese texts as the *Taoji* [A discussion of pottery], by Jiang Qi, which mentions porcelain manufacture at kilns near Jingdezhen. Liu Xinyuan (1983) has examined the recent finds from the kiln, and he concludes that the *Taoji* was written during the Southern Song dynasty, between 1214 and 1234.

The *Taoji* states that a kind of ware called *qingbai* porcelain was manufactured at the Jingdezhen kilns. There is sharp disagreement among scholars about the meaning of this term; many say it can be equated with what is nowadays referred to as *yingqing* ware—a kind of early Chinese porcelain with a glaze that has a shadowy blue tinge but does not feature underglaze decoration. In 1959, the Chinese porcelain expert Chen Wanli conducted an extensive study of first-hand sources that used the term *qingbai;* he concludes that it should not be confused with *yingqing* and that it was actually an abbreviation for what is today called blue and white.

This is highly significant, because the blue and white porcelain retrieved from the Hutian kiln site closely resembles blue and white pieces that the Chinese exported across the ancient land and maritime Silk Road to distant countries (Liu Xinyuan and Bai Kun, 1980). Many blue and white pieces may have passed overland through Jin and Xia hands to areas in central Asia, and on into the Middle East. More important, the Chinese of the Southern Song dynasty had mastered the use of the magnetic compass and built sophisticated oceangoing vessels that travelled with ceramic exports to such places as the Philippines, Java, Indonesia, southern India, and beyond—in the direction of the Persian Gulf and the east coast of Africa. We know that the Chinese of the twelfth century had considerable knowledge of distant countries: their resources are demonstrated in such works as the *Lingwai Daida* [A discourse on regions beyond the southern mountains], by Zhou Qufei (written in 1178) and the *Zhufanzhi* [A description of foreign peoples], by Zhao Rukuo (completed in 1225).

Twentieth-century archaeological discoveries all along the Silk Road have consistently pointed to the impact of Chinese ceramics on the ancient world. Most scholars have assumed that, unlike other Chinese ceramics exported, all the unmarked blue and white porcelains recovered are products of the Yuan dynasty (1279 to 1368). However, this is a view that fails to take into account certain historical events. For example, archaeological exploration of the ancient medieval marketplace of Fostat in Egypt has revealed a wide variety of ancient Chinese blue and white objects. Fostat, established in A.D. 641, was a thriving commercial center in the eleventh and twelfth centuries but was all but destroyed in 1168. Although it enjoyed some economic recovery in the mid-thirteenth century, its centrality in Egyptian Islamic history had ended before the Yuan era.

Nishapur, which was located in modern-day northeastern Iran, is another case in point. This city was established in A.D. 430 and was utterly destroyed by Genghis Khan in 1221. The inhabitants began rebuilding, but the city was soon levelled again, this time by the violent earthquakes of 1267 and 1280. Chinese blue and white porcelain was retrieved from the ruins of Nishapur during explorations conducted by the New York Metropolitan Museum of Art in the 1930s; the chronology of Nishapur's misfortunes supports the hypothesis that these blue and white pieces predate the Yuan cultural era.

We must reexamine the notion that blue and white porcelain was invented, developed, and exported to the entire medieval world during the Yuan dynasty—

Figure 91 *(opposite)*. Blue and white porcelain *yuhuchun* ("wine") vase. Song era, 960 to 1279. Uncovered in 1988 in a tomb at Wutonghua, Wengniute Banner, north of Chifeng. Height 28 cm; diameter of mouth 8 cm, of footring 8.1 cm. Collection of Wengniute Banner Cultural Relics Management Office.

The body of this piece is very thin, and it is relatively light in weight. It was made using high-quality porcelaneous materials, glaze, and underglaze pigment. The body of the vase is adorned in underglaze blue with a dragon with raised head, bared teeth, and four-clawed talons; the dragon soars among the clouds. A comparable vase was exhibited in 1935 at Burlington House in London and was attributed to the Song by the renown British ceramics specialist R. L. Hobson.

Figure 92. Two of five blue and white porcelain stemcups. Song dynasty, 960 to 1279. Uncovered in 1978 in a hoard northwest of Hajingou Village, Dayingzi Commune, northeast of Chifeng. Left cup height 10.3 cm; diameter of mouth 12 cm. Right cup height 9.7 cm; diameter of mouth 11.4 cm. Collection of Chifeng Municipal Museum.

Both cups have a design of ten-drilled vine in underglaze blue on the inside rim and hidden designs of two striding dragons molded in low relief under the glaze on the inside of the bowl. The bottom of the bowl of the cup on the left is adorned with a cloud pattern in underglaze blue; the cup on the right has a flower cluster in the same position. The outside of the left cup bears two striding dragons with a curling cloud pattern between them in underglaze blue. The cup on the right has an underglaze blue design on the outside of phoenixes with a cloud pattern between them.

an era that lasted less than a century. Central to the idea that the manufacture of Chinese blue and white porcelain commenced during the Yuan cultural era are blue and white vases in the collection of the Percival David Foundation bearing a date of 1351. The artistic and technical sophistication of these vases suggests that they represent a rather mature stage of blue and white porcelain production in China, a stage that may have been reached only over a period of several centuries, not several decades.

Many scholars believe that it was only after the Mongol conquests that China gained the materials and technical expertise required to create the blue and white effect. Nevertheless, this view is contradicted by historical fact. By the time of the late Northern Song emperor Huizong (1101 to 1125), China was producing some of the most technically sophisticated ceramics the world has seen. Moreover, a close examination of Tang/Song records shows that by those eras the Chinese already had access to domestic and foreign sources of the cobalt-bearing minerals used to paint the blue underglaze designs characteristic of blue and white. On the basis of his study of Chinese records, Feng Yunlong (1992) has demonstrated that the gaolinite necessary to fortify the bodies of large porcelain vessels, such as the blue and white wine and fruit containers of Figures 89 and 90, was also first used in China before the Yuan cultural era, no later than the time of the Southern Song emperor Xiaozong's reign (1163 to 1189).

Some scholars assume that the invention of blue and white porcelain was the result of the Mongols' general support of the arts (Lee, 1968). There is no doubt that high-quality blue and white pieces were manufactured during the Yuan dynasty. But there is no clear evidence that the Mongols themselves prized ceramic products. An anecdote from the records of the Yuan dynasty gives indication of the Mongols' priorities. He Yongzu, a Chinese who was a diligent high official in the Yuan government, lived in a rented house and drank from blue porcelain cups; when the Yuan emperor heard of his state, he pitied the man and bestowed gold and silver cups upon him (Lee Yukuan, 1982).

There is also little evidence that the Mongols encouraged the manufacture of Chinese blue and white porcelain. In fact, as Julian Thomson (1987) points out, local gazetteer records of the Jingdezhen area compiled in 1325 make no mention of the mass manufacture of blue and white porcelain there. Most of the money pieces found in association with blue and white porcelain along the maritime Silk Road date from the Song rather than the Yuan dynasty. This fact has led some scholars to believe that Yuan exporters used Song cash or that the Yuan traded with paper currency which has been lost from archaeological contexts. This reasoning may be compelling, yet it scarcely impinges on independent evidence that the Song Chinese were producing high-quality blue and white and exporting it to the medieval world at least 120 years before the Yuan era. The archaeological work conducted in the 1960s by Leandro and Cecilia Locson at the Santa Ana and the Laguna de Bay sites in the Philippines is significant in this regard (Locsin and Locsin, 1988; Addis, 1967); they provide various objective archaeological criteria to demonstrate that blue and white was exported to the Philippines during the Song dynasty.

Archaeological discoveries are significant precisely because they provide physical evidence against which to test generally accepted assumptions about the history of art. I hope that the many discoveries in Inner Mongolia during the last several decades will provide impetus to revise the attributions of unmarked blue and white porcelain in the world's collections. In this way, the pioneering work of twentieth-century archaeologists shall have secured a foundation for deeper study of ancient East/West cultural contact that must be conducted in the century to come.

Figure 93 *(top)*. Rubbings of iron coins. Xia state, twelfth century. From a hoard of coins uncovered at Adulai Village, outside of Baotou. The left rubbing is of a coin from the Xia Qianyou reign period(1170 to 1190); the right is of the Xia Tiansheng reign period (1149 to 1169). Courtesy of Baotou Institute of Archaeology.

Figure 94 *(bottom)*. Blue and white porcelain cup. Southern Song dynasty, 1127 to 1279. Retrieved in 1983 and 1984 from the Xia inner city of the Heicheng site, Ejina Banner, Alashan League. Height 4.3 cm; diameter of mouth 8.1 cm, of footring 2.8 cm. Photograph courtesy of Institute of Archaeology, Huhehaote.
   The body is thin and of fine consistency; the transparent glaze has a light green tinge, and the underglaze has an uneven blackish-green color. Like the plate and jar of Figures 89 and 90, the cup is the product of the Raozhou district *Yutu* porcelain industry.

6

The Mongol Era and the Yuan Dynasty

At the beginning of the thirteenth century, the Mongol people emerged as a political force in the region north of the Gobi Desert. United under the leadership of Genghis (or Chinggis) Khan, they established the formidable Mongolian empire. In 1260, Genghis's grandson, Kubilai Khan, founded the Yuan dynasty, which persisted until the mid-fourteenth century. Without question, these events had a profound effect on historical developments in China and throughout the entire medieval world.

There are several schools of thought on the origins of the Mongol peoples. Scholars from Mongolia believe that the Mongols arose from the Xiongnu, while many Russian historians maintain that they descended from the Tujue (or Turks). However, most Chinese scholars believe that the Mongols were the descendants of a tribe called the Mengwu Shiwei, who originally resided in what is today northeastern China.

The problem is a complex one because, as we have seen in previous chapters, the confederations of the steppe were usually agglomerations of pastoral nomadic tribes of different ethnic and cultural origins. The Mongol confederation was no exception. As Lin Gan (1989) points out, the dominance of the steppe by the powerful Tujue empire during the Tang dynastic era has given rise to the linguistic argument that the Mongol language and hence the Mongols themselves were of Turkish origin. Notwithstanding, Lin explains that there are strong chronologic, geographic, linguistic, and cultural reasons to believe that the Mongols were the descendants of a branch of the Shiwei tribes of the Eastern Hu line.

The Shiwei were a metal- and leather-working people of very ancient origins. Some historians believe that they came to northeastern China at the end of the Xia dynastic era, when they fled north from Henan province after the Shang conquest. Zheng Yingde (1984) thinks that the term *Shiwei* is a transliteration of the name Xianbei, and that the word *Menggu*, or "Mongol,"

Opposite: Gold decoration for a saddle arch. Detail of Figure 101.

145

Archaeological sites of the Mongol era and the Yuan dynasty.

1. Heishantou city site, Eergunayou Banner, Hulunbeier League.
2. Aurug city site, Delgerkhan District, Khenity province, Mongolia.
3. Taiqing Palace, Qingdao, Shandong province.
4. Kaicheng city site, Guyuan District, Ningxia Autonomous Region.
5. Genghis Khan Memorial Shrine, Yijinhuoluo Banner, Yikezhao League.
6. Kara Khorum city site, Hangai Mountains, Mongolia.
7. Wujiacun, Wuchuan County, Wulanchabu League.
8. Alunsimu city site, Daerhanmao Mingan United Banner, Wulanchabu League.
9. Tomb, Baogedu Wusumu Hashatugacha, Xianghuang Banner, Xilinguole League.
10. Tomb, Wujiadi Village, Wuguquan Commune, Xinghe County, Wulanchabu League.
11. Mingshui tomb, Daerhanmao Mingan United Banner, Wulanchabu League.
12. Jininglu city site, Bayintala Commune, Chahaer Youyiqian Banner, Wulanchabu League.
13. Liangcheng tomb, Houdesheng Village, Liangcheng County, Huhehaote Municipal District.
14. Dadu, or Great Capital, Beijing.
15. Shangdu, or Upper Capital, Zhenglan Banner, Xilinguole League.

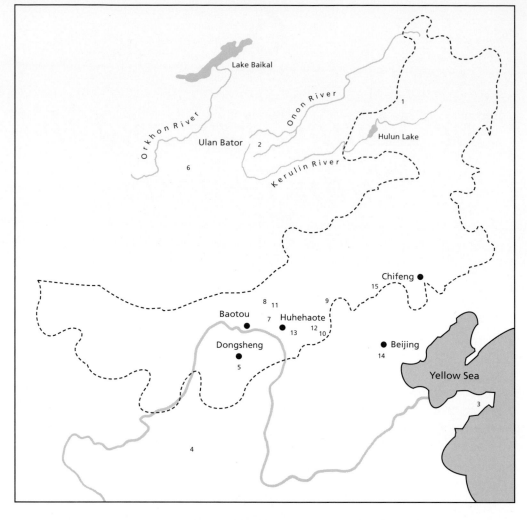

was derived from the name for Wuhuan chieftains and literally means "the brave fighter who knows no fear."

Zhao Yue (1991) agrees that the Mongols were the descendants of the Shiwei. He notes that in Mongolian the term *shiwei* means "forest lands," and he maintains that this name was given to or assumed by the tribe in ancient times when they were masters of the forests of the Hulunbeier area in northeastern Inner Mongolia. Zhao believes that these same forests were the birthplace of the Mongolian people. Indeed, Genghis Khan enfeoffed this land to his younger brothers, and Zhao sees this as evidence that he considered the Hulunbeier to be his ancestral homeland. Archaeologists have in fact found a number of ancient cities dating from the Mongol era in this region, the best preserved and most important of which is Heishantou, believed to be the city of Genghis's younger brother Jochikasar (Wang Tingdong, 1989).

According to Chinese records, by the time of the Tang dynasty (618 to 907), there were as many as nine different tribes with the name Shiwei living in northeastern China, and the Tang court had established a Shiwei Area Commander to oversee these peoples. Between the sixth and the eighth centuries, the early Mongol tribes also fell under the suzerainty of the Turks and the Uighur states at one time or another.

After the eighth century, the early Mongols (then called the Mengwu Shiwei) began to migrate steadily westward; they followed the Erguna River as they moved across the Hulunbeier steppe and finally settled along the upper reaches of the Onon and Kerulen rivers, where they engaged in nomadic pastoralism. After the tenth century, these peoples, among other tribal groups, were under the control of the Liao dynasty.

By the eleventh and twelfth centuries, the area now called the Mongolian

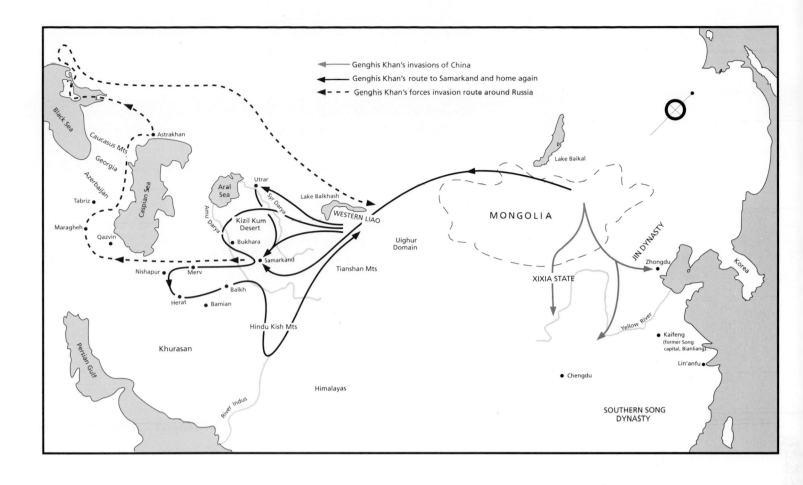

Plateau was home to many different tribes, the most influential of which—in addition to the Mongols themselves—were the Tatar, the Merkit, the Kerait, the Naiman, and the Onggut. These groups fought with each other, and abductions, raiding of livestock, and pillaging of property were frequent. It was in the midst of such precarious circumstances and social unrest that Genghis Khan grew to manhood.

Genghis Khan was born in the early 1160s, the son of the Kiyat-Borjigid chieftain Yisügei, and was named Temüjen because, at the time of his birth, his father had captured a Tatar chieftain of the same name. Legend has it that the newborn Temüjen had a large blood clot in the palm of his hand, an omen that he was destined to be a hero.

When Temüjen was a boy, his father was poisoned by a group of Tatars, and the Kiyat tribe broke up and scattered, abandoning their chief's family. Temüjen's mother, Ho'elun, was a brave and stalwart woman who persevered through the times of extreme hardship that followed, raising her children and stepchildren alone.

Early accounts of Temüjen glorify him: he was said to have been intelligent, brave, and an adept fighter, even from an early age, and as such a potential threat to the leaders of other tribes of the steppe. As a young man, Temüjen had just reestablished his clan when the Merkit tribe raided his encampment; although he eluded capture, his bride Börte was seized. Through an alliance with another tribe, the Kerait, Temüjen was able to defeat the Merkit and recover his wife (Urgunde, 1990).

The victory over the Merkit signalled the beginning of Temüjen's rise to power. In the years that followed, he repeatedly met perils and endured crises through force of character and willpower. In 1189, after he was elected leader of

Genghis Khan's invasion of China and the Khwarazm Shah's Empire. From Marshall, 1993; courtesy of University of California Press.

the Kiyat, he embarked on a series of military campaigns to unify the peoples of the steppe. One of his most important offensives was against the Naiman, a tribe that roamed from the Khangai Mountains to the region of the Greater Altai Mountains.

To check Temüjen's rising ambitions, the Naiman had attempted to make an alliance with the Onggut (called the *Wanggu* in Chinese) who resided in the area north of the Yinshan mountains in Inner Mongolia. The Onggut not only refused to enter this partnership but also pledged their allegiance to Temüjen and joined him in the fight that brought down the Naiman.

In 1206 Temüjen called for a *khuriltai,* a traditional meeting of tribal leaders to decide upon military and state matters. At this assembly, which was held at the head of the Onon River, Temüjen was acknowledged supreme leader and given the title of Genghis Khan (this honorific has been interpreted by scholars to mean "emperor of all emperors" or "oceanic ruler"). With his enthronement, Genghis Khan established the Mongolian Khanate and organized the beginnings of a state apparatus.

In the late 1960s, the Mongolian archaeologist K. Perlee discovered Genghis Khan's capital, Aurug, which is believed to be the place where the *khuriltai* was convened in 1206. It is located on a plain near Delgerkhan district, Khentiy province, approximately 240 kilometers (150 miles) east of Mongolia's capital of Ulan Bator. Recent Japanese survey and exploration at the site has revealed the foundations of dozens of ancient structures over a 40-hectare (100-acre) area. Among the structures are thirteen earth platforms thought to be palace remains (Hannam, 1993).

After his enthronement, Genghis Khan set out on a series of campaigns of conquest. His first target was the Xia state, which occupied the territories of western China through which trade passed between central China and central Asia. In 1209 the Mongols attacked the Xia capital at Zhongxingfu. Rather than incur death and heavy damages, the Xia emperor formally recognized Mongol authority and promised to pay tribute and send a daughter in marriage to the Mongol court. Having secured access to north China across the Yellow River into Shaanxi province, the Mongols then began an assault to bring down the Jin dynasty.

For almost 100 years, the Mongols had been under the nominal suzerainty of the Jin, much to their chagrin. However, toward the end of the twelfth century, the dynasty was beset by internal dissent and open rebellion. The Mongols were quite aware of these internal problems and other weaknesses, because in the early decades of the twelfth century many of the Jin's Qidan and Chinese officials had defected to the Mongols. Once their campaign against the Jin began, the Mongols were strengthened by additional defections from among the ordinary Qidan and Chinese subjects of the Jin.

By 1214, the Mongols had crossed north China and laid siege to the Jin capital of Zhongdu (at modern-day Beijing). Again, a peace accord was reached when the Jin offered to pay tribute and send imperial princesses for marriage into the Mongol court.

The campaigns in northern China were not the only ones conducted at this time. In 1217, to retaliate for the massacre of Mongol merchants and envoys by the sultan of Khwarazm, Genghis decided to lead troops and attack westward. In 1220, he divided his forces into four divisions and conquered many cities in central Asia. After capturing the important commercial center of Bukhara, the Mongols proceeded to overwhelm and sack Samarkand.

Most cities in the path of the Mongol onslaught were given the choice of unconditional surrender or utter destruction. If the officials of a city submitted but then later rebelled, the Mongols promptly returned to destroy it; such was the fate of Nishapur, where a Mongol general and envoy had been killed. The

Figure 95 *(opposite).* Portrait of Genghis Khan in his sixties, following his conquests. Painted by a Chinese artist on stretched silk. Courtesy of Palace Museum, Taipei, Taiwan.

太祖皇帝 即成吉思罕諱帖木真

欽差近侍劉仲祿奉
成吉思皇帝旨道與諸處官員
每
丘神仙應有底脩行底院舍等係
逐日念誦經文告天底人每與
皇帝祝壽萬萬歲者所據大小差
發稅賦都休教著者據
丘神仙底應係出家門人等隨處
院舍都教免了差發稅賦者其
外詐推出家影占差發底人每
告到官司治罪斷按主者奉到
如此不得違錯須至給付照用
右付神仙門下收執
照使所據神仙應係出家門下
精嚴住持院子底人等並免差
發稅賦准此
癸未羊兒年三月　日

宣差阿里鮮面奉
成吉思皇帝聖旨丘神仙奏
知來底公事是也煞好我
前時已有聖旨文字與你
來教你天下應有底出家
善人都管著者好底歹底
丘神仙你就便理會只你識
者奉到如此
癸未年九月二十四日
西域化胡歸順回至燕京
皇帝感勞郡賜金虎符牌曰
真人到處如朕親臨丘神
仙至漢地凡朕所有之城
池其欲居者居之掌管天
下道門事務以聽神仙處
置他人勿得干預宮觀差
役盡行蠲免所在官司常
切衛護
天樂道人李道謙書

Mongols came back to Nishapur and massacred all of the city's inhabitants—it is said that even the dogs and cats were slaughtered.

After they took Samarkand, Mongol forces moved on to attack Azerbaijan and Georgia. In 1223, one expedition crossed the Caucasus Mountains and defeated the Kipchak and the Russian army. These raids brought the Mongols over the Crimean Peninsula and as far west as the Dnieper River.

By then, Genghis Khan was in his sixties (Fig. 95) and had for a long time been interested in a Chinese Daoist monk from Shandong province named Changchun (or Qiuchuji), who was said to possess the secret of immortality. In 1221, Genghis sent a letter to Changchun summoning him to Samarkand.

Although over seventy at the time, the monk made the trek across central Asia to Samarkand and met with Genghis in 1222; his travels were recorded by a disciple in a work entitled *Changchun Zhenren xiyouji* [The journey to the west of the sage Changchun] (Wang Guowei, 1972). Two stone inscriptions from Shandong dated to 1223 confirm that the chronology of Genghis Khan's western campaigns is as recorded in surviving texts; they also show that Changchun's entreaties to Genghis had some influence. These inscriptions (Fig. 96) indicate that Genghis gave the monk royal dispensation to help the masses. Changchun returned to Shandong province and advocated various reforms, which—according to the inscriptions—included fostering belief in the Daoist religion, calling for reduced taxation, promoting peace among the people, and enforcing laws to prevent corruption and killing (Dong Zhuchen, 1986).

Several years after the raids in the far west, Genghis Khan returned to the Mongolian steppe and divided the lands he had conquered, creating several *ulus*, or appanages, for his first three sons. The oldest, Jochi, was given the most distant territories of conquest, which included the lands of the Kipchak, Khwarazm, and

Figure 96 *(opposite)*. Two stone inscriptions at the Laoshan Taiqing Palace in Qingdao, Shandong province. The inscriptions, which date to 1223, concern the Daoist monk Changchun's historical relations with Genghis Khan. Courtesy of Inner Mongolia Museum, Huhehaote.

Figure 97. Modern-day shrine to Genghis Khan located 15 km east of Atengxirezhen, Yijinhuoluo Banner, Yikezhao League, south of Dongsheng. A shrine has been located in the Yijinhuoluo Banner since the early Qing dynasty (1616 to 1911); the current structure was completed in 1956. Photograph by Kong Qun.

Figure 98. Ruins of the Mongol capital of Kara Khorum, built by the son of Genghis Khan in the early twelfth century at the foot of the Hangai mountains on the upper Orkhon River, Mongolia. *Left,* one of a pair of large granite tortoises on the edge of the suburb outside the eastern gates of the city. *Center,* remains of stone bases of wooden pillars at the eastern gates. *Right,* outer walls of the Erdeni Tzu lamasary at Khujirt built in the sixteenth century near the Kara Khorum site. Many of the remains of the palace compound were cleared to provide material to build the monastery. *Far right,* a plan of the palace and its surrounding structures, as revealed by the 1948 and 1949 excavations of Russian archaeologists, showing location of *A,* main palace, *B,* private apartments, *C-F,* storehouses or treasuries, *G,* possible site of Khan's yurt, *H,* gate guardhouse and other buildings, and *I,* stone tortoise. Photographs courtesy of Elga Stephans and Helle Girey, Institute of Archaeology, University of California, Los Angeles. Plan from Phillips, 1969.

Kangli. This appanage, which had its capital at Sarai, north of the Caspian Sea, was called the Kipchak Khanate, or the Khanate of the Golden Horde. The second son, Chaghatai, received the central Asian lands of the Western Liao and nominal supervision of the Uighurs (de Rachewiltz, 1983), who had inhabited the region of modern-day Xinjiang province and had submitted to the Mongols in 1209. This appanage, with its capital at Almalik on the Ili River, was called the Chaghatai Khanate. Ögödei, the third son, was granted the lands of the Naiman; this was called the Ögödei Khanate and had its capital at Emil, north of Lake Balkash.

Meanwhile, the Xia, who had earlier made peace with the Mongols after a long struggle between pro- and anti-Mongol factions at their court, changed their minds and tried to form an alliance with the Jin against the Mongols. The Jin had, moreover, relocated their capital south to Kaifeng in modern-day Henan province. Genghis interpreted these moves as acts of aggression; he held council with his generals after his return to the steppe and decided to finish the Xia once and for all. In 1226, he personally led the attack on the Xia, and the next year, Mongol troops surrounded the Xia capital of Zhongxingfu (in present-day Ningxia).

In the same year, 1227, Genghis Khan died in the Liupan mountains near the Xia capital; he was in his mid-sixties. Tradition has it that, according to his last wishes, his death was kept secret, and the siege of Zhongxingfu was continued. When the Xia king finally surrendered, he was executed and the city's inhabitants massacred.

Of interest are extensive structural remains recently uncovered near Kaicheng in southern Ningxia. Based upon preliminary findings, Zhuang Dianyi (1993) believes that the structures were built during the Yuan dynasty by the third son of

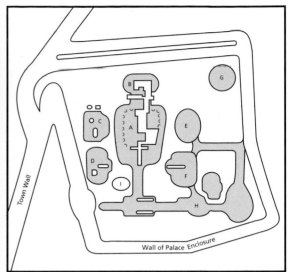

Kubilai Khan. Surveys and excavations are currently being carried out to determine if these structures were built upon the site where Genghis Khan took up residence in the summer of 1227, just prior to his death.

After Genghis Khan's death, messengers were sent to all Mongol khanates to summon princes and tribal chieftains to attend his burial rites as well as a *khuriltai* to choose the successor to the throne. According to contemporary accounts, in the summer of 1227, a great procession led by the Khan's Imperial Guard set off from northern Inner Mongolia and proceeded north into the Mongolian steppe with the body of Genghis Khan in a carriage drawn by fifteen oxen. As the procession moved through the countryside, every animal and person in its path was killed, as dictated by old traditions, to ensure secrecy and to provide chattel for the deceased in the afterworld. Then the Khan's body was buried secretly, supposedly at Burkhan-kaldun, with his yurt and other funerary wares. The exact location of the burial was vigorously guarded at the time and is still unknown.

According to legend, Genghis Khan had passed through the Ordos area during his final campaign and had been so taken with the beautiful grasslands that he dropped his horsewhip. When attendants went to fetch it, Genghis told them to let it be and expressed a desire to be buried in these Ordos grasslands. The attendants buried the horsewhip on the spot and erected a ceremonial stone tumulus over it. In modern times, a shrine to Genghis Khan's memory has been built in the Ordos region where this incident is purported to have occurred (Fig. 97). Its curators, men who claim direct descent from Genghis Khan, welcome the thousands of Mongol people who come to the shrine each year to pay homage to Genghis Khan, to participate in traditional ceremonies, and to seek blessings.

After the burial of Genghis Khan, his youngest son Tolui became regent in charge of Mongol affairs of the state and army. In 1229, Tolui convened a *khuriltai*

Figure 99 *(left)*. Imprint of bronze Mongol seal, thirteenth century. Collected in 1974 at Wujiacun Village, Wuchuan County, Wulanchabu League. Seal height 5.5 cm; face 10.9 cm square. Collection of Inner Mongolia Museum, Huhehaote.

The characters *shang* ("superior") and *wang* ("king") are incised on the seal's knob. The fourteen-character inscription on the face, shown here, is in intaglio "nine-fold" script (an ornate Chinese writing used exclusively for seals) and reads "Seal of the Commander-in-Chief of Hebei dispatched by the Princess Regent." In the center of the seal are two lines of Uighur script that are unclear but appear to read "Seal of the Commander-in-Chief."

Figure 100 *(right)*. Pounded-earth walls of the Onggut city of Alunsimu, located on the steppelands of Daerhanmao Mingan United Banner, Wulanchabu League. Photograph by Kong Qun.

The walls, which date from the twelfth century, stand over 2 meters

on the banks of the Kerulen River. At this meeting, in accordance with the wishes of Genghis Khan, Tolui's older brother, Ögödei, was elected Great Khan. In the next few years, Ögödei completed the conquest of the Jin dynasty, through an alliance with the Chinese Southern Song state, and ordered the resumption of the western campaigns under the leadership of his nephew Batu (the son of the then-deceased Jochi). First, the lands west of the Ural River were conquered; then the Mongol forces routed the Bulgars along the middle of the Volga, suppressed the Kipchak north of the Caspian Sea, and occupied Russia. The Mongols also penetrated the borders of present-day Poland, Hungary, and Austria. But these western campaigns came to a temporary halt in 1241, when Ögödei died.

Eleven years later, Tolui's oldest son Möngke was elected Great Khan, and he soon ordered his younger brother Hülegü to resume the western offensives. Hülegü's armies defeated the Isma'iliyah (known in the West as the Assassins) within modern-day Iran's borders and captured Baghdad. In 1259, they overran the Syrian cities of Aleppo, Homs, and Damascus; Aleppo fell to a catapult bombardment and suffered a 6-day massacre (Turnbull and McBride, 1980). The Mongols then founded the Il-khan state, the fourth of the khanates that they established.

While he was Khan, Ögödei had built a city, Kara Khorum (called *Helin* in Chinese), at the foot of the Khangai Mountains on the upper Orkhon River in Mongolia. During Möngke's time, it became a thriving economic and political center for the Mongol empire. The city site was excavated in 1948 and 1949 by Russian archaeologists, who retrieved tiles, glazed architectural ornaments, pottery, coins, and metalwork.

Kara Khorum was basically oblong and approximately 2,500 meters (north to south) by 1,500 meters (8,200 by 4,900 feet); it apparently had a suburb

Figure 101. Front arch decoration from a set of six gold facings for a saddle. Mongols, thirteenth to fourteenth centuries. Unearthed in 1988 at Baogedu Wusumu Hashatugacha, Xianghuang Banner, Xilinguole League. Height 21.8 cm; width 22.5 cm; weight 193.4 grams. Collection of Inner Mongolia Museum, Huhehaote.

The saddle ornaments were retrieved from the tomb of a Mongol noblewoman who was 17 to 19 years old at the time of her death. They were made of hammered gold leaf and designed to fit over a wooden saddle *(reconstruction at right)*. The central motif of the front arch ornament is a reclining deer set in a lozenge; the background is of entwined peonies.

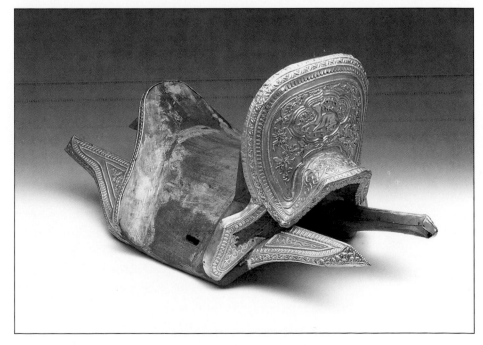

Figure 102. Detail of a porcelain tile facsimile of a late Yuan-era painting, showing Börte, the wife of Genghis Khan, wearing the *guguguan* hat reserved for Mongol noblewomen. Courtesy of Genghis Khan Shrine, Yijinhuoluo Banner.

outside its eastern gates. The remains of several structures were noted or uncovered near these gates (Fig. 98). Further excavation south of the gates in 1950 revealed a store of metal products, mainly agricultural implements (Phillips, 1969).

One of the primary goals of the Russian exploration was to excavate Kara Khorum's palace and its surrounding structures. They found that the palace was built on a raised earth platform and set in a court, which was surrounded by walls constructed of clay, sand, and pebbles and estimated to have been 4 to 5 meters high (13 to 16 feet). The outermost wall was about 250 by 225 meters (820 by 740 feet).

During the thirteenth century, after the Mongol incursions into Eastern Europe, the Christian West sent emissaries to Mongolia, primarily for the purpose of gathering information that would be useful in dealing with the Mongol threat (Richard, 1969). The most successful of these missions was led by John of Plano Caprini, who arrived at Kara Khorum in 1246. He left a detailed account of his visit to the Mongols in his *Historia Mongolorum,* which he submitted to Pope Innocent IV after his return in 1247 (Dawson, 1955).

Perhaps because they did not consider the conquest of Europe worth their while, the Mongols never renewed their campaigns there after the death of Ögödei in 1241. However, Marco Polo and other westerners—many of whom were Christian missionaries—continued to travel to the Mongols. One of the missionary visitors was Wilhelm van Ruysbroeck (also known as William of Rubruck), a Franciscan who went supplied with letters of introduction from the French king Louis IX. Ruysbroeck arrived in Kara Khorum in 1254 and, like Caprini, wrote an account of his travels upon his return to Europe a year later (Dawson, 1955); his records of the Mongol capital, as well as those of other eye witnesses, coincide with the finds of twentieth-century archaeologists (Phillips, 1969).

Archaeological fieldwork conducted to the south of Kara Khorum, in the Inner Mongolia Autonomous Region, has considerably increased our knowledge of the material culture of the Mongol era, especially that of the Onggut tribes. These people, descendants of the Turks of central Asia, had relocated to the Yinshan mountains in present-day Inner Mongolia toward the end of the Tang dynastic era. During the Jin dynasty they were a powerful force on the northern frontier, and they had helped Genghis Khan defeat the Naiman, his principal adversary on the Mongolian steppe. The Onggut later played a crucial military role in the Mongol conquest of the Jin dynasty.

Because the Onggut tribes had served his people, Genghis Khan decreed that the sons of the Onggut leader would be married into the Mongol court and become imperial sons-in-law. From Genghis's time until the collapse of the Yuan dynasty, the two groups maintained conjugal relations, and the Onggut became one of the central components of the Mongol elite. As Yi You (1982) points out, this close association led to the Onggut's adoption of many of the Mongol customs, to the point that it is now virtually impossible to distinguish the artifacts of these groups from one another.

A bronze seal collected in 1974 at Wujiacun Village in Wuchuan County, Wulanchabu League, coincides with historical accounts of Onggut and Mongol relations. The seal's top knob bears two characters meaning "superior" and "king." The fourteen-character inscription on the seal's face (Fig. 99) is in intaglio "nine-fold" script (an ornate Chinese writing used exclusively for seals) and translates as "Seal of the Commander-in-Chief of Hebei dispatched by the Princess Regent." In the center of the seal are two lines of Uighur script that are unclear but appear to read "Seal of the Commander-in-Chief."

The seal was not found with other objects, but as Ding Xueyun (1984) points out, a variety of ancient cities, cultural sites, and tombs in the area where the seal was uncovered all date to the Jin and Yuan dynastic eras, during which the

Figure 103. Single-lugged gold cup. Mongol, thirteenth to fourteenth centuries. Retrieved in 1976 from Tomb #4, Wujiadi Village, Xinghe County, Wulanchabu League. Height 4.9 cm; diameter of mouth 12.1 cm, of base 7.9 cm; weight 188.9 grams. Collection of Inner Mongolia Museum, Huhehaote.

The flat-bottomed cup has a flower shape and a loop beneath its crescent-shaped handle. A strip of entwined honeysuckle and peony designs runs along the side of the cup and *(left)* on its handle and inside bowl.

region was occupied by the Onggut tribes. After extensive analysis of relevant texts, Ding concludes that this was an official seal issued to the commander-in-chief of Hebei by Genghis Khan's third daughter, Alaqa-beki, who was married to the Onggut chieftain and had held the position of "Princess Regent" since several years before Genghis departed on his western campaigns in 1217. Ding explains that although the center of Onggut government was in Inner Mongolia, the tribes' dominion extended across the northern frontier and included areas such as Hebei.

In Daerhanmao Mingan United Banner, several hundred kilometers northwest of Huhehaote, are the remains of Alunsimu, one of the most important of the ancient cities located on the Mongolian steppe. The city was built on the site of the Jin city of Andabaozi and became the governmental, economic, cultural, and religious center of the Onggut tribes.

Several groups of scholars visited the Alunsimu site in the 1920s and 1930s: Huang Wenbi went there in 1927, Japanese explorers began a survey in 1929, and Owen Lattimore conducted his own surveys in 1932. These inspections and later studies revealed that Alunsimu was basically rectangular and approximately 900 meters long (east to west) by 600 meters wide (3,000 by 2,000 feet). The portions of the pounded-earth city walls that remain stand over 2 meters (6 feet) high (Fig. 100). Within the walls are the foundations of about 100 structures and 17 courtyard compounds, and a variety of wide and well-organized streets and avenues are still distinguishable.

A little to the north of the city's center is a large courtyard area containing a string of structures on a foundation almost 3 meters (10 feet) high. It is from this location that pieces of a stone with a 600-character inscription were retrieved; the inscription dates from the Yuan era. A study of rubbings and photographs made of the stone in the early part of this century shows the inscription to be a detailed

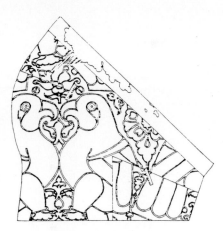

Figure 105. Design of brocade cowl. Mongol, thirteenth to fourteenth centuries. Unearthed in 1978 from Onggut tombs at Dasujixiang Mingshui, Daerhanmao Mingan United Banner. Length and width of cowl 36 cm. Collection of Inner Mongolia Museum, Huhehaote.

The motif is of two falcons or eagles facing each other with a rosette between them.

tribute to the activities of generations of Onggut kings. Deng Hongwei and Zhang Wenfang (1992) infer that the series of structures in Alunsimu where the stone was found was originally the palace compound of the Onggut kings.

Alunsimu was at the center of routes of communication and trade leading from the northern Mongolian steppe south through the Ordos and modern-day Ningxia to the Gansu Corridor and thence to the west. *Alunsimu* means "[the city] with a multitude of temples," and surveys there have charted the remains of Buddhist and Lamaist temples as well as Nestorian and Roman Catholic churches. Wang Shaohua (1992) maintains that Alunsimu was one of the first places in Asia where Christian churches were established.

One of the more remarkable Mongol-era discoveries in recent years is the tomb at Baogedu Wusumu Hashatugacha in Xilinguole League, which was exposed during a rainstorm in 1988. Archaeologists retrieved a number of gold and fabric artifacts there, including a wooden saddle fitted with ornaments of hammered gold leaf (Fig. 101). Professor Zhu Hong of Jilin University has analyzed the complete skeleton found in this tomb and determined that the interred was a woman between 17 and 19 years of age (Su Jun, 1993).

Six fragments of birch bark found in the Hashatugacha tomb suggest that the young woman buried there was a member of the Mongol nobility. Thin traces of coarse, loosely woven silk cling to the birch bark, and it is pierced with evenly spaced needle holes. Su Jun (1993) believes that the bark pieces originally formed part of a *guguguan*, the traditional hat worn by Mongol noblewomen (Fig. 102).

Four Mongol-era tombs discovered in 1976 at Wujiadi Village in Xinghe County, Wulanchabu League, have yielded gold, silver, iron, birch bark, and wooden artifacts. A flat-bottomed gold cup with a round loop beneath its crescent-shaped handle (Fig. 103) was retrieved from Tomb #4. This cup resembles the "ladles with thumb-rests *[yazhibei]*" that Marco Polo said were used in the great halls of Genghis Khan and Kubilai Khan to scoop wine out of large bronze jars (Latham, 1958). Gai Shanlin (1984) notes that the construction of the Wujiadi tombs compares closely with that of Onggut tombs uncovered very near Alunsimu; he believes that the interred were noblemen and cavalry warriors.

The Onggut tomb unearthed in 1978 at Dasujixiang Mingshui, Daerhanmao Mingan United Banner, has yielded a variety of artifacts (Figs. 104-107) dating from the Jin/Yuan eras, including several silk garments—a large gold brocade robe, a cowl with a brocade design of raptors, and leggings of a tapestry (or weft) weave *(kesi)*. Silk fabric remains have also been recovered from another Mongol-era site, the ruins of the city of Jininglu, which are about 30 kilometers (19 miles) southeast of modern-day Jining City in Chayouqian Banner (east of Huhehaote and near the Wujiadi tombs). A large half-sleeve vest (Fig. 108) has a printed gold pattern; another fabric piece bears an inscription indicating that it was used by a high military official stationed at Jininglu.

The weft-woven leggings (Fig. 106) clearly derive from central China and are perhaps products of the Southern Song. But the gold brocade and gold imprint silk fabrics (Figs. 104, 108) from these Onggut sites all appear to have been manufactured in the north; they are typical products of the Jin/Yuan era. Such fabrics, which are rarely recovered from Southern Song sites, were popular among the Mongol nobility. Marco Polo reported that at the time of his visits fabrics of these types were being manufactured in northeastern Inner Mongolia, near modern-day Chifeng (Latham, 1958).

It is possible, however, that many of the fabrics mentioned here were manufactured in Chinese central Asia. Xia Hexiu and Zhao Feng (1992) point out that the designs on the gold brocades from the Mingshui tomb are quite comparable to designs on silks found to the west of China along the Silk Road. A gold brocade robe comparable to the Mingshui piece was recovered at the Yanhu site in

the northern Tianshan mountains south of the modern-day city of Urumuchi in 1970. In analyzing the fabric remains from Yanhu, Wang Binghua (1973) explains that during the Song/Jin cultural era, the Uighur people of this area were famous for their gold brocade workmanship and that they introduced these products to China. During the Yuan dynasty, a special factory for the manufacture of gold brocade and gold imprint silk was established in central Asia. In short, there is reason to believe that the Mingshui tomb fabrics were made by Uighur craftsmen from central Asia.

Another important find is the Yuan-era tomb at Houdesheng Village in Liangcheng County; the tomb is on a mountainside southeast of Huhehaote and was revealed after several violent rainstorms. The walls and ceiling of the tomb are covered with frescoes, and a central mural shows the tomb's occupant in life (Fig. 109a). On the basis of the facial features and shape of the hat of this figure, Wang Dafang (1993) believes that he was a Mongol nobleman who lived in the Onggut region during the Yuan era. Among the scattered remains found within the tomb was a clay tile with a hand imprint (Fig. 109b). Similar pieces have been found at the Onggut city of Alunsimu, and Wang infers that the burial of such objects was an ancient Mongol shamanistic practice.

I N 1257 MÖNGKE had convened a *khuriltai* at which the Mongols decided to move against the Southern Song dynasty. Möngke led the troops in person but died of illness in 1259 during the attack on the city of Hezhou in modern-day Sichuan province. His younger brother Kubilai called a meeting of tribal leaders in 1260 in the city of Kaiping in modern-day Inner Mongolia and formally proclaimed himself Grand Khan and emperor of a

Figure 106. *Gesi* (tapestry or weft-woven) leggings. Mongol, thirteenth to fourteenth centuries. Unearthed in 1978 from Onggut tombs at Dasujixiang Mingshui, Daerhanmao Mingan United Banner. Length 82 cm; width 25 cm. Collection of Inner Mongolia Museum, Huhehaote.

The fabric pattern is of flowers on a purple ground; designs of leaves and lotus and peach flowers adorn the side. The two ribbons at the top of the leggings secured them to the wearer's leg.

new state, which he subsequently named *Da Yuan,* or "Great Yuan dynasty."

Kubilai's claim to the throne was contested by his younger brother Arigh-böke, who had been a high official during Möngke's rule, with duties that included the administration of Kara Khorum. The disagreement over succession led to conflict, and Kubilai used the old territories of the Xia to launch an economic blockade against Arigh-böke at Kara Khorum. In 1264, his brother surrendered and recognized Kubilai as the Great Khan; Arigh-böke died shortly thereafter.

With his leadership confirmed, Kubilai conducted a series of campaigns of conquest against southern China, Japan, Burma, and southeast Asia, the greatest and most successful of which was his assault on the Southern Song dynasty in southern China. By launching a massive attack and overcoming great difficulties, the Mongols finally vanquished the Southern Song capital of Lin'anfu, in modern-day Zhejiang province. Remnants of the Southern Song army continued to put up resistance until 1279, when they were completely wiped out. This victory unified all of China, ending several hundred years of division.

In 1276, the Yuan court relocated to their newly completed capital city of Dadu, or Great Capital, which was in an area that is part of modern-day Beijing and was one of the finest architectural and engineering accomplishments in Chinese history. A vast labor force had been amassed for the project, and two of its principal architects were Kubilai's Chinese ministers Liu Binzhong and Guo Shoujing.

Liu Binzhong, who had joined the Mongol court at Kara Khorum some 30 years earlier, had been a major architect in the construction of Kubilai's city, Kaiping; it was he who planned the overall layout of Dadu. Guo Shoujing opened up the Jinkou River, which had been dammed since the Jin dynasty, and thus rerouted the Lugou River to facilitate the transport of lumber and building materials from the western mountains. A painting housed in the Beijing Palace Museum depicts

Figure 107 *(opposite).* Gold stemcup. Mongol, thirteenth to fourteenth centuries. Unearthed in 1978 from Onggut tombs at Dasujixiang Mingshui, Daerhanmao Mingan United Banner. Height 12.5 cm; Diameter of mouth 10.8 cm, of base 6.5 cm; weight 174.1 grams. Collection of Inner Mongolia Museum, Huhehaote.

A pattern of entwined grass and leaf designs is incised around the mouth, and the outside of the bowl is decorated with curved lotus flowers, blooming Chinese crabapple, and peony. A lotus leaf design is incised around the lower edge of the stem, which was originally welded to the bowl.

Figure 108. Half-sleeve vest with pattern printed in gold and lining of yellow silk. Yuan dynasty, 1279 to 1368. Retrieved from a hoard of fabrics unearthed at Jininglu city site, Tuchengzi Village, Bayintala Commune, Chahaer Youyiqian Banner, Wulanchabu League, about 30 km southeast of Jining. Length 58 cm; width from cuff to cuff 107 cm. Collection of Inner Mongolia Museum, Huhehaote.

Figure 109. Central mural from a tomb uncovered in 1991 at Houdesheng Village, Liangcheng County, Huhehaote Municipal District, southeast of Huhehaote. Yuan dynasty, 1279 to 1368. Height 70 cm; width 210 cm.

The mural depicts the tomb's occupant, a Mongol nobleman, in life. The tomb also contained a clay tile *(below)* bearing the imprint of a human hand; this piece is now in the collection of the Inner Mongolia Museum, Huhehaote. Photographs by Kong Qun.

the results of Guo Shoujing's effort: wooden rafts float down the Lugou on their way to the Dadu construction site.

A number of important structures built in Dadu during the early Yuan era still stand today. Among them is the Tibetan Buddhist *Baita*, or "White Pagoda" (Fig. 110), in the western part of Beijing, which was designed and constructed by the Nepalese Anige between 1271 and 1279.

Kubilai had founded the city of Kaiping in Inner Mongolia prior to proclaiming himself leader of the Mongols, and after he became Great Khan he renamed it Shangdu, or Upper Capital (Figs. 111-113). During the Yuan dynasty, the Mongol emperors would travel from Dadu to Shangdu each summer to escape the heat of the Beijing area.

As emperor, Kubilai—unlike many of his predecessors—recognized that the Mongol state could no longer be maintained by military actions alone. He and his successors enacted vigorous political and economic reforms to regenerate China, which was in a state of chaos after the conquest. Kubilai reorganized the civil administration, established a special bureau in the government to promote agriculture, and actively fostered trade of all kinds. The Yuan dynasty set up ten "circuits," or provincial offices, within China to administer governmental affairs in the localities. These administrative divisions were an important innovation in political structuring, and they have been in use to this day (the Chinese term for province, *sheng,* derives from the word for these divisions).

In the cultural realm, Kubilai revivified the Chinese Hanlin Academy, an institution for pursuit of the arts and traditional learning that had existed since the Northern Song era. A special office to govern Buddhist affairs was also established. One of the more interesting of Kubilai's cultural reforms was his commissioning of a new Mongol written language.

The Mongol script in existence at the time was based upon the Uighur script, which was derived from Sogdian and ultimately from Aramaic. This script did not transcribe the sounds of the Chinese names, titles, and offices with great precision: what was needed was a more versatile alphabet (Rossabi, 1988). Kubilai commissioned the newly appointed head of the Office of Buddhist Affairs, a Tibetan lama named 'Phags-pa (Basiba in Chinese), to devise the new script. The monk worked with a team of scholars and other monks, and he presented the script to Kubilai in 1269. The alphabet was based upon Tibetan and contained forty-one letters (Yi Si, 1989).

Kubilai made efforts to encourage the use of the 'Phags-pa script (it had been named after its inventor), issuing various edicts to promulgate its use in official court documents (Rossabi, 1988). But it never succeeded in replacing the Uighur script or Chinese. Extant examples of the use of 'Phags-pa—which include stone inscriptions, Buddhist texts, seals, coins, metal tablets, paper money, and porcelains—are rather rare.

One piece featuring 'Phags-pa script is of particular historical interest; it is a square bronze official seal dating to Kubilai's time that was unearthed in Hulunbeier League, northeastern Inner Mongolia. The inscription on the seal's face reads "Seal of the Kipchak Battalion of the Imperial Army" (Fig. 114). The same phrase is etched on the top of the seal in Chinese, and the top bears an additional legend in Chinese, "Made by the Minister of Rites of the Department of State Affairs *[Shangshu Libu]*, third month of the twenty-fourth year of *zhiyuan*" (i.e., A.D. 1287).

During the reign of Genghis Khan and his successors, the Mongols had conducted several campaigns to subdue the Kipchak in the Caucasus mountains north of the Caspian Sea. When these people were finally conquered during the Yuan dynasty, their notoriously fierce warriors were organized into left and right divisions of a Kipchak Guard within the Imperial Army *(Qinjun)*, the most important Yuan military establishment. Like various other ethnic groups conquered by the Mongols, the Kipchak produced political and military figures who rose to prominence in the Yuan era; among them was the general Tugh Tugha, who took command of the ethnically diverse armies that were assembled by the Yuan between 1284 and 1286 and that included the Kipchak troops. The security of the Yuan throne after Kubilai's reign depended a great deal upon these elite military units (de Rachewiltz, 1983).

The Department of State Affairs that issued the Hulunbeier seal with Chinese and 'Phags-pa script legends was a top-level administrative agency in the Yuan central government; it operated under the Secretariat *(Zhongshusheng)*. The fact that the seal was uncovered in Hulunbeier League—an area that was the ancestral homeland of the Mongols and the site of cities founded by many of Genghis Khan's brothers and their descendants—reinforces its historical significance.

During the Yuan era, as in the years before the dynasty was founded, Christian missions travelled across central Asia from Europe. This is borne out by a stone carving found at the site of the Yuan-era city of Alimali, in Huocheng County along the northern Tianshan mountains close to the modern Sino-Kirghizian

Figure 110. The Tibetan Buddhist *Baita* ("White Pagoda") designed and constructed by the Nepalese Anige between 1271 and 1279. The structure stands in the Miaoying Temple compound inside Fuchengmen in the western section of modern-day Beijing. The Liao pagoda that had been constructed on this spot in 1096 was used as a foundation for the Baita.

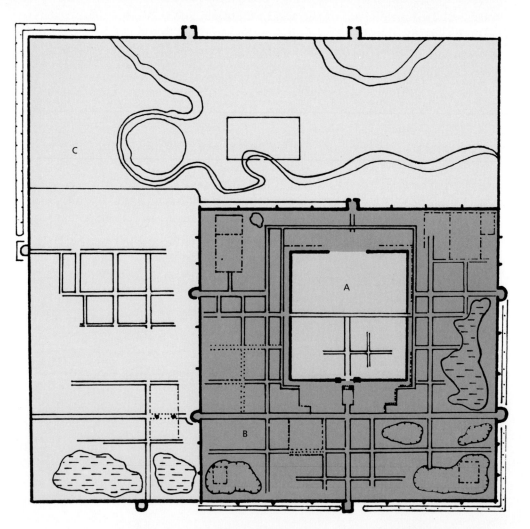

Figure 111 *(top)*. Marble architectural ornament. Yuan dynasty, 1279 to 1368. Found at Longguang Huayan Temple in the northeastern corner of Shangdu's Palace City. Height 31.5 cm; length 79 cm; width 33.5 cm. Collection of Inner Mongolia Museum, Huhehaote. Photograph by Kong Qun.

The ornament is carved in the shape of the head of a *chi* (hornless dragon).

Figure 112 *(right)*. Layout of Kaipingfu, the second Mongol capital, located in Xilinguole League, on the northern banks of the upper Luan River, about 250 km north of Beijing. The capital was completed in 1258, and Kubilai Khan made it his residence 2 years later; it was renamed *Shangdu* ("Upper Capital") in 1263. The city had three sectors: *A,* the Imperial City, *B,* the Palace City, and *C,* the Outer City. The site has been surveyed many times during the last century. Plan courtesy of Inner Mongolia Museum, Huhehaote.

166

border. A Christian cross is carved at the center of the stone, and there are inscriptions in Syriac (ancient Syrian) on either side of the cross. On the basis of a study by Huang Wenbi, Cheng Zhenguo (1985) dates the carving to the fourteenth century.

By the beginning of the fourteenth century, internecine fighting among the ruling elite had resulted in a progressive weakening of the Yuan state. Paralyzed by its own intrigues, the court was less and less able to control the provincial areas outside the capital. While the regular shipment of taxes and supplies were being disrupted by bandits, the provincial leaders began taking matters into their own hands. The corrupt and exploitative behavior of these authorities was compounded by natural disasters, and the populace (both Chinese and Mongol) was left with little recourse.

The result was an explosive outbreak of peasant uprisings that emanated from Anhui province after 1351. When the Yuan court did not intervene militarily, the various rebel groups began to vie with each other for control of southern China. Finally, Zhu Yuanzhang, the leader of one of these groups, marched toward the Yuan capital.

This eventually led to the Yuan dynasty's downfall in 1368: its last emperor, Shundi (*Toghon Temur* in Mongolian), withdrew from the Yuan Great Capital and returned to the Mongolian steppe. Zhu Yuanzhang captured the city without a fight and founded the Ming dynasty (1368 to 1644). After the fall of the Yuan, the Mongols established the Northern Yuan, and this state and the Ming dynasty struggled militarily into the fifteenth century. Based upon the recent discovery of dated documents, Guo Zhizhong and Li Yiyou (1987) conclude that the Heicheng garrison city was among the places occupied by the Northern Yuan state.

Of the four khanates that the Mongols had established in Eurasia, only the Khanate of the Golden Horde—the original appanage given by Genghis Khan to his oldest son Jochi—remained after the fall of the Yuan dynasty; it persisted into the late fifteenth century. Tamerlane, who was born in the early fourteenth century, claimed that he was the legitimate heir to the Chagahatai Khanate. In a series of campaigns in the late fourteenth and early fifteenth centuries, he conquered central Asia, portions of the Middle East, Armenia, Georgia, and southern Russian. The Timurid state that he established endured until the time of his great-grandson, who died in the late fifteenth century.

Figure 113 *(top)*. Structural and architectural remains uncovered within the Palace City (Fig. 112, B) of the Mongol capital Shangdu. These rare photographs taken by the Japanese in the 1940s show remains that are no longer extant. Courtesy of Inner Mongolia Museum, Huhehaote.

Figure 114 *(bottom)*. Imprint of a bronze seal. Yuan dynasty, 1279 to 1368. Unearthed in Hulunbeier League. Seal height 8.2 cm; face 7.3 cm square. Collection of Hulunbeier Cultural Relics Work Station.

The seal knob is trapezoidal, and the face bears an inscription in 'Phags-pa official script, which translates "Seal of the Kipchak Battalion of the Imperial Army." The same phrase is etched on the top of the seal in Chinese, as is an additional legend, "made by the Minister of Rites of the Department of State Affairs *[Shangshu Libu],*" third month of the twenty-fourth year of zhiyuan [i.e., A.D. 1287]).

References Cited

Abbreviations:

BMW: *Beifang minzu wenhua* [Journal of the Culture of the Northern Nationalities] 1992, supplementary issue (published by the Zhaowuda League Mongolian Teachers College).

BW: *Beifang wenwu* [Journal of Northern Antiquities].

BWZ: *Baotou wenwu ziliao* [Baotou Journal of Research Materials on Cultural Relics], (inner circle publication of the Baotou City Institute of Cultural Relics).

EE: Seamen, Gary (ed.), *Ecology and Empire*, Proceedings of the Soviet-American Academic Symposia in Conjunction with the exhibition, *Nomads: Masters of the Eurasian Steppe* (Ethnographics Press, Center for Visual Anthropology, University of Southern California, Los Angeles, 1989).

EWKW: *Eerduosi wenwu kaogu wenji* [Collected Essays on the Archaeology of the Ordos], (inner circle publication of the Institute of Cultural Relics, Yikezhao League, Inner Mongolia, 1981).

KG: *Kaogu* [Archaeology].

KGXB: *Kaogu xuebao* [Journal of Archaeological Studies].

LS: *Linhuang shiji* [Historical Remains of the Linhuang Area], inner circle publication of the Balinzuo Banner Institute of Cultural Relics, 1988.

NDKWYW: *Neimenggu dongbuqu kaoguxue wenhua yanjiu wenji* [Collected Essays on the Archaeological Research of Eastern Inner Mongolia], (Haiyang Press, Beijing, 1991).

NWK: *Neimenggu wenwu kaogu* [Inner Mongolian Journal of Archaeology and Cultural Relics].

NWS: *Neimenggu wenwu sanji* [Assorted Notes on the Cultural Relics of Inner Mongolia], (publication of the Mongolian Studies Association, Huhehaote City, 1979).

WLCBW: *Wulanchabu wenwu* [Journal of Cultural Relics of the Wulanchabu League], (inner circle publication).

WW: *Wenwu* [Journal of Cultural Relics], (note: this journal was called *Wenwu cankao ziliao* until December 1958).

ZBKW: *Zhongguo beifang kaogu wenji* [A Collection of Archaeological Treatises on the Northern China], (Cultural Relics Publishers, Beijing, 1990).

ZGB...: *Zhongguo gudai beifang minzu kaogu wenhua guoji xueshu yantaohui* [Proceedings of the International Academic Conference of Archaeological Cultures of the Northern Chinese Ancient Nations], (held in Huhehaote City, August 11-18, 1992).

ZMS: *Zhaowuda Mengzu shizhuan* [Journal of the Zhaowuda League], (published by Mongolian Teachers College).

Addis, J. M., "Chinese Porcelain Found in the Philippines," *Transactions of the Oriental Ceramic Society*, 37: 1967.

Alekseev, Valery P., "Some Aspects of the Study of Productive Forces in the Empire of Chinghiz Khan," in EE, 1991.

Allsen, Thomas T., "The Yuan Dynasty and the Uighurs of Turfan in the 13th Century," in Morris Rossabi (ed.), *China Among Equals* (University of California Press, Berkeley, 1983).

An Lu, "*Donghu zuxi de fumian zangsu ji xiangguan wenti* [Funerary Masks of the Eastern Hu Ethnic Line and Related Issues]," BW, 1: 1985.

An Zhimin and Zhen Naiwu, "*Neimenggu Ningchengxian Nanshengen 102 hao shiguomu* [The Stone Tomb #102 from the Ningcheng County Nanshangen Site, Inner Mongolia]," KG, 4: 1981.

Anthony, David W. and Dorcas R. Brown, "The Origins of Horseback Riding," *Antiquity* 65: 1991.

Artamonov, M. I., "Frozen Tombs of the Scythians," in *Old World Archaeology: Foundations of Civilization* (Readings from *Scientific American*), (W. H. Freeman and Co., San Francisco, 1965).

Bai Junpo, "*Neimenggu Ningcheng chutu Liaodai sancaihu* [A Three-Colored Glaze Pot Uncovered at Ningcheng County, Inner Mongolia]," WW, 3: 1984.

Basilov, Vladimir N. (ed.), *Nomads of Eurasia* (Natural History Museum of Los Angeles County and University of Washington Press, Seattle, 1989).

Beijing Cultural Relics Bureau, Institute of Archaeology, Chinese Academy of Sciences, "*Beijing Houyingfang Yuandai juzhi yizhi* [A Yuan Era Residence at Houyingfang, Beijing]," KG 6: 1972.

Bu Yangwu and Cheng Xi, "*Neimenggu diqu tong (tie) fu de faxian ji chubu yanjiu* [On the Discovery and Preliminary Research of Bronze (and Iron) Cauldrons in Inner Mongolia]," in ZGB..., 1992.

Campbell, Colin, "Search for Ancient Clues Links U. S. and Soviet Experts in Wary Exchange," *New York Times,* February 17, 1986.

Cen Rui, "*Mojie wen kaolue* [A Brief Investigation of the Capricornus Design]," WW, 10: 1983.

Chen Sixian, "*Shangduxian 'dayuan' tonghu yiyi* [On the Meaning and Significance of the 'Dayuan' Bronze Pot Inscription from the Shangdu County Hoard]," WCLBW, 3: 1989.

Chen Sixian, "*Dui Lipinyao yu Taoheqi Jinshipai de jidian renshi* [Several Issues Regarding the Gold Ornamental Plates Recovered from Lingpiyao and Taoheqi]," NWK, 3: 1984.

Chen Sixian, "*Xianbei kaoguzhong di xin keti—Xianbei, Xiboli, caoyuan sichou zhilu* [A New Subject in Xianbei Archaeology—Xianbei, Siberia, and the Silk Road of the Grasslands]," in NWS, 1979.

Chen Sixian and Zheng Long, "*Neimenggu Linhexian Gaoyoufang chutu de Xixia jinqi* [Xixia Gold Artifacts Unearthed at the Gaoyoufang City Site, Linhe County, Inner Mongolia]," WW, 11: 1987.

Chen Tangdong, "*Shangduxian chutu jiaocang tongqi tieqikao* [A Study of the Bronze and Iron Artifacts Unearthed from the Shangdu County Hoard]," NWK, 1: 1991.

Chen Tangdong and Lu Sixian, "*Xianbei dongwu xingzhuang shizhong fanying de Tuobashi zuyuan shenhua de chuangzao* [The Origin of Tuoba and the Creation of the Myth Reflected in the Animal-Design Ornamentation of the Xianbei]" in ZGB..., 1992.

Chen Wanli, "*Wo dui 'qingbai ciqi' de kanfa* [My Views on the Meaning of the Term 'Qingbai Porcelain']," WW, 6: 1959.

Chen Wanli, "*Wo duiyu Liaomu chutu jijian ciqi di yijian* [My Views on Several Ancient Ceramics Unearthed from Liao Tombs]," WW, 11: 1956.

Chen Yongzhi, "*Zuzhou shishi zaitan* [A Further Inquiry into the Stone Edifice at the Zuzhou City Site]" in NDKWYW, 1991.

Cheng Zhenguo, "*Xinjiang Alimali gucheng you faxian yikuai Jidujiao Shuliyawen keshi* [The Ancient Alimali City Site in Xinjiang Province Once Again Uncovers a Christian Stone Inscription with Syriac Writing]," WW, 4: 1985.

Dawson, Christopher, *The Mongol Mission: Narratives and Letters of the Franciscan Missionaries in Mongolia and China in the Thirteenth and Fourteenth Centuries* (Sheed & Ward, New York, 1955).

Deng Hongwei and Zhang Wenfang, "*Alunsimu gucheng yizhi* [The Remains of the Ancient Alunsimu City Site]," NWK, 1, 2: 1992.

Ding Xueyun, "*Jianguo gongzhu tongyin yu Wanggubu yicun* [The Seal of the Princess Regent and the Ancient Remains of the Onggut Tribe]," NWK, 3: 1984.

Dong Juan, "*Yinchuan Gangzijing Xixia yaozhi* [The Gangzijing Xixia Kiln Site at Yinchuan City, Ningxia Province]," WW, 8: 1978.

Dong Zhuchen, "*Chengjisi huangdi xi Qiuchuji shengzhi shikekao* [A Study of the Stone Inscriptions Recording the Imperial Dispensation Bestowed by Genghis Khan upon Qiuchuji]," WW, 5: 1986.

Dunnell, Ruth W., "Naming the Tangut Capital: Xingqing/Zhongxing and Related Matters," *Bulletin of Sung Yuan Studies,* 21: 1989.

Dunnell, Ruth W., "Who are the Tanguts? Remarks on Tangut Ethnogenesis and the Ethnonym Tangut," *Journal of Asian History*, 18, 1: 1984.

Feng Xianming, "*Youguan qinghua ciqi qiyuan de jige wenti* [Several Problems Concerning the Origins of Blue and White Porcelain]," WW, 4: 1980.

Feng Xianming, "*Woguo taoci fazhanzhong de jige wenti* [Several Problems Concerning the Development of Chinese Porcelain]," WW, 7: 1973.

Feng Yongqian, "'*Guan han xinguan' zikuan ciqi zhi yanjiu* [Research of Ancient Ceramics with the 'Guan and Xinguan' Marks]," in *Zhongguo gudai yaozhi diaocha fajue baogaoji* [Collected Reports of the Excavation of Ancient Chinese Kiln Sites], (Cultural Relics Press, Beijing, 1984).

Feng Yunlong, "*Gaolingshan zhi gaolingtu shikai niandaikao* [The Earliest Historical use of Gaoling Earth from Gaoling Mountain]," *Jingdezhen taoci xueyuan xuebao* [Journal of the Jingdezhen Institute of Ceramics], 13, 1: March 1992.

Gai Shanlin, "*Xinghexian Wujiadi gumu* [The Ancient Tomb at Wujiadi Village, Xinghe County]," NWK, 3: 1984.

Garner, Harry, *Oriental Blue and White* (Faber & Faber, London, 1954; 3rd ed., 1970).

Gu Feng and Xu Liangyu, "*Yangzhou xinchutu liangjian Tangdai qinghua ciwan canpian* [Two Tang Era Blue and White Porcelain Bowl Fragments Recently Uncovered at Yangzhou]," WW, 10: 1985.

Gu Juying, "*Wanbu Huayanjingta* [The Wanbu Huayanjing Pagoda]" in NWS, 1979.

Guo Suxin, "*Neimenggu Huhehaote Bei Wei mu* [The Northern Wei Tomb Unearthed in Huhehaote City, Inner Mongolia], WW, 5: 1977.

Guo Zhizhong and Li Yiyou, "*Neimenggu Heicheng kaogu fajue jiyao* [Essential Finds from the Recent Archaeological Explorations of the Ancient Heicheng City Site, Inner Mongolia]," WW, 7: 1987.

Hannam, Peter, "In Search of Genghis Khan," *Far Eastern Economic Review*, September, 1993.

He Lin, "*Guanyu 'shanyu heqin' wa* [Regarding the Tile with the 'Conjugal amity with the Shanyu' Inscription]," BWZ, 1: 1981, p. 52.

He Lin, "*Qiantan Baotou chutu de guhuobi* [A Brief Discussion of Ancient Coins Uncovered at Baotou City]," BWZ, 1: 1981, pp. 137-38.

Hirth, Friederick and W. W. Rockwill (translators and annotators), *Chau Ru-kuo: His Work on the Chinese and Arab Trade in the Twelfth and Thirteenth Centuries, Entitled Chu-fan-chi* (Printing office of the Imperial Academy of Sciences, St. Petersburg, 1911).

Hoang, Michael, *Genghis Khan* (New Amsterdam Books, New York, 1991).

(Song) Hong Hao, *Songmuo jiwen* [Records of Experience on the Pine Forest Plains], (Shangwu Press, Taipei, 1979).

Huang Weiwen and Weiqi, "*Salawusuhe de Hetaoren jiqi wenhua* [Ordos Man and His Culture in the Sjara-osso-gol River Region]" in EWKW, 1981.

Huang Wenbi, "*Yuan Alimali guchengkao* [A Study of the Yuan Era Ancient City of Alimali]," KG, 10: 1963.

Inner Mongolia Cultural Relics Team, Inner Mongolia Museum, "*Helingeer faxian yizuo Zhongyao de Dong Han bihuamu* [The Discovery of an Important Eastern Han Frescoed Tomb at Helingeer County]," WW, 1: 1974.

Inner Mongolia Institute of Archaeology and the Zhelimu League Museum, *Liao Chenguo gongzhumu* [Tomb of the Liao Princess of the State of Chen], (Cultural Relics Press, Beijing, 1993).

Jia Zhoujie et al., "*Yuan Shangdu diaocha baogao* [A Report on the Explorations of the Yuan Shangdu City]," WW, 5: 1977.

Jian Siqing, "*Guanyu Tangdai Hongzhouyao wenti* [Problems Concerning the Tang Era Hongzhou Kilns]," WW, 2: 1958.

Jin Fengyi, "*Xiajiadian shangceng wenhua jiqi zushu wenti* [Problems Regarding the Ethnic Identity of Xiajiadian Upper Period Culture]," KGXB, 2: 1987.

Jing Yongtian, "*Liao Shangjing fujin Foshi yizhi* [Buddhist Temple Sites in the Liao Upper Capital City Site Region]," in LS, 1988.

Jing Yongtian, "*Liao Shangjing chengzhi fujin Foshi yizhi ji huocangmu* [Buddhist Temples and Cremation Burials in the Liao Upper Capital City Site Region]," NWK, 3: 1984.

Jin Yongtian and Wang Jingzhi, "*Liaodai jiyaogu renwu yupai* [A Liao Era Jade Plaque with the Design of a Man Beating a Waist Drum]," in LS, 1988.

Jin Yufu, "*Liaoguo Fuma guowang muzhiming kaozheng* [Critical Study of the Stone Tomb Inscription from the Liao Tomb of the Commander Escort and Prince Titled to Protect the State]," KGXB, 3: 1956.

(Qing) Ke Shaowen, *Yuanshi* [Yuan Histories], (Zhonghua Shuju, Beijing, 1976).

Kessler, Adam T. "The *Erlitou* Site: Evidence for the Contemporaneity of Late Xia and Early Shang Kings," Doctoral Dissertation, University of California, 1989.

Kriukov, Michael V., and Vadim P. Kurylev, "The Origins of the Yurt: Evidence from Chinese Sources of the Third Century B.C. to the Thirteenth Century A. D." in EE, 1989.

Kwanten, Luc, *Imperial Nomads* (Philadelphia, University of Pennsylvania Press, 1979).

Latham, Ronald (trans.), *The Travels of Marco Polo* (Penguin Press, Middlesex, 1958).

Lee Yu-kuan, *A Study of Sung Underglaze Blue and Red Porcelains* (Yuzankaku Shuppan Co., Ltd., Tokyo, 1982).

Lee Yu-kuan, *Art Rugs from the Silk Route and Great Wall Areas* (Oriental House Ltd., Tokyo, 1980).

Lee Yu-kuan, *Oriental Lacquer Art* (Weatherhill, New York, 1972).

Lee, Sherman E., "The Art of the Yuan Dynasty (1279-1368)," in *Chinese Art under the Mongols: The Yuan Dynasty* (Cleveland Museum of Art, Cleveland, OH, 1968).

Li Fanwen, "*Xixia lingmu chutu canbei cuipian* [Collected Extant Stone Tablet Inscriptions from the Xixia Royal Tombs], (Cultural Relics Press, Beijing, 1984).

Li Wenxin and Zhu Zifang, in Liaoning Provincial Museum (ed.), *Liaoci xuanji* [Selected Works of Liao Ceramics], (Cultural Relics Press, Beijing, 1962).

Li Yiyuo, "*Liaodai Qidanren muzang zhidu gaishuo* [An Outline of Liao Dynastic Qidan Burial Institutions]," in NDKWYW, 1991.

Li Yiyou, "*Caoyuan sichou zhilushang de Jingdezhen qinghua ciqi—Heicheng chutu qinghua ciqi de niandai he laiyuan* [Jingdezhen Blue and White Porcelain on the Silk Road of the Grasslands—The Origin and Dating of Blue and White Porcelain Uncovered at the Heicheng Site]," 1988 draft based on field notes delivered to Dr. Adam Kessler of the Natural History Museum of Los Angeles County in 1991.

Li Yiyou, "*Lindong di Liao Shangjing yizhi* [The Site of the Liao Upper Capital at Lindong]," in *Neimenggu Wenwu Ziliao Xuanji* [Collected Research Source Materials on the Cultural Relics of Inner Mongolia], (People's Press of Inner Mongolia, Huhehaote City, 1964).

Li Zuozhi, "*Huhehaoteshi dongjiao chutu de jijian Yuandai ciqi* [Several Yuan Era Ceramics Unearthed in the Eastern Suburbs of Huhehaote City], WW, 5:1977.

Lin Gan, *Donghushi* [The History of the Eastern Hu], (People's Press of Inner Mongolia, Huhehaote City, 1989).

Lin Gan, *Zhaojun yu Zhaojunmu* [Zhaojun and Zhaojun's Tomb], (People's Press of Inner Mongolia, Huhehaote City, 1979).

Lin Gan, *Xiongnushi* [Xiongnu History], (People's Press of Inner Mongolia, Huhehaote City, 1977).

Lin Meicun, "*Kaituo sichou zhilu de xianqu—Tuhuoluoren* [Pioneers in the Expansion of Silk Road Frontiers—The Tuhuoluo People], WW, 1: 1989.

Lin Yun, "*Dui Nanshangen M102 chutu kewen guban de yixie kanfa* [Some Remarks on the Bone Slip with Carved Designs from Tomb #2 of the Nanshangen Site]," in NDKWYW, 1991.

Liu Guanmin, "*Neimenggu Chifengshi Dadianzi mudi shuyao* [An Account of Essential Facts Concerning the Graveyard Finds from the Chifeng City Dadianzi Site in Inner Mongolia]," KG, 4: 1992.

Liu Guanmin and Xu Guangji, "*Neimenggu dongbu diqu qingtong shidai de liangzhong wenhua* [Two Bronze Age Culture-Types from the Regions of Eastern Inner Mongolia," NWK, 1981, inaugural issue.

Liu Huan-zhen, "*Zhongguo Neimenggu Baotou Yenjialiang chutu de qinghua taociqi* [Blue and White Porcelain Artifacts Unearthed from the Baotou Yenjialiang Site, Inner Mongolian Autonomous Region, China]" in *1989 Gudai taoci Kexue jishu guoji taolunhui*

[Proceedings of the Scientific Symposium on Ancient Pottery and Ceramics], (Shanghai, 1989).

Liu Xinyuan, "*Jiangqi 'Taoji' zhuzuo shidai kaobian* [A Study of the Date of Authorship of Jiangqi's `Taoji']," Part II, *Wenshi* [Journal of Literature and History], 19: 1983.

Liu Xinyuan and Bai Kun, "*Jingdezhen Hutianyao kaocha jiyao* [Essential Discoveries from the Survey Explorations of the Hutian Kiln Site at Jingdezhen]," WW, 11: 1980.

Liu Yiman, "*Yinxu qingtongdao* [Bronze Knives from the Yinxu Site]," KG, 2: 1993.

Locsin, Leandro, and Cecilia Locsin, *Oriental Ceramics Discovered in the Philippines* (C. E. Tuttle & Co., Rutland, Vermont, 1968).

Lubec, G. et al., "Use of Silk in Ancient Egypt," *Nature*, 6415: March 1993, p. 25.

Ma Changshou, *Beidi yu Xiongnu* [The Northern Di and the Xiongnu], (Sanlian Press, Beijing, 1962).

Ma Wenkuan, "*Liaomu Liaota chutu di Yisilan boli—jiantan Liao yu Yisilan shijie de guanxi* [On Islamic Glass Unearthed from Liao Tombs and Pagodas—A Discussion of Liao Relations with the Islamic World," in ZGB..., 1992.

Maenchen-Helfen, Otto J., *The World of the Huns* (University of California Press, Berkeley, 1973).

Medley, Margaret, *Yuan Porcelain and Stoneware* (Pitman Publishers, London, 1974).

Mongolian Studies Center of the University of Inner Mongolia (ed.), *Neimenggu wenwu guji jianshu* [A Brief Description of the Ancient Cultural Remains of Inner Mongolia], (People's Press of Inner Mongolia, Huhehaote City, 1977).

Morgan, David, *The Mongols* (Blackwell, Cambridge, 1986).

Northeastern Cultural Relics Team, Institute of Archaeology, Academy of Science, "*Ningchengxian Nanshangen de shiguomu* [The Stone Tomb Burial at the Ningcheng County Nanshangen Site]," KGXB, 2: 1973.

Onon, Urgunge (translator and annotator), *The History and Life of Chinggis Khan* (The Secret History of the Mongols), (E. J. Brill, Leiden, 1990).

Pan Xingrong and Yi Zuo, "*Yuan Jininglu gucheng chutu de jiaocang sizhiwu ji qita* [The Hoard of Ancient Silk Fabrics Uncovered at the Yuan Jininglu Ancient City and other Matters]," WW, 8: 1979.

Phillips, E. D., *The Mongols* (Praeger, New York, 1969).

Qi Dongfang, "*Zhongguo zaoqi madeng de youguan wenti* [Regarding the Early Use of the Horse Stirrup in China]," WW, 4: 1993.

Qiao Shaoqin, "*Guanyu beifang youmu wenhua qiyuan de tantao* [Regarding the Origins of Northern Nomadic Cultures]," NWK, 1 & 2: 1992.

Qin Weibo, "*Guanyu Xianbei zaoqi zai renshi* [A Reconsideration of Early Xianbei Culture]," BW, 3: 1988.

Rachewiltz, Igor de, "Turks under the Mongols, A Preliminary Investigation of Turco-Mongol Relations in the 13th and 14th Centuries" in Morris Rossabi (ed.), *China Among Equals* (University of California Press, Berkeley, 1983).

Ratchnevsky, Paul, *Genghis Khan: His Life and Legacy* (Blackwell Ltd., Oxford, 1991).

Richard, Jean, "The Mongols and the Franks," *Journal of Asian History*, 3, 1: 1969.

Rossabi, Morris, *Khubilai Khan* (University of California Press, Berkeley, 1988).

(Qing) Ruan Yuan [ed.], *Shisanjing zhushu* [The Collated and Annotated Thirteen Classics], (Jinzhang Tushuju Cangban, Shanghai, 1926).

Sang Jianxin, "*Hangzhoushi faxian de Yuandai ciqi jiaocang* [A Hoard of Yuan Era Ceramics Uncovered at Hangzhou City]," WW, 11: 1989.

Sarianidi, V. I., "The Treasure of Golden Hill," *American Journal of Archaeology*, 84, 2: April 1980.

Shi Jinpo, "*Zangzu wenhua he Xia wangchao de lishi yuanyuan* [On the Historical Origins of Tibetan Culture and the Xixia State]," *Zhongguo Xizang* [Chinese Journal of Tibetan Studies], 2: 1989.

Shi Jinpo et al., *Xixia wenwu* [Xixia Cultural Relics], (Cultural Relics Press, Beijing, 1988).

Shuowen jiezi gulin (Shangwu Press, Taipei, 1959).

(Han) Si Maqian, *Shiji* [Records of the Historian], (Zhonghua Press, Beijing, 1959).

Sinor, Denis, "The Inner Asian Warriors," *Journal of the American Oriental Society*, 101.2: 1981.

Stein, Aurel, *Innermost Asia*, vol. I, (Claredon Press, Oxford, 1928).

Su Bai, "*Shengle, Pingcheng yidai de Tuoba Xianbei—Bei Wei yizhi* [The Tuoba Xianbei of the Shengle and Pingcheng Area—Ancient Remains of the Northern Wei Dynasty]," WW, 11: 1977.

Su Bai, "*Dongbei, Neimenggu diqu de Xianbei yiji* [Xianbei Remains in Northeastern China and Inner Mongolia]," WW, 5: 1977, fig. 1.

Su He, "*Cong Zhaomeng faxian de daxing qingtongqi shilun beifang de zaoqi qingtong wenming* [A Discussion of Early Northern Bronze Age Cultures from the Point of View of the Large Bronze Vessels Retrieved in the Zhaowuda League Area]," NWK, 2: 1982.

Su Jun, "*Guanyu Neimenggu Xilinguolemeng Xianghuangqi Baogeduwu Lasumu Hashatu Gacha yimu chutu wenwu shidai de chubu fenxi* [Preliminary Notes on the Periodization of the Hashatu Tomb, at Baogeduwu, Lasumu Hashatu, Xianghuang Banner, Xilinguole League]," essay based on field notes delivered in 1993 to Dr. Adam Kessler of the Natural History Museum of Los Angeles County.

Sun Jinyi et al., *Nuzhenshi* [A History of the Jurchen], (Jilin Historical Press, Changchun City, 1987).

Talat Tekin, *A Grammar of Orkhon Turkic*, Uralic and Altaic Series, vol. 69, (University of Indiana Press, Bloomington, 1968).

Tang Xizi, *Han Wei liang Jin Nanbeichao Fojiaoshi* [History of Buddhism during the Han, Wei, and Jin North and Southern Dynasty Era], (Dingwen Shuju, Taipei, 1982).

Thompson, Julian, "Decorative Motifs on Blue and White in the S. C. Ko Collection," in *The S.C. Ko Tianminlou Collection*, part I (Hong Kong, 1987).

Tian Guangjin, "*Neimenggu shiqi shidai—qingtong shidai kaogu faxian he yanjiu* [Inner Mongolia's Neolithic—Archaeological Discoveries and Research of Bronze Age Cultures]," NWK, 1 & 2: 1992.

Tian Guangjin, "*Xigoupan Handai Xiongnu mudi* [Record of the Archaeological Exploration of the Han Era Xiongnu Graveyard at the Xigoupan Site]" in *Eerduosi qingtongqi* [Ordos Bronzes], (Cultural Relics Press, Beijing, 1986).

Tian Guangjin and Guo Suxin, "*Zailun Eerduosishi qingtongqi de yuanliu* [A Further Discussion on the Origins of Ordos Style Bronzes]," in ZGB..., 1992.

Tian Guangjin and Guo Suxin, *Eerduosi qingtongqi* [Ordos Bronzes], (Cultural Relics Press, Beijing, 1986).

Tian Guangjin and Guo Suxin, "*Xigoupan Xiongnumu* [The Xiongnu Tombs at the Xigoupan Site]," WW, 7: 1980.

Tian Guanglin, "*Caoyuan sichou yanjiu* [Research on the Silk Road of the Grasslands]," *Sichoushi yanjiu* [Journal of Silk Historical Research], 9, 1: April, 1992.

Tian Guanglin and Zhang Jianhua, "*Qidan zangsu yanjiu* [The Research of Qidan Burial Practices]," BMW, 1992.

Tian Jindong, "Beijing Liangxiang faxian de yichu Yuandai jiaocang [A Hoard of Yuan Era Ceramics Uncovered at Liangxiang, Beijing]," WW, 6: 1972.

(Yuan) Tuo Tuo, *Songshi* [The Song Histories], (Zhonghua Shuju, Shanghai, 1977).

(Yuan) Tuo Tuo, *Liaoshi* [Liao Histories], (Zhonghua Shuju, Beijing, 1974).

Turnbull, S. R. and Angus McBride, *The Mongols* (Osprey Publishing Ltd., London, 1980).

Wang Binghua, "*Yanhu gumu* [The Ancient Tombs Uncovered at Yanhu, Wulumuqi City]," WW, 10: 1973.

Wang Dafang, "*Guanyu Liangcheng Yuanmu de rending*" [On the Verification of the Liangcheng Yuan Tomb], essay based on field notes delivered in 1993 to Dr. Adam Kessler of the Natural History Museum of Los Angeles County.

(Qing) Wang Guowei (annotator), *Changchun zhenren xiyouji* [The Journey to the West of the Sage Changchun], (Guangwen Shuju, Taipei, 1972).

(Qing) Wang Guowei, "*Guifang Kunyi Xianyunkao* [A Study of the Guifang and Xianyun Tribes]," in *Guantang Jilin* (Zhonghua Press, Beijing, 1959).

(Qing) Wang Guowei, "*Hufukao* [A Study on the Clothing of the Hu Peoples]," in *Guantang Jilin* (Zhonghua Press, Beijing, 1959).

Wang Huide, "*Guanyu Xiajiadian xiaceng wenhua gucheng de jige wenti* [Several Issues About Xiajiadian Lower Period Culture-type Ancient City Sites]," BMW, 1992.

Wang Huide, "*Niao tuteng de lanshang—jiantan Dongyi wenhua* [The Origins of the Bird Totem—and a Discussion of Dongyi Culture]," ZMS, 3: 1990.

Wang Longgeng, "*Baotou Zhaojunmu de chuanshuo* [Legendary Accounts of the Zhaojun Tomb in the Baotou Area]," BWZ, 1: 1981.

Wang Shaohua, "*Engami Namio kaocha Alunsimu gucheng suiji* [Professor Engami Namio's Surveys of the Ancient Alunsimu City Site]," NWK, 1, 2: 1992.

Wang Tingdong (ed.), *Neimenggu Zizhiqu zhongdian wenwu baohu danwei jieshao* [An Introduction to Ancient Cultural Sites Under the Protection of the Inner Mongolian Autonomous Region], (People's Press of Inner Mongolia, Huhehaote City, 1989).

Wang Weixiang, "*Qidan dazi yu Qidan dazibei canshi* [Qidan Great Script and Fragments of Stelae with Qidan Great Script]," in LS, 1988.

Wang Yuping, "*Neimeng Yimeng nanbu jiushiqi shidai wenhua de xin shouhuo* [New Paleolithic Finds from the Southern Regions of the Yikezhao League in Inner Mongolia]," KG, 10: 1961.

Wang Yuping, "*Yimeng Salawusuhe kaogu diaocha jianbao* [Preliminary Report on Archaeological Surveys of the Sjara-ossogol River Region, Yikezhao League]," WW, 4: 1957.

Watt, James C. Y., "The Arts of Ancient China," *The Metropolitan Museum of Art Bulletin*, Summer, 1990 (reprint).

Wei Changyou, "*Liao Shangjing yizhi* [The Process of the Liao Upper Capital's Construction]," in LS, 1988.

(Northern Qi) Wei Shou, *Weishu* [The Northern Wei Histories], (Zhonghua Press, Beijing, 1974).

Wilford, John Noble, "New Finds Suggest Even Earlier Trade on Fabled Silk Road," *New York Times*, March 16, 1993.

Wittfogel, Karl A., and Feng Chia-sheng, "History of Chinese Society: Liao (907-1125)," *Transactions of the American Philosophical Society*, New Series, 36: 1946.

Wu En, "*Lun Xiongnu kaogu yanjiuzhong de jige wenti* [Several Problems in the Research of Xiongnu Archaeology]," KGXB, 4: 1990.

Wu En, "*Yin zhi Zhouchu de beifang qingtongqi* [Northern Bronzes from the Yin and Early Zhou Dynastic Era]," KGXB, 2: 1985.

Wu Rukang, "*Hetao renlei dinggu han gugu huashi* [Cranium and Femur Fossils of Ordos Man]," *Gu jizhui dongwu xuebao* [Journal of Ancient Vertebratology], 2, 4: 1958.

Wu Tianchi, *Xixia shigao* [Xixia History], expanded ed. (People's Press of Sichuan Province, Chengdu City, 1982).

Xia Hexiu and Zhao Feng, "*Damaoqi Dasujixiang Mingshui mudi chutu de sizhipin* [Ancient Fabrics Uncovered at the Mingshui Tomb, Dasujixiang, Damao Banner]," NWK, 1 & 2: 1992.

Xia Nai, "*Cong Xuanhua Liaomu de xingtulun ershibasu han Huangdao shiergong* [A Discussion of Constellations and the Zodiac based upon the Stellar Diagrams in the Xuanhua Liao Tomb]," KGXB, 2: 1976.

Xiang Chunsong, "*Neimenggu Wengniuteqi Liaodai Guangdegongmu* [The Liao Tomb at Guangdegong, Wengniute Banner, Inner Mongolia]," BW, 4: 1989.

Xiang Chunsong, "*Neimenggu Jiefanyingzi Liaomu fajue jianbao* [Preliminary Report on the Excavation of a Liao Tomb at the Jiefangyingzi Commune, Inner Mongolia]," KG, 4: 1979.

Xu Xinguo, "*Qinghaisheng Huzhutuzu Zizhixian Dong Han muzang chutu wenwu* [Artifacts Unearthed from an Eastern Han Tomb at the Huzhu Tuzu Autonomous County, Qinghai Province]," WW, 2: 1981.

Xu Zhongshu, "*Chenhou siqi kaoshi* [An Explication and Analysis of the Four Chenhou Vessels], *Guoli zhongyang yanjiuyuan lishi yuyan yanjiusuo jikan* [Bulletin of the Institute of History and Philology, Academia Sinica], 3, 4: 1933.

Yang Guozhong and Liu Zhongfu, "*1980 nianqiu Henan Yanshi Erlitou yizhi fajue jianbao* [A Brief Report of the 1980 Excavations of the Yanshi Erlitou Site, Henan Province]," KG, 3: 1983.

Yang Wenxian and Zhou Kun, "*Zhongguo de 'Langong'—Tangdai lancai yu qinghuaci* [Blue Palace of China, Tang's Blue Pigment and Blue and White Porcelain]," in *Zhongguo gud ai taoci kexue jishu dierjie guoji taolunhui* [Proceedings of the 2nd International Conference on Ancient Chinese Pottery and Porcelain], (Chinese Academic Publishers, Beijing, 1985), #A-17.

Yi Si, "*Yuandai dishi Basisba* [The Yuan Era Emperor, a Follower of Basiba]," *Zhongguo xizang* [Chinese Journal of Tibetan Studies], 2: 1989.

Zhang Bozhong, "*Neimenggu Tongliaoxian Erlinchang Liaomu* [The Liao Tomb at Erlinchang, Tongliao County, Inner Mongolia]," WW, 3: 1985.

Zhang Bozhong, "*Qidan zaoqi wenhua tansuo* [The Search for Early Qidan Culture]," KG, 2: 1984.

Zhang Bozhong, "*Huolinhe kuangqu fujin faxian de Xi Zhou tongqi* [Western Zhou Era Bronzes Uncovered in the Huolinhe River Mining Region]," NWK, 2: 1982.

Zhang Nairen, Tian Guanglin, and Wang Huide, *Liaohai qiguan* [Ancient Wonders of the Liao River Region], (People's Press of Tianjing, Hebei Province, 1989).

Zhang Songbo and Feng Lei, "*Zuzhou shishi tansuo* [An Inquiry into the Stone Edifice at the Zuzhou City Site]" in NDKWYW, 1991.

Zhang Yu, "*Caoyuan sichou zhilu—Qidan yu xiyu* [The Silk Route of the Grasslands—the Qidan and Central Asia]" in NDKWYW, 1991.

Zhang Zhongpei, "*Xiajiadian xiaceng yanjiu* [Research on Xiajiadian Lower Period Culture]" in ZBKW, 1990.

Zhang Zhongpei, "*Zhukaigou yicun jiqi xiangguan wenti* [The Zhukaigou Site Remains and Related Problems]" in ZBKW, 1990.

Zhao Guodong, "*Chifeng diqu you faxian liangchu yanhua* [The Discovery of Two New Rock Art Sites in the Chifeng Area]," NWK, 1, 2: 1992.

(Song) Zhao Rukuo, *Zhufanzhi* [A Description of Foreign Peoples], in Wang Yunwu (ed.), *Congshu jicheng* (Shangwu Press, Shanghai, 1936), Volume 3272.

Zhao Yue, "*Youmu minzu de lishi yaolan—Hulunbeier shaoshu minzu yicun jianshu* [The Cradle of Pastoral Nomadic Peoples in Ancient Times—A Brief Description of the Cultural Remains of the Minority Peoples of the Hulunbeier Banner Region]," NWK, 1: 1991.

Zheng Shaozong, "*Chifengxian Dayingzi Liaomu fajue baogao* [A Brief Report on the Excavation of the Liao Tomb at Dayingzi, Chifeng County]," KG, 3: 1956.

Zheng Yingde, "*Shilun Shiwei shi Menggu zuyuan* [A Discussion of the Shiwei Tribes as the Origins of the Mongols]" in Hui Minghui (ed.), *Beifang minzu guanxishi luncong* [Collected Essays on the Historical Relations of Northern Peoples], (People's Press of Inner Mongolia, Huhehaote City, 1984).

Zhong Kang et al., "*Xixia bahaoling fajue jianbao* [A Brief Report on the Excavation of the Xixia Royal Tomb #8]," WW, 8: 1978.

Zhou Heng, *Xia, Shang, Zhou kaogu lunwenji* [Collected Essays on Xia Shang Zhou Dynastic Archaeology], (Cultural Relics Publishers, Beijing, 1980).

(Song) Zhou Qufei, *Lingwai daida* (A discourse on Regions Beyond the Southern Mountains), in Wang Yunwu (ed.), *Congshu jicheng* (Shangwu Press, Shanghai, 1936), Volume 3118.

Zhu Boquan, "*Zaoqi Qinghuaqi de zhongyao faxian* [Critical Discoveries of Early Blue and White Porcelain Vessels]," WW, 4: 1980.

Zhu Qingze and Li Penggui, "*Cong Meng Jin zhanzheng kan Chengjisihan de zhanlue zhanshu* [A Study of the Military Strategy and Art of Genghis Khan from the Point of View of the Mongol/Jin Wars]," in *Zhongguo Menggu shixuehui lunwen xuanji, 1983* [Proceeding of the 1983 Chinese Symposium on Mongolian Historical Studies], (People's Press of Inner Mongolia, Huhehaote City, 1987).

(Qing) Zhu Youzeng (Annotator), *Yizhoushu* [History of the Zhou], (Shangwu Press, Taipei, 1971).

Zhuang Dianyi, "*Chengjisihan siyu hedi?* [Where was Genghis Khan Buried?]," *Guangmin Ribao* [Guangmin Daily], August 8, 1993.

Index

An "f" following a page number indicates that an illustration related to the subject appears on the page; an "m" indicates a map.

Editor and Book Project Manager: Robin A. Simpson
Book Design and Typography: Dana Levy, Perpetua Press
Production Coordinator: Letitia Burns O'Connor, Perpetua Press
Design Assistance and Mechanicals: D.J. Choi
Computer Typography Assistance: Brenda Johnson-Grau
Photography Assistance: Richard Hink
Bibliography Editing: Kathy Talley-Jones
Cartography: Ron Hasler
Index: Academic Indexing Service, Berkeley